eat better
live better
feel better

Alkalize your life . . .
one delicious recipe
at a time

Julie Cove

Certified Holistic Nutritionist,
Certified Plant-based Cook

appetite
by RANDOM HOUSE

For John, Louis, Elliott,
and Amelia, my precious family.
Thank you for being my inspiration
to learn how to heal myself so I could
share this wisdom with you.
My wish is for you to be free
from illness to enjoy this wonderful
life to the fullest.

Appetite by Random House® and colophon are registered trademarks of Penguin Random House LLC.

Library and Archives of Canada Cataloguing in Publication Date

ISBN 978-0-14-752976-3
eBook ISBN 978-0-449-016077

Illustrations by Rose Cowles
Doilies on pages iv, 101, 129, 151, 181, 207, 241, 275, by angiemakes.com
Photos of Julie on pages 4, 29, 31 and 34 by Yvonne Becker
Photos of Julie in her studio on pages vi and 89 by Kelly Brown
Live blood photos on page 15 courtesy of Maureen Fontaine, Certified Darkfield Microscopist

Printed and bound in China

Published in Canada by Appetite by Random House®,
a division of Penguin Random House Canada Limited

www.penguinrandomhouse.ca

10 9 8 7 6 5 4 3 2 1

CONTENTS

eat better
live better
feel better

Welcome. I'm So Glad You Are Here!

The way you think, the way you behave, the way you
eat, can influence your life by 30-50 years.
—Deepak Chopra

 A few years ago, I was so consumed with back pain from a herniated disk that I lay in bed for months! I had tried chiropractic massage, acupuncture, even surgery—all without success. Only then did I discover the alkaline lifestyle, which completely healed my back pain and led me in a direction I never could have anticipated. I was sooo amazed and excited by the results that I started to read everything I could find about this lifestyle. Soon after, I started a blog so I could spread the alkaline word, which inspired me to become a certified holistic nutritionist and then a certified plant-based cook! The Aries in me wants to shout the news from the mountaintop, which is really what I'm doing by writing this book. So welcome, my friend, I've been waiting a long time to meet you.

To understand why the acid-alkaline balance of the body is so important, it helps to know that all living things are dependent on a balanced pH level. The pH is a measure of the concentration of hydrogen, and it is measured on a scale, where 0 is very acidic, 7 is neutral, and 14 is very alkaline.

Human bodies are alkaline by design, and the terrain in which our cells exist is the environment that must be pH-balanced. In other words, the pH level of our internal fluids—our blood and tissues—affects every cell in our body and is the most important measurement for maintaining our health.

Healthy blood has a pH of 7.365, and the body will do all that it can to maintain this level. However, when we eat a lot of acidic foods or experience a lot of stress, our blood pH can start to drop in very small

PH CHART

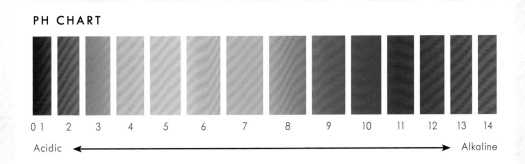

0 1   2   3   4   5   6   7   8   9   10   11   12   13   14

Acidic ⟵   ⟶ Alkaline

increments, which has compounding effects throughout the body. The body then has to put buffering minerals into the blood to restore the blood pH balance to its slightly alkaline state. Over time, if the body cannot adequately neutralize the acids, they accumulate, causing inflammation, which can leave us feeling fatigued, irritable, bloated, or, like me, in acute pain. By balancing out the acids with alkalizing foods, regular exercise, minimal stress, and positive thinking, we gain energy and enjoy better health. What's not to like?

This lifestyle has worked wonders for my own health and the health of my husband and three kids—and it's still working! It's not a trendy diet or a quick-fix plan; *it's a way of living and eating that supports the body—naturally.* All you have to do is understand how the body is designed, then pay attention to the signs it sends you and adjust your habits accordingly.

My ultimate goal is to inspire you to take charge of your health. My secondary goal is to tantalize you with delicious food that is simple, nourishing, and pretty (my fetish), and that will, of course, alkalize and energize your body—for life! This book explains the "why" and guides you through the "how"; and it contains a four-step program to help you—the very same plan that's helped me and my family find long-term energy and health—plus more than 100 of my favorite recipes for tasty, healthy food that will support your lifestyle shift. These recipes are jam-packed with whole foods and lots of veggies. You won't find dairy, eggs, meat (there's one fish recipe), refined sugar, or wheat, and

there's very little gluten. My intention is to share this alkaline lifestyle to help you discover optimal health without feeling like you're missing out on old favorites!

Don't be intimidated by any of the information or recipes. The bottom line is: eat your alkalizing veggies, whichever way you like 'em, and balance your plate with a little acidic food! Play with the recipes: use them as guides and don't fuss too much about the measurements. Worrying about what to eat all the time can cause acidity in your body, so find your groove and just go with it, check in, regain balance. Simple.

However you ended up with this book, you are in the right place. This is the future of health, and I want to be your inspiration on this path to optimal well-being. It will be an amazing journey, and I wish you all the best as you navigate it. Check out the resource section and read, research, and learn all you can. Knowledge will empower you to build a stronger commitment to take charge of your own health. Flip through the pages, find your starting point, and then dig in. Say hi on my blog, www.alkalinesister.com, and let me know how you made out.

A green juice cheer to you from your Alkaline Sister,

Julie

My Wake-up Call

 I tend to overthink and overdo things, and then become overwhelmed. But I've discovered that life can be simple. All of us have the power to choose, and what we choose dictates the change we want to experience. It's a lesson I've learned the hard way.

For many years I suffered from frequent colds, sinus infections, and back spasms. I was a busy mother, wife, and shopkeeper, and I saw my health as the doctor's responsibility, like most of us do. But then the bomb dropped. The universe delivered to me an excruciatingly painful bulging disk at my lowest vertebra. It brings tears to my eyes remembering how helpless I felt lying flat on my back, unable to stand for more than a few minutes before the pressure built up and I felt like I was being stabbed. I tried every modality possible to stop the pain—from acupuncture, laser light therapy, water therapy, and physiotherapy to osteopathy, traditional Chinese medicine, chiropractic therapy, massage, cortisone shots, prescription drugs, and, finally, non-invasive out-of-country million-dollar surgery!

After none of these techniques healed my poor herniated disk, and when a CT scan that I had to practically beg for showed my disk unchanged from 18 months prior, a chance meeting led me to alkaline health coaches. They helped me to realize that *I needed to heal from the inside out* with my own therapy of self-love, determination, visualization, **nutrition**, self-counsel, and exercise. They could guide me, but I needed to do the work a*nd I needed to really want to heal.*

Once I woke up to this realization, I was determined to take control! Somehow I convinced my sister Yvonne to join me in my alkaline lifestyle. Immediately, we learned to make alkaline meals, ingested nutritional supplements almost hourly, and drank gallons of water. Within 3 months, I was finally pain-free and off all my medications. And much to my surprise, I found I had lost 40 pounds. I was alive again!

This journey has given me an amazing gift of insight into how a sick body can reverse the symptoms of disease to become healthy and vibrant. I want to show you how to take responsibility for your own health by following a simple alkaline lifestyle. Simply put, it means:

- going back to basic whole foods and fresh local produce
- focusing on how the foods we eat nourish our mind and body
- finding joy in preparing food and sharing meals
- listening to our bodies and being mindful of what we eat
- balancing our daily meals with alkaline foods
- enjoying some form of daily exercise
- resting and relaxing every single day
- minimizing the stress in our lives

What I've also learned is this: *the body is an amazing machine.* It is incredibly resilient and it can take a lot of abuse before it finally gives in. It also has an amazing ability to heal when you are patient and give it what it needs. Whether you go cold turkey or make a slow transition will determine how quickly you reclaim your health, regain your energy and well-being, and find your natural body weight.

Is the Alkaline Lifestyle for You?

With so many natural therapies and diets available, why choose the alkaline lifestyle? I get asked this question all the time, and the simple answer is that it works. If you need some more reasons, here are a few:

1. **It's sustainable and long-lasting.** Some solutions work well in the short-term, but the guidelines are so strict that you're bound to fail at some point. And when you do, your problems will just come back again—sometimes worse than before. When you live an alkaline lifestyle, however, you consume a higher volume of alkaline foods and fluids than acidic foods, and embrace exercise, rest, and positivity as a way of life, all of which bring your body's pH–acid versus alkaline–into balance and keep it there.

2. **It's healing.** An acidic body is one that is breaking down and showing symptoms of ill health—whether it be a cold, a rash, diabetes, or cancer (see sidebar, page 7). High levels of stress, negative thoughts, lack of exercise, shallow breathing, and poor nutrition are all acid-forming. Changing your diet will improve your body's pH levels and reduce your symptoms to a certain degree, but you must also manage and balance the other pieces of the puzzle to achieve optimal health. As your body releases its acids, you will naturally find the body weight that is healthy for you—either by losing the extra fat cells that have protected your vital organs from overacidity or by properly absorbing the nutrients that will allow you to build lean muscle and healthy tissue. You will also find that you increase your stamina, regain your vibrancy, improve your digestion, ease or eliminate your symptoms, and reclaim your glowing self. This is why I talk about alkalizing your lifestyle, not your diet.

3. **It's economical.** Some programs depend on expensive special foods. With this one, all you need are some fresh veggies, a juicer and/or a blender, and a bit of time. Homegrown veggies are best, but organic ones from the farmers' market or your local grocery store are good too. If you can't afford organic, buy whatever produce is freshest, most nutritious, and to your liking. I like to support my body by using natural supplements, such as alkaline mineral salts, vitamins and minerals, and sometimes enzymes, because they leave me feeling even more vibrant and energetic. Some people prefer not to supplement, and that's fine, although it's very beneficial while regaining balance and speeds up the process immensely. It's true that some of these powders, liquids, and capsules can be expensive, but they're a whole lot cheaper than prescription drugs and long-term health care!

4. **It's simple and flexible.** If you don't like kale, that's not a problem. If your kids won't eat lemons, that's okay. If you want to visit a restaurant with friends, don't worry. Adopting an alkaline lifestyle and keeping disease at bay while living in a vibrant body is completely doable! Enjoy your favorite comfort foods from time to time. Once you understand how the alkaline lifestyle works, you'll know how to find and return to a state of alkaline balance. Just check in with your body, balance your food choices, alkalize, and carry on. Simple as that.

WHAT EXACTLY IS THE ALKALINE LIFESTYLE?

The 4 steps in the next section will help you to set your intention: transition from where you are now (Inspire), cleanse your body (Desire), release deep-rooted acids and toxins (Aspire), and finally establish the routines and practices that enable you to maintain a healthy, balanced alkaline lifestyle (Acquire). When you choose alkaline, here's what you're aiming for.

Nutrition

- **Ideally, 75% of each daily meal should be alkaline foods (see the Alkaline Food Chart, pages 8–9).** Basically these are vegetables—lots of green ones, mostly raw but some warmed and served whole, juiced, or blended, and extremely low-sugar fruit, like lemons, limes, avocados, and tomatoes.
- **The 25% acidic balance can be made up of raw or cooked foods.** You can choose from whole grains, seeds, nuts, legumes, low sugar fruits, plant proteins—and a tiny bit of fresh wild salmon. Use the handy Alkaline Food Chart (pages 8–9) to guide you.
- **Hydrate with 3–4 quarts of alkaline or filtered water throughout the day, every day.** Consuming the purest filtered water you can means less harm to the body from contaminants while eliminating the need for your body to cleanse impurities from regular tap water. Consuming alkalized water means you substantially boost your body's

ability to release acids, thus there is immense benefit to filtering and alkalizing your water. (Learn how to alkalize your water on page 43.) Adding powdered greens is very energizing and releases unwanted toxins; it's a super way to release fat cells too.

Exercise

- **Move your body with daily exercise.** Choose activities such as walking, light jogging, swimming, biking, yoga, tai chi, or rebounding that move your body gently without overstressing it and causing excessive lactic acids to form.

Mental, Emotional, and Spiritual Habits

- **Take charge of your stress and emotions.** When you start to get anxious, frustrated, or angry, adjust your course of action or change the way you respond to situations. Get support, if you need it.
- **Embrace your own health.** Instead of relying on your doctor, take responsibility for your own well-being by monitoring your body and choosing prevention over illness and disease.
- **Live life to the fullest.** Be present, capture the joy around you, and follow your passion.
- **Find your personal harmony.** Learn to live joyfully and to truly love and accept yourself for the wonderful person you are. This is alkaline living at its best!

 ## WHERE SHOULD YOU START?

The alkaline lifestyle is effective because it can support you, no matter where you are with your health. Most people start with **Step 1, the Inspire stage**, because it's a great way to transition gently into this new lifestyle. The goal is to introduce more alkaline foods into your diet, but there are no strict requirements for when or how much.

Some people will want to start with **Step 2, the**

Desire stage. If you have a chronic health issue or you're very ill, you'll want to step up the amount of alkaline foods in your diet as quickly as you can. As with any new health program, consult your holistic health practitioner before you dive right in, but by committing to eating only alkaline foods, you'll be putting only healthy nutrients into your body. A sick body can only benefit from the good stuff!

If you're already eating an abundance of alkaline foods, you might want to skip straight to **Step 4, the Acquire stage.** There, you'll learn to hone and complement your alkaline eating habits with exercise, positive thinking, and emotional balance.

And what about **Step 3, the Aspire stage?** Most people get there from Steps 1 or 2, but it could be your starting place if you're ill but not quite ready to commit to only juices and blended drinks as in the Desire stage.

To decide where you should start, check the list of symptoms below. If you have 3 or more nagging symptoms, you may want to start with Desire. If you have only 1 or 2 not too serious symptoms, maybe lean into the Inspire stage and carry on through each stage successively. Confirm your choice by flipping to the next section of the book. Look for the step you think you'd like to begin with and read the information provided: find out who it's recommended for, how long it might take, and what you'll be aiming for. If in doubt, think about starting with the Inspire stage, and begin a slow lifestyle transition. If you are really ill or have chronic ailments, you might start, as I did, with the Desire stage, but that means going "cold turkey," which is definitely not for everyone! No matter where you decide to begin, check in with your holistic health-care provider. Let them know what you are planning so they can help monitor your progress, support your efforts, and ensure you're on the path to optimal health that is right for you.

Once you've chosen a starting point, adjust your course as needed. Follow the guidelines to stay focused and on track to a more alkaline body, but customize as needed. Ready? Let's start your alkaline journey!

ARE YOU SUFFERING FROM OVERACIDITY?

It's pretty easy to tell when your body is holding on to more acids than it can release. If you suffer from ANY symptoms of ill health, that's a dead giveaway. Dr. Robert O. Young defines 7 stages of degeneration along the road from health to ill-health (acidosis): low energy, irritation, mucus buildup, inflammation, plaque buildup, ulceration, and chronic disease.

If you have even a few of these symptoms, you could most likely benefit from alkalizing your lifestyle. Be honest with yourself and imagine how you'd feel if you no longer felt or experienced these symptoms.

SYMPTOMS OF OVERACIDITY

ARE YOU EXPERIENCING ANY OF THE FOLLOWING?	DO YOU HAVE ANY OF THE FOLLOWING?	DO YOU ...?
❑ Low energy levels/fatigue	❑ Excess weight	❑ Drink coffee/sodas for energy
❑ Brain fog	❑ Fewer than 2 bowel movements/day	❑ Smoke cigarettes
❑ Poor memory	❑ Gas after meals	❑ Eat a lot of sweets, processed, fried or fast foods
❑ Lack of concentration	❑ Indigestion	❑ Drink tap water
❑ Sleepiness after eating	❑ Bad breath	❑ Often exercise excessively
❑ Bloating after meals	❑ Poor skin—acne or skin rashes	❑ Take medications, either prescription or over-the-counter
❑ Mood swings	❑ Constant yeast infections	❑ Use stimulants or drugs
❑ Depression	❑ Mercury fillings	❑ Live in a polluted environment or near a power station or major power lines
❑ Allergies	❑ Joint pain	
❑ Food sensitivities	❑ Cravings for sugar	❑ Look way older than your age
❑ Frequent headaches	❑ Cravings for salt	❑ Cook with a microwave
❑ Coated tongue	❑ Thyroid issues	❑ Carry a lot of stress
❑ Blood-sugar crashes	❑ Strong body odor	
❑ A recent loss or trauma	❑ Frequent need to urinate	

Did you answer yes to any of the above? If so, maybe it's time to give the alkaline lifestyle a shot! The beauty is that you *can* reverse the negative effects of an unhealthy diet and lifestyle if you sincerely have the will to do so. I challenge you to try this lifestyle for 30 days and then decide if you can give up all that you've gained. I have a hunch you'll keep on alkalizing!

ALKALINE FOOD CHART

HIGHLY ALKALINE FOODS

ADD TO YOUR PLATE AS OFTEN AS YOU CAN

veg
- Alfalfa Grass
- Barley Grass
- Broccoli
- Cucumbers
- Dandelion
- Fresh Vegetable Juice
- Jicama
- Kale
- Kamut Grass
- Kelp
- Parsley
- Radishes (black)
- Sea Veg, (kombu, nori, agar, etc.)
- Soy Lecithin (pure)
- Soy Nuts (soaked, dried)
- Soy Sprouts
- Spinach
- Sprouted Legumes
- Sprouted Seeds (sunflower, buckwheat, pumpkin, etc.)
- Sprouts (alfalfa, radish, pea, etc.)
- Wheatgrass

misc.
- Alkaline Water
- Celtic Sea Salt
- Green Drink Powder
- Himalayan Salt
- Mineral Salts

MODERATELY ALKALINE FOODS

veg
- Artichokes
- Arugula/Rocket
- Asparagus
- Broccoli
- Butter Beans

HEAP YOUR PLATE WITH 70–100%

- Cauliflower
- Celery
- Collard Greens
- Endive
- Green Beans
- Green Cabbage
- Horseradish
- Lettuce
- Mustard Greens
- Parsnip
- Peppers, Hot (fresh)
- Pumpkin (raw)
- Radishes (red, white)
- Savoy Cabbage
- Squash (all kinds, raw)
- Spring Greens
- Turnips
- Watercress
- White Cabbage

fruit
- Avocados
- Cherries, Sour
- Lemons (fresh)
- Limes
- Tomatoes (raw)

nuts/seeds
- Hemp Hearts
- Hemp Mylk

oils
- Borage Oil
- Evening Primrose Oil
- Flaxseed Oil

misc.
- Bee Pollen
- Chia/Salba
- Quinoa
- Tea (herbal)

herbs & spices
- Basil
- Cayenne Pepper
- Garlic
- Ginger
- Ginseng
- Oregano
- Sorrel
- Thyme

MILDLY ALKALINE FOODS

ENJOY ON YOUR PLATE OFTEN

veg
- Aubergine/Eggplant
- Beets
- Bell Peppers
- Bok Choy
- Brussels Sprouts
- Carrots
- Cauliflower
- Horseradish (fresh)
- Kohlrabi
- Leeks
- New Potatoes
- Onions (red, white)
- Peas (fresh)
- Red Cabbage
- Rhubarb Stalks
- Rutabaga/Swede
- Yams
- Zucchini

fruit
- Coconuts (fresh)
- Grapefruit (white)

nuts/seeds
- Almond Butter (raw)
- Almond Mylk
- Almonds
- Buckwheat
- Pine Nuts (raw)

oils
- Coconut Oil (raw)
- Fish Oil
- Olive Oil
- Sesame Oil

grains/legumes
- 100% Buckwheat Pasta
- Lentils
- Spelt (grain, flour, sprouted bread)
- White/Navy Beans

most herbs & spices, including:
- Caraway Seeds
- Chives

- Cumin Seeds
- Fennel Seeds

misc.
- Bee Pollen
- Bottled Water (Fiji, Hawaiian, Evian)
- Chicory
- Stevia, green dried

in moderation
- Goat's Milk
- Raw Honey
- Soy Beans/Edamame (organic, fresh, frozen)
- Tofu (organic)

NEUTRAL–MILDLY ACIDIC FOODS

ACCENT YOUR PLATE

veg
- Cooked Vegetables
- Frozen Vegetables
- Sweet Potatoes

fruit
- Acai Berries
- Cantaloupe
- Coconut Mylk
- Currants (fresh)
- Dates (fresh)
- Dragonfruit
- Figs (fresh)
- Goji Berries
- Nectarines
- Pomegranates
- Watermelons

nuts/seeds
- Brazil Nuts
- Flax Seeds
- Hazelnuts (Filberts)
- Macadamia Nuts (raw)
- Pecans
- Pumpkin Seeds
- Sesame Seeds
- Sunflower Seeds
- Walnuts

oils
- Cod Liver Oil
- Grapeseed Oil

grains/legumes
- Amaranth
- Basmati Rice
- Black Beans
- Bulgur Wheat
- Chickpeas/Garbanzo Beans
- Kidney Beans/most beans
- Millet

misc.
- Apple Cider Vinegar
- Hummus
- Rice Mylk
- Tea (green)
- Protein Powders (rice, soy, hemp)

use caution
- Raw Unpasteurized Dairy Milk
- Yogurt (unsweetened)
- Grass-fed Whey Protein Powder

MODERATELY ACIDIC FOODS

JUST ADD A LITTLE TO YOUR PLATE

veg
- Canned Vegetables

fruit*
- Apples
- Apricots
- Bananas (ripe)
- Black Currants
- Blackberries
- Blueberries
- Cherries, sweet
- Cranberries
- Dates (dried)
- Figs (dried)
- Fruit Juice (natural)
- Gooseberries (ripe)
- Grapefruit (pink)
- Grapes (ripe)
- Guavas
- Italian Plums
- Mandarin Oranges
- Mangos
- Mangosteens
- Nectarines
- Oranges
- Papaya
- Peaches
- Pears
- Pineapples
- Raspberries
- Rose Hips
- Strawberries
- Sugar Cane (fresh)
- Tangerines

- Tomatoes (canned purée)

*enjoy 1-2 pc fruit per day as part of your daily acidic consumption once you are alkaline balanced

nuts/seeds
- Cashews
- Pistachios

oils
- Sunflower Oil

misc.
- Soy Cheese
- Soy Sauce/Tamari
- Tap Water

grains/legumes
- Barley
- Brown Rice
- Kamut
- Oats
- Rye Bread
- Wheat Kernel (organic)
- Whole-grain Pasta/Couscous (organic)
- Whole-grain Sprouted Bread/Tortillas (yeast free)

meat
- Buffalo Meat
- Chicken
- Liver
- Ocean Fish
- Oysters
- Wild Freshwater Fish

avoid these
- Alcohol Sugars (xylitol, sorbitol, etc.)
- Beet Sugars
- Butter
- Cereals (most boxed)
- Cheese (all varieties, from all milks)
- Corn, Corn Tortillas
- Corn Oil
- Fruit Juice
- Ketchup
- Margarine
- Mayonnaise
- Milk, Pasteurized
- Molasses
- Pasteurized Juices
- Peanuts/Peanut Butter
- Quark
- Sauerkraut
- Soda/Pop
- Sourdough Bread
- Sugar Cane (dried)
- Tempeh
- Yogurt (sweetened)

HIGHLY ACIDIC FOODS   SKIP YOUR PLATE OR USE EXTREME CAUTION

beverages
- Alcohol (beer, wine, spirits)
- Cocoa
- Coffee
- Fruit Juices (sweetened)
- Tea (black)

sweets
- Artificial Sweeteners
- Brown Rice Syrup
- Candy
- Canned Fruit
- Chocolates
- Dried Fruit
- Jams/Jellies
- Syrup

animal/seafood
- Beef
- Deli Meats
- Eggs
- Farmed Fish
- Pork
- Sardines/Tuna (canned)
- Shellfish
- Veal

misc.
- Deep-fried Foods
- Miso
- Mushrooms
- Pickled Vegetables
- Vinegar
- Yeast

The 4-Step Program

INSPIRE

Easing Your Way into the Alkaline Lifestyle

In a nutshell, you could easily transition to
this lifestyle diet just by increasing your
raw greens or gently warmed veggies to 75% on
your plate at lunch and dinner and adding a
fresh veggie juice in the morning.

Start here if:

- you are curious about this lifestyle and are interested in seeing if it might make a difference for you

- you want to slowly ease into an alkaline lifestyle

- you are craving energy and vibrancy

- you are experiencing ongoing pain and/or minor symptoms of ill-health

- you are carrying excess weight or are underweight

- you eat too many processed foods

Begin with:

- a 50/50 balance of alkaline veggies to acidic foods at each meal, then move to 60/40, and finally a 75/25 balance, which would then lead you to the Acquire stage. Choose from any of the recipes in this book.

Plan on:

- 4–12 weeks in this stage as you slowly lean in to alkaline meals

Think of this Inspire stage as a new beginning. Identifying WHY you want to alkalize and WHAT you hope to achieve is a good place to begin. And you might ask how it's possible to alkalize the blood if it's already alkaline. The answer is that the pH of our blood is kind of like our body temperature—it fluctuates. It's difficult to tell when the pH of our blood is out of whack because this situation is so dangerous that the body immediately reacts by buffering any imbalance. When we deviate from our ideal blood pH by even the smallest amount, the body responds by informing us with signs and symptoms of ill-health. That's its job. Your job is to listen and decide what changes to make to help your body feel how you'd like it to feel.

Your body constantly buffers any acidity in the blood's pH with 4 primary alkaline minerals: calcium, magnesium, potassium and, sodium. If it is not getting these key minerals from alkaline foods, it draws on its emergency sources: your bones and your tissues. As it depletes these mineral stores, symptoms of ill-health start to emerge. Your body fluids will also reflect your acidic state (see box below). The acidic fluids become a breeding ground for microorganisms that proliferate and contribute even more acid to your body, causing inflammation. By alkalizing your lifestyle you'll give your body the buffers it needs so it doesn't have to borrow from its emergency sources, *and* you'll reduce the number of acids in your body overall, creating a more alkaline environment where your cells can thrive. The end result? You'll reclaim your glowing self, increase your stamina, regain your vibrancy, improve your digestion, ease or eliminate your symptoms, and return to a healthy body weight.

The easiest way to check your acidity is to test the pH of your urine and saliva. When there's too much acidity in the body—because of stress, a poor diet, environmental toxins, inactivity, or even too much waste from our own metabolic processes—the body goes into high gear to balance the pH and release as much of the acid as it is able to buffer. The 4 main channels for elimination are the skin, lungs, urinary tract, and colon. When there are a lot of acids in your body, they will be present in your urine and saliva.

1. ASSESS YOUR CURRENT HEALTH

TRY THIS: Measure Your pH

1. Go to your local health store and buy a roll of yellow litmus paper.
2. Find a notebook and a pen and place them in the bathroom.

First thing in the morning, before you eat or drink anything, and then a couple times during the day (around 2 hours after meals, but be consistent about the times if you can), test your saliva. To do this, place a small amount of saliva on the litmus paper (do not put the litmus paper directly on your tongue). Within 10–30 seconds, the paper will change color. Match the color on the paper with the scale that came with it to determine your pH. Record your pH measurement in your notebook, along with the date and time.

> ### ALKALINE BY DESIGN
>
> - The pH of our BLOOD is meant to stay at 7.365, slightly alkaline.
>
> - The pH of our URINE is ideal at 7.2–8.4 and around 8–8.2 during a deep cleanse.
>
> - The pH of our SALIVA should be around 7.2–7.5, and no more than 8.4.

3. Next, test your urine during your second pee of the day, before you have anything to eat, but after a glass of plain water. To do this, wet the litmus paper with just a few drops from your urine stream. Record your pH measurement in your notebook, along with the date and time. Once you begin your transition, you will repeat these tests for 2–3 days (see chart on page 30) to get a sense of how acidic you are. Thirty days of testing is ideal to identify trends and to monitor your improvement.

4. Finally, check your pH score against the chart on page 30. If your score is low, your body is most likely in need of alkalizing and may be overly acidic. This may help you to determine what stage to begin with or how quickly you choose to alkalize your lifestyle.

If you have the opportunity, follow up your saliva and urine pH monitoring with a *live blood analysis*. Make an appointment with a trained microscopist (see Resources). They will take a small sample of your blood and look at it under a high-powered microscope to see what's happening at the cellular level. Healthy blood cells are uniform in shape, size, and color, and live for 120 days in alkaline-balanced plasma. They carry a negative electrical charge, which allows them to circulate freely through our veins. Unhealthy cells circulating in unhealthy plasma appear broken or squashed, and will stick together and die as they lose their electrical charge.

You don't need to have a live blood analysis to know that your body is unhealthy—skin rashes, bloating, pain, and other symptoms will tell you that—but seeing the polluted cellular waste floating around in my blood gave me the motivation I needed to start drinking alkaline greens powders and green juices. I could see that the high electrical charge from these alkaline drinks helped my blood cells to stay healthy and heal my body.

Live blood analysis reveals not only the health of your blood but also the overall condition of your immune system; any imbalances in your hormones and blood sugar; the presence of parasites, mycotoxins, heavy metals, or cholesterol; and any difficulties with digestion and proper absorption of fats, proteins, and other nutrients. It is not a diagnostic tool. It's a good way to assess your current health and then check your progress after 2–4 months of alkalizing your lifestyle.

BLOOD BEFORE, DURING, AND AFTER ALKALIZING THE BODY

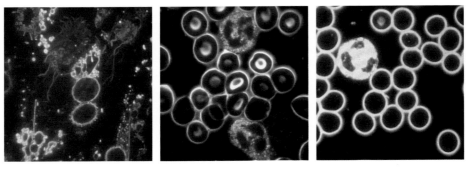

VERY UNHEALTHY   UNHEALTHY   HEALTHY

Digestion starts in the mouth, where teeth chew the food into smaller pieces and salivary glands produce enzymes to start breaking it down into molecules. The tongue moves the food to the back of the throat and down into the esophagus, which gently pushes the food toward the stomach. All of this happens in a matter of seconds!

Once the food moves into the stomach, a sphincter (or muscle) prevents it from flowing back up. Instead, the food is mixed with gastric juices that continue to break down the molecules and kill any bacteria. It may remain here from 4—5 hours with limited nutrient absorption occurring.

From the stomach, the food moves through another sphincter into the small intestine, which averages around 23 feet long, where it is further broken down into basic nutrients. More than 90% of nutrient absorption happens here.

By the time the food passes through another sphincter and reaches the large intestine, which is about 5 feet long, it is mostly waste material, although some water and minerals are still absorbed into the body over the next couple of hours as the waste becomes more solid. Waste then transits through the colon over 30—40 hours, before finally being excreted through the rectum and anus. The entire digestion process takes 40—50 hours.

The Human Digestive System

2. LEARN ABOUT YOUR BODY

Now that you have tested, measured, and understood your body's pH level, it helps to understand what is happening and why so that you'll have a better idea of whether you want to ease into the alkaline lifestyle or go cold turkey like I did. Before you make any final decisions, however, consult with your health-care practitioner and read on to understand how changing your diet affects your metabolism, your digestion, and, ultimately, the health of your cells.

While conventional medicine treats symptoms, the alkaline lifestyle looks at the whole body and treats the root cause—that is, the acidity level of the whole body, which is what's causing the imbalance. Once your body is efficiently buffering and then releasing your excessive acids, the inflammation will begin to subside. As you provide your body with the nutrients it needs to heal—physically, mentally, and spiritually—it will ultimately be able to repair itself and prevent reoccurence. Addressing overacidity is also the answer to the prevention of ill health, for good!

As a nutritionist, I know that food is the delivery method of most key nutrients necessary for optimal wellness, which is why understanding how acidity affects digestion is such an important part of understanding the alkaline lifestyle.

EPIGENETICS

If you have a degenerative medical condition, you most likely created it from within. You may have inherited a genetic weakness that you nurtured with your lifestyle over many years, and the ailment appeared once your body was highly acidic. Fortunately, you can nurture a clean body environment that won't allow disease to thrive. The study of how your internal terrain determines the fate of your cells is called *epigenetics*.

When the body is constantly bombarded with acids it tucks them away in your fatty tissues (and we gain weight when they need more storage space). It also dumps the acids into the lymphatic system, which will do its best to help out; when they're not released due to a lack of exercise, the lymph dumps them back into the blood, triggering a vicious cycle. And when we run low on our stock of acid-buffering minerals and we aren't nourishing our body with lots of alkaline mineral-rich foods, deficiencies occur and serious health problems arise, such as osteoporosis, bone cancer, liver disease, and kidney disease.

The goal of the alkaline lifestyle is to support the body's efforts to maintain its delicate blood and tissue pH by continuously supplying enough buffering minerals to counter the acidic substances the body faces every day.

THE FACTS: Digestion and Gut Health

Digestion is the process that moves food into the body through the gastro-intestinal tract—often called the digestive system—and eliminates waste through the intestines. When this delivery system is working smoothly, enzymes help to break down the nutrients in the food we've eaten into the molecules—fat, proteins, and carbohydrates—that nourish, energize, and heal the body. Through this biochemical process known as metabolism, the fats become fatty acids, the proteins become amino acids, and the carbohydrates become simple sugars, nutrients that the body stores in the liver, muscles, and fat until they're needed to build and restore

cells. Our digestive system, particularly the layer of cells that lines our gut, also protects our entire immune system from the toxins we ingest, which puts it at the core of the health of every other system in the body.

Metabolism and digestion create acids that are naturally buffered when our body is in balance. However, a poor diet, a lot of stress, or excessive exercise can trigger poor digestion. The villi—cellular projections that line the small intestine and increase the surface area for maximum nutrient absorption—can become clogged with acids and mucus. When this happens, not only can nutrients not be properly absorbed but

bacteria and yeast such as *Candida* begin to thrive. They can multiply so quickly that they invade the cell walls of the intestine, creating inflammation, and permeate the villi, causing leaky gut, a condition that occurs when undigested food particles pass into the bloodstream. As we've seen, when our cells, tissues, and organs (our inner terrain) become overly acidic and our body is constantly trying to balance the pH of our blood, inflammation, illness, and disease ensue.

Early signs of overacidity are reflected in your digestive health and should not be left unaddressed. If you are experiencing any of the symptoms in the table, it's important to discuss them with your health-care provider or a holistic nutritionist A protocol of supplements tailored to suit your individual needs would greatly enhance the success of your alkaline journey and speed up your healing. (See also page 41.)

The bottom line: Symptoms of poor digestion are the direct result of an overly acidic lifestyle. Until you regain your alkaline balance, you will find it difficult to get a handle on your symptoms, heal your digestive system, and control the growth of *Candida* and other yeasts in your body. You may also experience such symptoms as fatigue, poor memory, headaches, shortness of breath, joint pain, arthritis, myalgia, environmental illnesses, infection (especially chronic and fungal ones), and pancreatic insufficiency. *Alkalize your food and lifestyle choices and your symptoms will diminish.*

EAT FOR HEALTH AND VITALITY

By eating mindfully, being present in the moment, and appreciating your food and enjoying it socially, you can maximize food's healing and nourishing qualities. What and how you eat are the keys to your physical, emotional, spiritual, and social well-being.

ADDRESSING DIGESTIVE SYMPTOMS OF OVERACIDITY

SYMPTOM(S) →	POSSIBLE CAUSE(S) →	POSSIBLE REMEDY
Bloating, gas, and constipation	• Too few enzymes to properly digest your food (eating too fast, eating too many cooked foods) • Too many different foods in one meal	Practice proper food combining; take digestive enzymes with meals
Heartburn, low energy after meals, smelly bowel movements	• Too little hydrochloric acid (HCL) to digest animal proteins	Take a betaine HCL supplement (page 62) with meals containing animal proteins
Candida (yeast infections and overgrowth) and constipation	• Too many unhealthy bacteria in the gut that allow yeast and fungi to flourish	Purchase an anti-candida supplement kit (see Resources) to combat yeast overgrowth; follow my 4 step program
Food sensitivities and allergies (skin rashes, diarrhea, urinary tract infections, asthma, nausea, etc.)	• A leaky gut that allows undigested food molecules, especially fats and proteins, to escape into the bloodstream where they do not belong • An overload of toxins in the body, which are being pushed out any way possible to protect the vital organs and functions from damage	Do a cleanse to flush toxins from the body
Chronic inflammation of portions of the digestive tract (irritable bowel syndrome (IBS), celiac disease, Crohn's disease, arthritis, etc.)	• Overgrowth of microorganisms due to excessive sticky mucus formed by acidic foods	Follow a supplement protocol from your holistic health—care provider to suit your individual needs; alkalizing your lifestyle will also help immensely

THE CASE FOR CALCIUM

People often ask where I get my calcium since I skip dairy. They don't realize how much calcium—one of the 4 primary alkaline minerals (calcium, magnesium, potassium, and sodium)—is in vegetables, especially the really green ones. The recommended daily allowance for most adults is between 1000 mg and 2000 mg.

• Broccoli comes in at 103 mg/100 g (just under 1 cup)

• Kale at a whopping 249 mg/100g (just under 1 cup)

• Collard greens at 250 mg/100 g (just under 1 cup)

You certainly won't be missing out on your calcium with a diet high in greens. If you are very acidic, I highly recommend a supplement that contains a balanced ratio of alkaline minerals, including calcium to help the body release excess acids.

3. SET YOUR INTENTION

Guess what I love the most about this alkaline lifestyle? That it's a journey. It's a day-to-day approach, choosing health over illness. It's starting from where you are and beginning to make choices that maintain a balance between what you love and what serves your well-being. It's being aware of and knowing how to choose the right path, and when you end up on a side road that doesn't serve you, it's recognizing that and being empowered to get back on track.

Taking responsibility for your health is how you will avoid a nasty diagnosis or escape the one you have. But it isn't easy. Habits are hard to break. Thinking differently takes time, and we often have to be in enough pain that we're forced to make a change. That was me: I made a conscious choice because I *had* to. If you are not experiencing illness but recognize your diet is not optimal, NOW is the time to make the gradual change—before you are in panic mode! Take the first step. Who knows where the awareness will lead? If you are conquering a serious diagnosis, be diligent. Give your body what it needs—the alkaline environment to release the acids, build new cells, and repair the damage—and it will respond.

If you had a condition last year and you still have it this year, it is because you are continually neglecting to provide the nutrients your body needs to build healthier cells to heal your condition. Keep in mind that emotional, mental, and spiritual issues and your stress levels play a role here too.

Ideally, your goal in this Inspire stage is to slowly increase your alkaline intake to 50 percent alkaline-forming foods, with 50 percent acidic-forming foods. If you already do this, then shoot for 60/40 or higher. This gradual progression will help you to create sustainable change while slowly allowing your body to release built-up acidity and toxins as you transition from your existing diet. You can stay here as long as you like, but perhaps give yourself 4–12 weeks to transition.

> ### RENEWAL TIME FOR CELLS
>
> If you improve your nutrient intake, you will quickly regenerate healthy cells.
> - Intestinal lining: 2–3 days
> - Skin: 2–4 weeks
> - Lung cells: 2–3 weeks
> - Red blood cells: 4 months
> - Liver: 6 months

Remember, if you are really ill, consider heading directly to the Desire stage (Step 2, page 33) to give your digestive tract a rest. Consuming only vegetable juices and blended smoothies allows the intestinal lining time to rebuild and heal with a huge boost of concentrated nutrients. Whichever approach you choose—and either is a good option—just consult with your naturopath or health-care practitioner before you begin to be sure you are taking a balanced approach for your overall health. As you set your intention, remember that you are not alone. Many others have worked through their diagnoses and found their way back to a healthy body and a vibrant life. You can do it!

If you do need help, don't be shy. Sometimes we need a little helping hand. I sure did! Enlist an alkaline consultant (see Resources) to support and guide you if you have a more serious medical condition. Encourage a family member or a friend to join you. Know that an alkaline lifestyle will serve you well and guide your

choices, allowing you to live vibrantly. But you have to *want* the benefits, so set your intention, make the commitment by writing it in your alkaline journal, and let's go create some new habits. Remember, Rome wasn't built in a day: replacing old habits with permanent new ones can take up to a year. But it's doable. I'm proof of that, and you can be too!

4. START YOUR TRANSITION

"The area of greatest misunderstanding and confusion in the field of nutrition is the failure to properly understand and interpret the symptoms and changes that follow the beginning of a better nutritional program. What is meant by a better nutritional program? It is the introduction of foods of higher quality in place of lower-quality ones." —Stanley S. Bass

Imagine you are living in an exotic place, tasting new-to-you, delicious, fresh foods that bring you energy. You'd want more. Approach your transition to the alkaline lifestyle this way. Each time you add a new food, make it something delicious, prepare it in a way you like, and even fancy it up with a garnish or by serving it in your favorite pretty bowl. Somehow, food just tastes better to me this way. Or invite a friend to come and taste-test your new recipe. The idea is to find the joy in making these additions to your diet so they become easy for you to embrace.

As you add the new, slowly phase out the old. Initially, don't worry so much about cutting stuff out. Add the good stuff in and then slowly weed out the not-so-good stuff, eliminating it week by week.

To add in:

1. Eat more and more veggies each day. Add nice big salads, serve steamed veggies with meals, snack on raw veggies between meals.
2. Discover new veggies. Check out the Top 10 Alkaline Foods (page 60) and the Alkaline Food Chart (pages 8–9), and try to get your hands on veggies you've never tried before. Need a recipe? Check the Guide to the Recipes (pages 98–99).
3. Get yourself a good blender to make blended greens and green smoothies.
4. Buy a juicer (see page 45) so you can start juicing your veggies, even if it's just on the weekends.
5. Drink more water. Start with 8 glasses per day and work toward 12–16.

To weed out:

1. Day by day and week by week, try to reduce your consumption of drinks and foods that you know are highly acidic and are not serving you, such as alcohol, sweet fruits, dairy, meats, fermented foods, and processed foods.
2. Month by month, try to eliminate these acidic foods completely or make them only rare indulgences. You may find you are no longer interested in them.
3. As often as possible, replace coffee, caffeinated tea (including green tea), alcohol, fruit juice, and soda with water, green juice, or greens powder.

GIVE STEVIA A CHANCE!

You'll notice I recommend stevia often but it's for your own good, especially if you have a sweet tooth. Try the alcohol-free version for less aftertaste and/or blend with another low-glycemic sweetener. You'll reduce your sugar intake immensely if you do and regain an alkaline balance that much faster!

ALKALINE FOOD PYRAMID

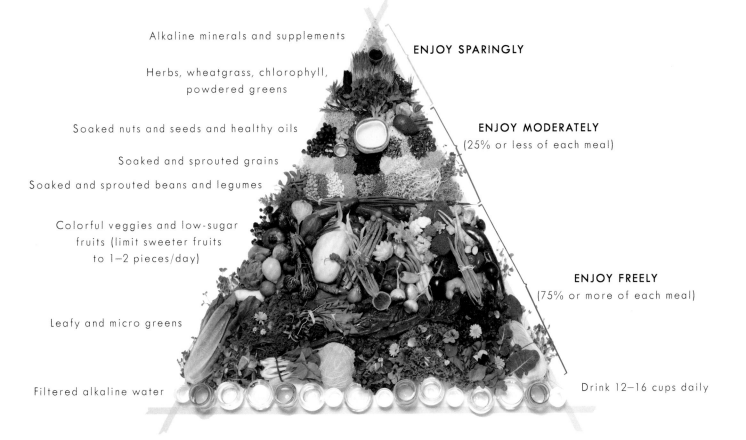

Alkaline minerals and supplements

ENJOY SPARINGLY

Herbs, wheatgrass, chlorophyll, powdered greens

ENJOY MODERATELY
(25% or less of each meal)

Soaked nuts and seeds and healthy oils

Soaked and sprouted grains

Soaked and sprouted beans and legumes

Colorful veggies and low-sugar fruits (limit sweeter fruits to 1–2 pieces/day)

ENJOY FREELY
(75% or more of each meal)

Leafy and micro greens

Filtered alkaline water

Drink 12–16 cups daily

What Foods Are Alkaline?

Need some help? Acidic foods are one or all of the following: processed, low in water content, high in sugar, made from animals, fermented, fried, and overcooked. Alkaline foods are whole, plant-based foods that are high in water content, high in alkaline minerals, and very low in sugar (or have trace amounts).

It can be confusing at first. Cooked foods are more acidic than raw because heat reduces the number of active enzymes; although acidic outside the body, lemons are alkaline in the body because they contain lots of alkaline minerals and little sugar; and even though they are high in water content, bananas and mangos are acidic because they are also very high in

sugar. What healthier choices could you make?

If you are not used to eating whole, unprocessed foods, lean into this Inspire stage at your own pace. **The *three* most important changes you can make to your diet are ADDING more greens and veggies, INCREASING your water intake, and REDUCING the amount of sugar.** The body does not differentiate between natural sugars—like those in fruit, fruit juices, grains, and high-carbohydrate foods—and refined sugars—such as those in pastries, chocolate bars, snack foods, and sodas. When sugars break down, the end products are glucose, fructose, and sucrose, and each behaves the same way in the body regardless of the source. It's acidic, period. Our body does need a bit of glucose to fuel our energy furnaces, but we should only have about *1 teaspoon of glucose circulating in the body at any one time.* So cut out the refined sugars and choose fruits and vegetables that are very low in fructose and other sugars. Once you zap the yeast and your pH is more stable, your sugar cravings will subside and you will be more in control of any indulgence in sweeter fruits.

The good news is that with an alkaline lifestyle, you can completely forget about counting calories or worrying about carbohydrates, fats, and even sugars because it will provide the nutrients in a balance that is ideal for your body to maintain its proper functioning and avoid disease. Consuming abundant quantities of greens and veggies daily is how humans used to eat, and it's what you're aiming for now.

HOW MUCH SUGAR IS IN MY FRUIT?

LOW FRUCTOSE					MODERATE FRUCTOSE					HIGH FRUCTOSE				
FRUIT	F	G	S	T	FRUIT	F	G	S	T	FRUIT	F	G	S	T
Limes	0.2	0.2	0	0.4	Strawberries	2.5	2.2	1.0	5.8	Pomegranates	4.7	5.0	0.4	10.1
Avocados	0.2	0.5	0.1	0.9	Oranges	2.5	2.2	4.2	9.2	Persimmons	5.56	-	-	18.6
Cranberries	0.63	-	-	4.0	Bananas	2.7	4.2	6.5	15.6	Cherries, sweet	6.2	8.1	0.2	14.6
Apricots	0.7	1.6	5.2	9.3	Honeydew Melons	2.96	-	-	7.65	Pears	6.4	1.9	1.8	10.5
Lemons	0.8	1.0	0.6	2.5	Raspberries	3.2	3.5	2.8	9.5	Apples	7.6	2.3	3.3	13.3
Grapefruit	1.2	1.3	3.4	6.2	Dragonfruit	3.2	-	-	8.0	Grapes	7.6	6.5	0.2	18.1
Nectarines	1.37	1.2	6.2	8.77	Cherries, sour	3.3	4.2	0.5	8.1	Jackfruit	9.19	-	-	31.8
Peaches	1.53	1.2	5.6	8.33	Watermelons	3.3	1.6	3.6	9.0	Dried Prunes	12.45	-	-	36.2
Clementines	1.64	-	-	9.5	Blueberries	3.6	3.5	0.2	7.3	Dried Apricots	12.47	-	-	53.4
Plums	1.8	2.7	3.0	7.5	Papayas	3.73	-	-	5.9	Dried Dates (Noor, Deglet)	19.56	-	-	63.0
Cantaloupe	1.8	1.2	5.4	8.7	Blackberries	4.1	3.1	0.4	8.1	Dried Figs	22.93	-	-	50.3
Guavas	1.9	1.2	1.0	6.0	Kiwi	4.3	5.0	1.1	10.5	Raisins	29.68	-	-	59
Pineapples	2.1	2.9	3.1	11.9	Mangos	4.68	0.7	9.9	15.28	Dried Dates (Medjool)	31.95	-	-	64.0

F = Fructose G = Glucose S = Sucrose T = Total Sugars per 100 g

• The body is designed to get energy primarily from glucose and very little from fructose. Fructose is not readily used for energy by your body's cells and takes a long time for the body to convert it into energy. The brain and the muscles all need glucose, not fructose, to function. Excess fructose is converted directly to fat cells.

5. PREPARE FOR THE UNEXPECTED!

If you had a highly acidic diet before, the more diligent you are about adding alkalizing foods to your menus, the more quickly and more often your body will start to release toxins from your body. At the same time, it will build up alkaline buffers to better neutralize acids rather than tucking them away in your tissues.

As you incorporate more alkaline foods, don't be alarmed by changes in your body. You might need to empty your bowels more often, your nose might start to drip, and your skin could break out. You might taste flavors differently and you might even become cranky. Vegetables contain more water than most foods, so you are bound to see changes at the beginning of the cleansing process. If the effects are too harsh, by all means pull back a little on your intake of veggies but don't give up! Your body is designed to metabolize alkaline foods; it is just out of practice!

TRY THIS: Tips to Help Your Body Adapt

1. Drink a glass of water with lemon to alkalize and gently release the toxins more quickly. Dilute your veggie juice with water, by half or more.
2. Consume your veggies throughout the day instead of in one large serving.
3. Practice proper **food combining** to facilitate proper digestion and maximum absorption of nutrients:

   - **Eat fewer different foods at one meal** to make it easier for your body to process them. Initially, choose 3–4 at most.
   - **Consume vegetables with a high water content and low sugar content with everything!** Enjoy them with proteins, healthy oils, and healthy starches.
   - **Limit animal proteins.** If you do eat them, choose organic and eat them only with vegetables that have a high water content: maybe fish with a nice salad and steamed veggies instead of rice or potatoes.
   - **Get your regular doses of healthy fats but enjoy them with green leafy vegetables and low-sugar fruits** like avocado, tomato, lemon, and lime for optimal assimilation. Avoid combining them with acidic animal proteins.
   - **Avoid combining mildly acidic starches with fruit.** For example, enjoy brown rice or sweet potatoes with alkalizing vegetables and/or low-sugar fruits like avocado, tomatoes, lemons, and limes. When your digestion is stronger, you may be able to manage a few berries on a spelt porridge.
   - **Eat fruit on its own or in extreme moderation,** as in salad greens with a few raspberries on top. All varieties of melon are best eaten alone.

Eat more green!

ALKALINE SUBSTITUTES FOR POPULAR ACIDIC FOODS

	INSTEAD OF THESE (ACIDIC)	ENJOY THESE (MORE ALKALINE)
Highly processed foods	• Processed foods are highly addictive and full of chemicals, but largely devoid of nutrients	• Homemade foods • Locally produced artisanal products you can trust
Sugar	• Highly refined sugars poison the blood with acids • All artificial sweeteners are poisonous and carcinogenic and cause aging and dehydration	• Stevia, lucuma, chicory root powder (also called inulin), or yacón syrup in moderation • Coconut nectar or maple syrup in extreme moderation
Table salt	• Iodized salts are laden with chemicals and stripped of minerals	• Himalayan salt, unrefined sea salt, Celtic sea salt
Dairy milk	• Cow's milk is mucus-forming and often full of hormones and antibiotics	• Almond mylk, hemp mylk, hazelnut mylk, coconut mylk
Dairy yogurt	• Dairy yogurt is mucus-forming and often full of hormones and antibiotics	• Unsweetened natural almond mylk yogurt, unsweetened natural coconut mylk yogurt
Dairy cheese	• Dairy cheese is mucus-forming and often full of very concentrated hormones and antibiotics	• Nut cheese (yeast-free), rice mylk cheese (yeast-free)
Animal proteins	• Animal products are highly acidic and take time to digest • Conventional meats are full of hormones and antibiotics and may contain GMOs	• Legumes, nuts, and seeds, organic tofu in moderation • Fresh wild salmon in moderation • Organic or wild meats to a maximum of 4 oz in 1 day, no more than 1–2 times per week
Eggs	• Eggs are highly acidic • Conventional eggs often contain hormones and antibiotics and carry bacteria such as *salmonella*	• Chia seed gel, flax seed gel • Agar agar • Local, organic pastured eggs, preferably not corn-fed, no more than 2–3 times per month
Simple carbohydrates	• Highly refined carbs, e.g., breads, break down into sugars and yeast	• Complex carbs such as whole grains and sprouted grains, no more than 20–30% of your daily intake
Oils	• Processed oils, e.g., corn, canola, safflower, butter, and margarine, are often oxidized, hydrogenated, and too high in omega-6 fatty acids • Many oils are nutritionally destroyed by heat and can cause cell damage	• Coconut oil, cold-pressed organic olive oil, hemp oil, avocado oil, flax oil, grapeseed oil, fish oil
Conventional produce	• Conventional produce is full of pesticides and herbicides and may be genetically modified (GMO)	• Homegrown veggies • Organic or locally grown, unsprayed farm produce (contain 25% more nutrients)
High-sugar and overripe fruits	• Sugar feeds yeasts, which are highly acidic • Improperly digested sugars ferment quickly in the body and contribute to acidity	• Veggies, soaked nuts, seeds • Very low-sugar fruits, such as lemons, limes, white grapefruit, avocados, tomatoes, young coconuts • Moderately low-sugar fruits such as berries, cantaloupes, watermelons, green apples, no more than 1–2 servings and properly food combined

	INSTEAD OF THESE (ACIDIC) →	ENJOY THESE (MORE ALKALINE)
Tap water	• Additives such as chlorine and fluoride are very acidic and damage vital minerals • Often contains contaminants such as pharmaceuticals	• Filtered pure clean water, alkalized and ionized • Add lemon juice to further alkalize
Irradiated dried herbs and spices	• Radiation depletes the nutrients	• Organic dried spices and herbs, choose fresh, if possible
Coffee, caffeinated tea, soda pop	• Caffeine, including that found in green tea, damages cells in the small intestine, which leads to improper nutrient absorption • It takes 8 glasses of water to neutralize the acids in 1 cup of coffee and 32 glasses to neutralize soda pop!	• Filtered pure clean water, alkalized and ionized (add lemon juice to further alkalize) • Herbal teas • Chicory root coffee replacement • A little raw cacao or carob, if desired
Alcohol	• Fermented yeasts are toxic to the brain, dehydrating, and very damaging to the liver • It takes 8 glasses of water to neutralize the acids in 1 glass of wine!	• Flavored waters (page 119) and carbonated water in moderation • Freshly juiced vegetables and fruit make nice cocktails too!
Vinegar and fermented foods	• Soy sauce, cooking wines, tamari, and most condiments contain yeast and fungus	• Lemon and lime juice • Bragg Liquid Aminos • Coconut aminos
Mushrooms and fungus	• These contain mycotoxins and are poisonous to the body, even in low doses like the edible ones	• Sun-dried tomatoes for flavor • Nuts, seeds, and legumes as accents
Peanuts	• These contain mycotoxins, fungus, and toxic molds called aflatoxins and are highly allergenic	• Almonds, brazil nuts, hazelnuts, pecans
Corn	• This food contains large amounts of mycotoxins and fungus and is highly allergenic	• Choose only organic, local, fresh (picked the same day) corn and eat it in extreme moderation (i.e., 4–5 cobs over the season)
Blue green algae, spirulina, chlorella	• These contain toxins, and they thrive in acidic ponds and obtain vitamin B12 from bird droppings	• Wheatgrass, barley grass, oat grass • Super-greens powder or liquid chlorophyll • Broccoli greens powder
Microwaved foods	• Electromagnetic radiation destroys nutrients	• Use a dehydrator to dry or warm food to a maximum temperature of 118°F to maintain its life force • Use a high-speed blender to warm soups to 118°F, if desired • Use the lowest temperatures for cooking
Stored foods	• Wheat, potatoes, and eggs harbor fungus and aflatoxins due to prolonged and improper storage beyond their growing season	• Spelt, kamut • New organic potatoes in moderation • Organic sprouted grains • Fresh, local, organic, pastured eggs in moderation

So, to recap: Keep animal proteins away from acidic starchy foods and keep fruit away from pretty much everything to avoid fermentation in the gut.

Acknowledge your cravings whenever you experience them, but beat them with these strategies:

- Drink a glass of lemon water instead of eating something.
- Replace sweets with snacks sweetened with stevia or cinnamon.
- Replace crunchy chips or crackers with kale chips or crunchy vegetables.
- Replace creamy butters, yogurts, and milks with smoothies, nut mylks, or avocado pudding.
- Replace unhealthy salty snacks with raw nuts tossed with olive oil and Himalayan salt, or use flavor salts spray (see Resources) on your tongue.
- Enjoy cinnamon to balance your blood sugar levels and alleviate cravings.
- Distract yourself with a cup of herbal tea, a book, or a room full of candles.
- Brush your teeth after dinner so you won't be tempted to eat again.
- Take your own raw nuts, nutritious wraps, and bottled water when traveling or even just leaving the house!
- Choose herbal teas or, in a pinch, a decaf almond mylk latte when going for coffee with friends.
- Recognize which emotions trigger your cravings and work with your health practitioner to address them.

FERMENTED FOODS = TOXINS

Yeast, fungus, and mold are found in fermented foods such as alcohol, vinegars, soy sauces, tempeh, and kombucha. Our ancestors may have eaten a small amount of naturally fermented foods and discovered that the probiotic bacteria helped their digestion. Today, however, our diets are highly acidic and our bodies are overgrown with yeast. In this environment, excessive use of fermented foods creates sticky mucus that escalates symptoms of disease. They can also colonize in the gut, overwhelming and crowding out the healthy bacteria there. Alternatively, probiotic supplements inoculate healthy bacteria without yeast, fungus, and mold and can be beneficial for short-term use.

So why do we keep hearing about the health benefits of fermented foods? If you are bloated, gassy, burping, and experiencing stomachaches, 1–2 teaspoons of organic apple cider vinegar or a small serving of naturally fermented sauerkraut used therapeutically with your meals can improve your digestion over a few days. Once your lifestyle is alkaline balanced, you won't need these fermented foods and avoiding these types of foods is recommended.

This Inspire stage is all about getting used to eating more alkaline foods. You'll find that the more you begin to add, the less you will desire your old favorites. This may happen slowly, which is fine, but chances are that just being aware of the effects of acidic foods will help you to make better food choices. Be sure to find your path on this journey in a way that empowers you instead of limiting and restricting yourself. Listen to your body, look for the positive changes to your health, and let those be your guide for adopting this alkaline lifestyle.

6. EMBRACE THE BENEFITS

I'm the first to admit that I'm not a perfect alkavorian. My goal is to feel great each and every day and know that I am truly healthy inside and out, which is why I still monitor my success maybe once or twice a month (never obsessively) with home pH tests and a few times per year with my live blood analysis. As you transition to this lifestyle, monitor the changes in your body by measuring the pH of your saliva and your urine. I suggest following the schedule in the chart on page 30. At the very least, test your morning pH daily (steps 1–3) and note your progress for 30 days. After that, only test your pH periodically.

Since the Inspire stage is designed to help you ease into the alkaline lifestyle, it might take some time to notice the benefits if you are highly acidic. But bit by bit, you should start to feel a little more energized and a little less bloated, think more clearly, and experience fewer mood swings. You may shed a few pounds and taste more subtle flavors. If your symptoms of ill-health don't disappear overnight, don't be discouraged. Know that your body intuitively knows how to heal itself and that balancing your pH will lead to proper cell growth, better overall health, and a much-improved quality of life.

Balance
your ph!

MONITOR YOUR BODY'S PH

STEP	WHAT	WHEN	OPTIMAL PH	WHAT'S HAPPENING
#1	Daybreak saliva	Upon rising: Before doing, or eating, or drinking anything at all, or even brushing your teeth	7.0–7.2+	Shows how effective your body's response is to acidic foods you may have consumed in the last 24 hrs, your emotional state, and your lifestyle overall. This is when the body's pH is typically the lowest, as it is releasing excess acids.
#2	Daybreak urine	Upon rising: Before doing, or eating, or drinking anything at all	7.0+	Shows how many accumulated acids your body's buffers collected and sent to your bladder overnight from your lifestyle as well as from your body's natural functions, such as digestion. This pH should improve from your daybreak urine test.
#3	2nd urine	While you get ready for the day: After drinking a glass of water but before eating anything	7.2+	Shows directly whether your alkaline buffers are working effectively or whether they are very depleted and need support; this is the most important measure of the day as your body has flushed overnight acids and now has leveled out.
#4	Post-meal saliva	5 mins after eating an alkaline breakfast	7.2–8.4	Your daybreak saliva score should improve.
#5	Post-meal urine	5 mins after eating an alkaline breakfast	7.2–8.4	Your daybreak urine score should improve.
#6	Midday saliva and urine	Mid-afternoon: About 1 hr away from food and drink (plain water is fine)	7.2–8.4	You are looking to maintain a level pH.
*	Quick saliva test 1	Eat a handful of almonds at any time of day and then test your saliva immediately	8.4	Shows, in an alkaline-balanced person, that your alkaline buffers are working effectively and that you have adequate reserves.
*	Quick saliva test 2	Eat a piece of high-sugar fruit, such as pineapple, or worse yet, some sugar		If your saliva skyrockets to 8.0, it shows your buffers are highly depleted and are scrambling to balance this acidic intake.

7. WHAT'S NEXT?

Once you become aware of your power to heal and the ability to guide your own well-being, you will probably become more conscious of the world around you. My journey, which started as a means to heal my back, led to complete relief from pain and massive weight loss. I became acutely aware of my food sources: I started to choose unprocessed, local, organic, sustainable, fairly traded, and non-GMO whenever possible, and gradually eliminated all meat and animal products from my own diet, though my family still eats some organic meat. I also began to switch up and eliminate the chemical cleaners and potions in my home and to be more selective with my personal care products. I even switched careers to get rid of my stressors and follow my new passion for nutrition!

As a family, we are now far better at recycling at home because we are more conscious of our planet. We exercise more often and we choose our restaurants based on how locally they shop for their ingredients and how wholesome the food is. We even travel differently: we choose more eco-conscious hotels with healthier restaurant options and we tote our chia seeds with us! Our entire outlook on living an alkaline lifestyle has expanded. Personally, my intention is to BE the example, to LIVE the lifestyle to inspire others to do the same. I'm certainly not perfect at it, but I am living proof of the difference it can make.

Are you inspired to continue alkalizing and to make it your lifestyle? Stick with the Inspire stage for as long as you need, but when you're ready, read on to learn how to fully cleanse your body and set yourself up for long-term, life-affirming health.

TRY THESE 3 RECIPES
to get inspired!!

Lean into Green Juice (page 105)

Simmered Quinoa with Spiced Almond Mylk and Sweet Potatoes (page 133)

Angel Hair Zucchini Pesto with Roasted Cherry Tomatoes (page 171)

DESIRE

Cleansing and Detoxifying Your Body

Juicing and blending your food gives
your digestive tract the little nap it needs
to rejuvenate. A healthy digestive tract is
vital for reaching optimal wellness.

Start here if:

- you have just successfully completed the Inspire stage and are ready to deep-clean your body (way to go!)

- you are motivated and ready to make a significant, immediate, positive change to your current lifestyle and want to get down to business!

- you have a medical condition and the support of your health-care practitioner and perhaps an alkaline coach to fast-track the alkalizing process

- you are living an alkaline lifestyle but have done a bit too much zigging and zagging and need to regain your alkaline balance

Aim for:

- 100% juiced or blended alkaline foods at every meal. Emphasize purely alkaline juices—after all, this is the veggie juice feast!

Plan on:

- 1–3 days, or as long as 1–2 weeks (supervised), depending on your current state of health. If you currently eat a lot of processed foods, I highly recommend at least 2–5 days of "pre-cleanse" in the Inspire stage, gradually adding in veggies and increasing your water intake before you begin.

A word of caution: If you are pregnant or nursing, it is *not* advisable to cleanse and detox your body, as toxins are released from tissues into the blood, which will flow through the placenta or reach your baby via your breast milk. Eat a balanced alkaline diet during and after your pregnancy, but save the juice feast until after you are through breastfeeding. Don't be afraid to include one or two green juices or green smoothies per day, though.

Think of the Desire stage as giving your digestive tract a break. When you're short on sleep, you feel burnt out, sluggish, and grumpy, right? Even when it's healthy, your digestive tract is always working away in the background. It labors even when you sleep, only at a much slower pace. So, if you're eating lots of acids, you're making it work extra hard all the time and it never gets a nap, which is why it often starts to get irritable.

Consuming pure alkaline juices and blended vegetables gives your digestive tract the well-deserved little rest it needs from breaking down foods so it can take out the trash that's been accumulating and heal. This is the way to make a fresh start for a clean, alkaline-balanced environment. But it can be a shock! My first veggie juice feast lasted a full 3 days. I didn't find it easy, but I can honestly say that it's the best thing I ever did for my health. I still do regular feasts—sometimes just for a day, sometimes much longer—and it always makes me feel squeaky clean and re-energized.

If you are highly acidic, flushing your body with all that healthy, nourishing liquid is going to get your body revved up. It's going to escort as many acids and toxins as it can from your body—and quickly, before that supply of healing fluids comes to an end. So try to get lots of rest and stay close to the washroom to get rid of all those nasties. Prepare yourself mentally by making a commitment to your health so that you transition from the feast right into new healthy lifestyle habits instead of returning to your old ones. Once you've experienced the benefits of a cleanse, though, you'll likely be back for more!

1. EDUCATE YOURSELF

Juice Cleanses 101

Juice cleanses and fasts have been used for centuries by people wanting to improve and optimize their health. So, it's safe to say that if some folks consider it a "fad," then it's been a very long-lasting one indeed! Of course, we have learned a lot over time about how best to go about doing them safely and obtaining maximum benefit from them.

This veggie juice feast is not about starving the body, it's about feeding it with much-needed nutrients that help remove accumulated toxins. It means nourishing the body with the juice of a wide variety of vegetables and low-sugar fruits that contain live enzymes and readily absorbed micronutrients and macronutrients (vitamins and minerals) and phytonutrients (also called healthy plant chemicals)—and that would need nearly 20 times what you could possibly eat in solid form in one sitting. It's considered a type of fast because your body is not obtaining fiber, or the protein or calories it may be used to. There's no restriction on the number of juices you can have; the goal is to consume juices as you become hungry throughout the day rather than just drinking as much as you can.

The combination of eliminating all processed foods and sugars and consuming only juiced vegetables instead of solid foods gives the digestive system a real break and an opportunity to heal. So even though they are good for you, try to minimize the amount of carrots, beets, or sweet potatoes you consume during this stage. These veggies are high in sugars and/or starches that are acid-forming. During this step, avoid fruit for the same reason. The focus here is on consuming water, vitamins, minerals, phytonutrients, live enzymes, and healthy fats—all of which are found in alkaline veggies. Incorporating blended vegetables alongside the juices is recommended if you choose to cleanse for longer than 3 days or if drinking juices alone is too hard.

4 ALKALINE ESSENTIALS TO RAISE & MAINTAIN YOUR PH LEVEL

To function properly and buffer acids, especially during a feast, the body needs the following every day:

- **chlorophyll:** aim for at least 70% green veggies (the balance in a variety of other colors, e.g., tomatoes, fennel, purple cabbage) at every meal, every day. Try fresh green leafy vegetables like spinach, sprouts, and kale, and fresh green vegetables like broccoli, peas, and asparagus. In addition, have a daily ounce of fresh wheatgrass, or substitute 1 teaspoon of greens powder per 4 cups of water, 3–4 times per day.

- **water:** aim for a minimum of 12–16 eight-ounce glasses per day.

- **healthy oils:** aim for 3 tablespoons per day (1 tablespoon per meal) of raw, plant-based oil, like olive, coconut, avocado or grapeseed. In addition, have 1 teaspoon per day of omega oil, like flax, hemp or fish. Avoid heating all oils, except grapeseed and coconut.

- **alkaline mineral salts:** aim for 1 teaspoon twice per day, upon rising and at bedtime, with a balanced blend of the 4 primary alkaline minerals, calcium, magnesium, potassium, and sodium (see Resources).

THE FACTS: Elimination of Acids and Toxins

How exactly does the detoxification process work? The body creates acidic waste as a byproduct of its normal functioning. Toxins and acids are also brought into our bodies or created inside us by the air we breathe, the food we eat, the water we drink, and the thoughts we think. Many of these acidic substances are processed and eliminated regularly by the lungs, the skin, the liver and kidneys, the intestines, and the lymph nodes. Our body binds some of the toxins that accumulate in our cells with fat cells to keep them from interfering with our vital organs. Most of the time, the body simply eliminates these acids and toxins on its own. However, when it is completely overloaded and can no longer manage, we begin to feel the uncomfortable effects of overacidity (page 7).

As our nutrient absorption is compromised by these excessive acids and toxins, mucoid plaque builds

up on the colon walls (dehydration and constipation also contribute to plaque). This plaque hardens, and narrows the passages, making it difficult for the muscles in the colon to fully contract and relax, an action called peristalsis that moves food through the colon, and this causes more plaque to accumulate, which can lead to some serious health problems in the colon.

Showering the colon with hydration and nutrition helps to break down the buildup so that the concentrated nutrients can reach the organs that require support and properly nourish all the cells in your body. Consuming juices and blended veggies also means digestive energies can be redirected to cleansing, metabolizing, nourishing, and building healthy new cells to support your alkaline journey. But remember, your body never stops eliminating acids—it is built to detoxify! Here's what's going on in your body when you embark on a veggie feast.

DAYS 1 TO 3: Purifying the Colon and the Blood

- all the nourishing alkaline fluids will move solids through the digestive tract, loosening and showering away plaque and other debris that prevents proper nutrient absorption
- nutrient-rich vegetable juices will flood all your cells with nourishing vitamins and minerals, which allows the blood cells to safely release and expel their toxins and the intestinal lining to create healthy new cells
- your urine and saliva pH will most likely measure below 7.2, especially on the morning tests, indicating that your body is indeed releasing acids; this is to be expected—note it in your journal
- adding alkaline-buffering mineral supplements (page 41) will help to neutralize (buffer) even more acids and carry them from the body
- your blood begins to release acids and toxins

- nutrient-rich vegetable juices continue to flood your cells with nourishing vitamins and minerals, which allows your cell tissue to safely release its toxins into the bloodstream
- your urine and saliva pH may still measure below 7.2 on the various tests, indicating that your body is continuing to release acids; you may also see it begin to improve, which is to be expected—note it in your journal
- the vitamins, minerals, and other nutrients will begin to enter the cells, tissues, and organs to heal and help produce healthy new cells
- all the alkaline fluids will continue to dislodge compacted waste from your colon, release and expel the toxins from your bloodstream and lymphatic system, and discourage acids from accumulating in the body
- as the more deeply rooted acids and toxins are trapped in your cells and then released and carried away as part of the cleansing cycle, they will show up as debris in your bloodstream as they are filtered through and sometimes appear as sadness, anger, depression, frustration, and/or pains or other symptoms from past injuries or illness

- if you are experiencing chronic symptoms, inflammation, or pain, it can be very helpful to carry on with your veggie feast beyond 7 days to release and expel the deep-seated acids and toxins that are contributing to your distress; be sure to have a professional health practitioner monitor your progress, and perhaps join a cleansing support group
- nutrient-rich juices, as well as blended veggies, continue to hydrate your cells and nourish them with micronutrients, protein, fat, carbohydrates, and electrolytes to further release and expel the toxins found deep in your cell tissue
- your urine and saliva pH may still measure below 7.2 on the various tests and will gradually begin to climb as you continue cleansing and releasing acids, depending on your degree of acidity
- the vitamins, minerals, and other nutrients will continue to facilitate the renewal of healthy new cells in your intestinal lining (to improve digestion); in your blood, tissues, and organs (to ease your symptoms); and in your skin (to make you glow!)

2. SET YOUR INTENTION

This Desire step is all or nothing: it means consuming 100% alkaline, nothing less. By committing to this veggie feast, you are choosing to clean up the toxins in your body and start living with energy, clarity, and optimal health. How long you follow this veggie feast is up to you. Even if you only do 1 or 2 days, give yourself a pat on the back. No matter how long you decide to cleanse for or how successful you are, your body will most certainly be cleaner than when you started!

Feasting for 3 full days will cleanse your blood right now. To continue to see the benefits of your cleansing efforts, maintain a high-alkaline diet by moving into the Aspire stage, and continue to hydrate well to allow your tissues to slowly release their acidic load. If you plan to do a 3-day feast, start on a Friday so your most intense detoxifying happens over the weekend.

Maintaining this veggie feast for longer than 3 days will eliminate the toxins in your tissues more quickly (and perhaps more intensely) and cleanse the acidic load that gets dumped into the blood from the tissues. The longer you go, the more quickly and effectively your body lets go of the acids, especially those buried deep in the tissues, and keeps cleansing the blood. If you plan to do a 7-day veggie feast (or longer), start on a Wednesday so your lower-energy days fall on the weekend. If you can take some days off work during this time, that's even better.

Either way is fine. You can choose before you begin or decide along the way what feels right for your veggie feast. As you release acids and toxins, pay attention to how you feel, how your pH measures, and how much support, pampering, and rest you are giving your body. Cleansing too fast and for too long can be harmful to the body. Follow your body's cues and adjust accordingly by slowing it down, stopping altogether for the time being, or carrying right on. If you plan to continue beyond 7 days, or if you are healing from a serious illness, consult with your health-care practitioner, a holistic nutritionist, and perhaps an alkaline consultant (see Resources) for proper support and guidance. However long you choose to cleanse, the veggie feast is an important part of alkalizing your lifestyle.

3. GET READY TO FEAST ON VEGGIES!

The more work you can do ahead of time to get ready for your cleanse, the easier it should be. Having all your tools and foods on hand; enlisting support from family, friends, and co-workers; and knowing what to expect can help you get the most from your veggie juice feast.

TRY THIS: Turn Your Kitchen into a Veggie-Feasting Zone!

1. Dust off, borrow, or buy a good-quality juicer, blender, or NutriBullet (see Resources).
2. Stock up on lots of fresh, local, organic, raw, mostly green veggies from your garden, the farmers' market, or your produce store.
3. To save time, wash, cut, and pack 4–5 days' worth of veggies in reusable green vegetable bags.

TRY THIS: 3 Ways to Prepare Your Mind and Body for the Veggie Feast

1. Assess your current alkalinity by measuring the pH of your urine and saliva. Record the results in your notebook.
2. Affirm your commitment to undertaking a deep cleanse and enlist the support of friends and family. Write your intention in your notebook.
3. Begin to clean up your diet by introducing green salads and raw veggie sticks, drinking more water, and cutting back on sugars such as fruit juices and breads. Stick with this pre-cleanse for 2–3 days. (If you discover that this is too tricky for you, return to the Inspire stage and lean into these eliminations more gradually. At the same time, make your very best effort and imagine how you'll feel once your symptoms begin to subside.)

SCHEDULE FOR A 3-DAY PRE-CLEANSE

ADD ⟶ ELIMINATE

	ADD	ELIMINATE
DAY 1	• 1–2 glasses of water • At least 1 raw green salad • A good night's rest	• All meats, poultry, and seafood • At least 50% of your usual processed foods (e.g., cheese, most condiments, storebought sauces and spreads, frozen foods, pastries, and desserts)
DAY 2	• 1–2 glasses more of water • At least 2 raw green salads • Stevia	• All refined sugars, including fructose, glucose, sucrose, and lactose • Maple syrup, honey, and natural fruit juices • All sugar substitutes such as sucralose and aspartame
DAY 3	• 1–2 glasses more of water • At least 2 raw green salads • At least 1 portion of steamed vegetables	• 100% of your usual processed foods (e.g., breads, crackers, pastas and cereals, butter and margarine, coffee and tea)

To supplement or not to supplement?

Many folks believe that using supplements during a cleanse is unnecessary because the juices and smoothies are already high in nutrients. However, the goal of the veggie feast is to super-alkalize your body, dump acids from your cells and tissues, and empty the colon of accumulated waste. Yes, the juices and smoothies *will* nourish your body, but the 4 key alkaline supplements (page 41) will jump-start the release of acids while helping you to maintain a healthy alkaline balance. As my alkaline coach said, "What might take 3 years to detox with whole healthy foods can be hastened to 3 months with alkaline supplements and a veggie feast!!" They worked wonders for me, and I still use them every day. But of course, you *can* cleanse without supplements and still get good results, so don't panic if you can't find these or choose not to use them.

TRY THIS: Boost Your Veggie Feast Results with Alkaline Supplements

1. Stock your cupboard with the 4 key alkalizing supplements: pHour salts (alkaline mineral salts), greens powder, healthy oils, and liquid vitamins and minerals. See Resources or visit your local natural foods store.

2. To help remove the harmful mucoid plaque that builds up on the colon with an acidic lifestyle, try a mild herbal laxative or a bulking laxative such as 1 tablespoon ground flax or chia seeds stirred into your juice or smoothie once each day. These fibers can really help get things moving, so reduce the amount or take it on alternating days if you find it too effective. Or sip a laxative tea for an even gentler nudge. Check with your health-care provider before using any laxative.

3. Introduce these supplements as directed by your health-care provider.

4 KEY ALKALINE SUPPLEMENTS

SUPPLEMENT →	DESCRIPTION →	REASON FOR USE →	RECOMMENDED DOSAGE
Mineral salts (see Resources)	A combination of 4 powerful carbonate salts (sodium bicarbonate, magnesium chloride, potassium bicarbonate, and calcium chloride)	To build up and maintain the body's supply of alkaline-buffering minerals, which support the release of acids	1 tsp, added to 1 cup of water, twice per day
Greens powder	A blend of vitamin- and mineral-rich concentrated greens (emphasize grasses rather than spirulina or chlorella)	To alkalize, energize, and nourish cells as they balance the body's pH level, especially the blood cells	1 tsp per 4 cups of water (aim for 12–16 cups of water per day)
Healthy oils	Any or a combination of cold-pressed organic oils, such as flax, hemp, coconut, olive, avocado oil, and/or a high-quality fish oil	To bind with acids and escort them from the body and to provide the body with essential fatty acids (omega-3, 6, and 9) that support brain health and provide energy	2–3 Tbsp per day, by the spoonful or added to blended drinks, with a minimum of 1 tsp per day of omega oil, like fish, flax or hemp
Liquid vitamins and minerals or colloidal vitamins and minerals	Any or a combination of vitamins, minerals, and fatty acids, such as the B-complex, including cobalamin (vitamin B12), ascorbic acid (vitamin C), chromium, and caprylic acid	To deliver easily absorbed essential nutrients to the body to support detoxification, healthy cell renewal, and proper functioning of the body	Taken under the tongue, as directed by your holistic health-care provider

ADDITIONAL ALKALINE SUPPLEMENT: DURING CLEANSE ONLY

SUPPLEMENT →	DESCRIPTION →	REASON FOR USE →	RECOMMENDED DOSAGE
Laxatives and fiber	A mild supplement preparation containing 1 or more of magnesium oxide, slippery elm, marshmallow, and ginger root, OR 1 Tbsp ground flax or chia seeds, hydrated, OR a mild laxative tea of dandelion root, chickweed, or milk thistle	• To help loosen colon mucus, break it up, and then bind to fecal matter, allowing for easier elimination and release • Fiber binds to released toxins and flushes them out	As directed on the package for teas and herbal laxatives, or stir 1 Tbsp ground flax or chia seeds into your juice or smoothie once each day

4. PREPARE FOR THE UNEXPECTED!

Each of us is unique and our bodies all deal differently with the process of detoxing. As the body releases acids and toxins from the blood and, especially, from deep within the tissues, we can anticipate some discomfort. Exactly how much and what kind varies from person to person.

Initially, you may feel hunger pangs. If you do, then drink more veggie juice or blended veggies. You should never go hungry! Your body is getting fewer dense calories than usual but it will be soaking up the nutrients it has been craving. Because these drinks are essentially pre-digested, especially the juice, it doesn't take a lot of effort to metabolize them, which means that your stomach will empty quickly and you may feel hungry once again.

After my daily morning juice, I am usually ready for something else within 15–30 minutes. That's when I drink some alkaline water, followed by a smoothie. In this Desire stage, you can consume as many alkaline veggie drinks as you like, but be sure to dilute your juice with at least 25% water—to avoid an intense release of toxins. Pure, filtered, mineralized, and alkaline water is the healthiest, most beneficial water we can drink: make alkaline water using a charcoal filter, reverse osmosis filter, or ionizing filter. In a pinch, use filtered water and add alkalizing minerals, a squeeze of lemon juice, or a salt sole (see sidebar, page 43). In a real pinch, drink regular water, rather than none at all.

Since the cleanse is about cleaning your digestive tract, including your colon, you will want to be near the washroom during your veggie feast, especially if it's your first one. You could be in there 7–10 times every day during the feast. Everyone's response time is different; if things don't start to move on the first day, you should see progress on the second and the third days. If not, you'll want to try using the fiber

supplement or a natural laxative to get things going. It's not a pretty thing, but let go, acids, let go!

The toxins and acids will choose to escape via your sweat, breath, urine, and feces, You may experience skin rashes, acne, bad breath, diarrhea, flu- and cold-like symptoms, or headaches. Generally, wherever your body has a genetic weakness or a historic pattern of illness, the toxins will try to escape via that weakness. This response to releasing acids is called a *healing crisis*. A mild crisis is normal, but it should not be unbearable. The more acidic the body, the more likely it is that a crisis will occur as there is more to detox.

You can choose how quickly to detox, but don't suppress the release of these toxins. If your symptoms become too much, slow down the process by drinking more water with lemon juice, paring back or spacing out your supplements, and perhaps incorporating more blended veggies instead of juiced ones. If you end up with a skin rash, let it run its course, opting for natural soothing remedies rather than running out for pharmaceuticals. It will pass.

After the first 3 days, you may experience an emotional cleansing too. You might start to cry out of the

---

HYDRATE FOR LIFE

Water makes up:

- 90% of our lungs
- 84% of our blood (and 98% of our blood plasma)
- 76% of our brain

Water is also critical to our digestion, circulation, and elimination processes.

Every day, the average person *loses 10 cups (2.5 liters)* of water through daily living. So eating veggies with a high water content and *hydrating with 12–16 cups of alkaline water* are absolutely key to carrying nutrients to our cells, eliminating toxins from the body, and balancing our blood pH.

blue, become irritable, or swing wildly between joy and anger. This is normal, so warn your family and then let your body flow with these emotions. Journaling during the cleanse is an effective way to process emotional experiences. If you choose to cleanse for longer than 3 days, you may find that old injuries or health issues resurface for a brief time and then subside as your body flushes the fascia (connective tissues) where those memories are buried.

Three to 7 days is an effective length of time for a juice cleanse (although you can go longer with supervision). The release is generally most intense in the first few days. If you are highly acidic when you begin to take your alkaline juices and supplements, your pH should drop—theoretically. However, what often happens is that your alkaline-buffering minerals are on high alert, working their butts off to buffer and escort the strong acids out of your body without harming your tissues along the way! So your pH will show an alkaline measure since these buffers are very present in your urine. If you are only minimally acidic, the opposite may occur. Your pH will show very low, at around 6.8, indicating that your buffers are not being called upon since there isn't much acid-buffering work to do. As you lessen your toxic load and become more alkaline balanced, your pH measurements will show trends that are more reflective of your daily choices.

A word of caution: Whatever your circumstance, if you want to cleanse for 2 weeks or more, do so only under the guidance of your health practitioner, an alkaline coach, or an experienced juice feasting group that offers regular monitoring and communication for support and motivation (see Resources).

MAKE YOUR OWN HOMEMADE ALKALINE WATER

A salt sole is not only a cool thing I learned to make in nutrition school, it's a concentrated mineral salt solution that supports health in myriad ways. By taking 1 teaspoon in a glass of filtered water each morning, you are adding 84 essential ionized minerals to help stabilize your pH and your oxidative stress levels. It can also dissolve and eliminate sediments, such as arthritis calcifications and kidney and gall bladder stones, while reducing your cravings for addictive foods. Salt is a natural anti-bacterial and fungicide—and it doesn't spoil or go bad.

How to Make It and How to Take It

- Fill a quart-sized mason jar ⅓ full with unrefined natural salt and fill it with filtered water, leaving 2 inches of space at the top.

- Cover the solution with a plastic (not metal) storage cap, shake it, and allow it to sit for 24 hours.

- If all the salt crystals have dissolved, add a little more salt. When the salt no longer dissolves, the sole is ready.

- Add 1 teaspoon of this salt sole to an 8-ounce glass of filtered water each morning. Taste it. If it tastes like saltwater, it is perfect. If it's too salty, dilute it with some plain filtered water. Add a squeeze of fresh lemon juice and you now have mineralized alkaline water.

- Store your sole, covered, at room temperature. Its anti-bacterial and anti-fungal properties will help it last indefinitely.

WILD ABOUT WHEATGRASS?

Did you know that a 2-ounce shot of wheatgrass is equivalent to 5 pounds of vegetables? It is a detoxing powerhouse for the liver and the blood, helps to neutralize acids and toxins, and is a complete protein, but it is an acquired taste. Try a shot at a juice bar, press your own and add it to your favorite juice recipe, or look for freeze-dried wheatgrass powder (see Resources) or frozen shots at your health food store.

5. START YOUR VEGGIE FEAST

Let's get serious! As you begin your veggie feast, think about a team of housecleaners all suited up in pretty aprons and fancy rubber gloves and scrubbing out your tissues, blood, and digestive tract to get them squeaky clean. Plan juices full of the alkaline veggies you love most that will nourish you and taste great. Surround yourself with people who support your choice to get healthy and ask them to help you stay on track. And remember, you are doing this for YOU. Now, let's get rolling!

You'll be whipping up quite a few juices over the next few days (and, I hope, over the rest of your life!), so it helps to understand how to make the most of them. Although juicing removes most of the insoluble fiber, it allows you to ingest a much more concentrated, easily assimilated form of enzymes, minerals, vitamins, and phytonutrients. These will alkalize the body and buffer acids much more quickly and effectively than solid foods while also giving your digestive tract a break. You may also choose to blend some of your green drinks (particularly after Day 3) and leave the fiber in. Blending pre-digests the veggies so your digestive tract still gets a break. However, the more juicing you can do, the more effective the cleanse. Here are some tips for making the most nutritious, best-tasting juices and smoothies possible:

- **Drink the juice immediately** or as soon as possible to avoid nutrient loss, as the molecules oxidize very quickly once exposed to air.
- **To store juice for just a few hours (unless you have an auger or twin-gear juicer),** ensure you have lemon or lime juice in it, make sure that the container is airtight and filled right to the top, and keep it refrigerated. Add ½ teaspoon vitamin C crystals or camu camu powder (rich in vitamin C) dissolved in a couple of ounces of water to help preserve it better.

- **Make smoothies ahead of time and refrigerate** them for up to 12 hours. The fiber in them extends their shelf life, as does lemon or lime juice, but they are best consumed right away.
- **Use the widest variety of fresh produce possible and change up the greens** to get a range of beneficial micronutrients and not too many of any one kind.
- If you need to, especially when starting out, **sweeten the juice or smoothie with a couple of drops of liquid stevia** and cut the bitterness with lemon juice. You will still have a perfectly alkaline drink.
- **Wash veggies well and leave their peels on** to retain essential phytonutrients just beneath the skin, unless they are tough or overly bitter or heavily waxed, but **peel citrus fruits** to expose the white pith below the skin, which contains valuable bioflavonoids. Lemons and limes (and their pith) add flavor, alkalize, and help to preserve the veggies in juice.
- **Add unpeeled fresh ginger** to juice for flavor, a little heat, and anti-inflammatory properties. **Fresh chili** adds spice and helps with blood circulation; rinsed, unpeeled **turmeric root** has anti-inflammatory, anti-oxidant, and anti-cancer properties; and rinsed, unpeeled **burdock root** expels toxins from the blood.

As you follow the cleanse, check in with your body. If you are up for the challenge, choose more juices and fewer fiber-filled blended recipes, but remember, this veggie feast is not a contest! It is designed to give your digestive tract a real rest and shower the colon with concentrated nutrients. If you can, try to stick with the raw vegetable juices for 3 days or more and you'll be more likely to notice the benefits. However, if you feel you want or need to eat more textured alkaline foods rather than sticking only to liquids, you can. Follow your body's cues if it needs something to chew! And if you need a treat or want to switch up the flavors a bit in the afternoon, don't be afraid to indulge in a delicious Chai-spiced Hemp Mylk (page 121)!

5 REASONS TO DRINK YOUR GREEN JUICE EVERY DAY!

1. It is the easiest way to incorporate way more veggies into your diet and will increase your consumption significantly.

2. Fresh juices suppress your appetite for acidic foods and help to curb cravings.

3. Vegetable juices can help to stabilize blood sugar levels. They have far less sugar than fruit juices and about 50% fewer calories if you go easy on the carrots and beets.

4. Most vegetables will improve the health of your skin, hair, and nails, giving you a noticeable glow and freshness.

5. Green juices provide crucial nutrients and buffering acids that alkalize your body and can single-handedly transform your current health picture—for the better!

ALL JUICES AND SMOOTHIES ARE NOT CREATED EQUAL

The flavor and nutritional value of your juice are affected by the machine that creates it.

- For speed and economy, choose a *centrifugal ejection juicer* (such as the Breville or the Juice Man) that spins and shreds foods to extract their juice. These are easy to use and easy to clean but subject foods to heat, and the juice oxidizes and loses its nutritional value quickly. Consume the juice within 30 minutes.

- If you have a bit more to spend, try a *masticating juicer* (like the Hurom or the Omega), which presses and squeezes foods at low speed to extract the juice. These produce a greater yield with a more concentrated, flavorful juice that oxidizes less quickly, but large fibrous vegetables require more prepping and chopping before juicing. Consume this juice within 24 hours (best the same day).

- If money is no object, a high-powered *twin-gear juicer* (such as the Angel or the Green Star) is very versatile. These yield the most flavorful and nutrient-dense juice and more of it (and they will also mince, chop, and make nut mylks). Refrigerate this juice for up to 72 hours!

- Choose a *blender* that is strong enough to pulverize almost anything without overheating or blowing out the motor. A high-speed Vitamix or Blendtec is ideal, but a more economical, less-powerful blender like a NutriBullet is designed to work well too. (A handheld immersion blender will also handle soups in a pinch.)

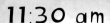

good morning

3-DAY CLEANSE

For a longer cleanse, return to Day 1 and follow the schedule again.

7 am

1. Measure the pH of your urine and saliva (page 30).
2. Drink 8 oz of pure water* at room temperature or warmed, mixed with a good squeeze of fresh lemon juice.
3. Take 1 Tbsp pHour salts mixed in 8 oz water.
4. Take your liquid vitamins and minerals with 3 Tbsp aloe vera, as directed by your holistic nutritionist.
5. Go for a walk or do some yoga stretches.

Day 2 repeat **Day 3** repeat

8 am

1. Drink 16–20 oz of green juice with 1 Tbsp healthy oil, either stirred in, by the spoonful, or taken in capsules.
2. With your meal, take any capsule supplements your health-care provider has recommended.

Day 2 Try Family Green Juice (page 102)
Day 3 Try Alkaline Green Juice (page 105)

11:30 am

Take a fiber supplement to maximize the cleansing of your bowels.

Day 2 repeat **Day 3** repeat

10–10:30am

Drink 16–20 oz of green juice.

Day 2 Drink 16–20 oz of green juice. Or try Creamy Avocado Breakfast Juice Blend (page 108)

Day 3 Drink 16–20 oz of green juice. Or try Lemon–Lime Green Goodness (page 107)

30–60 mins after breakfast

Mix 1 Tbsp greens powder with 12–16 cups of filtered, alkaline water (as per instructions on product) and sip it throughout the morning. The more you can drink, the less you will feel the side effects of detoxification.

Day 2 repeat **Day 3** repeat

NOON

1. Drink 16–20 oz of green juice.
2. With your meal, take any capsule supplements your health-care provider has recommended.

Day 2 Try Creamy Dill and Spinach Detox Soup (page 184)

Day 3 Try Sweet Garlicky Veg Juice (page 104)

1–3:30 pm

Mix 1 Tbsp greens powder with 4–8 cups of filtered, alkaline water and sip it throughout the afternoon.

Day 2 repeat **Day 3** repeat

3:30 pm

Drink 8–12 oz of a nut mylk drink (optional).
2. Go for a walk or do some yoga stretches.

Day 2 Try Chia Mint Smoothie (page 115)

Day 3 Try Lemon–Lime Chia Fresca (page 120)

30–60 mins before bedtime

If you feel hungry, make one more 8–10 oz juice.

Day 2 Lean into Green Juice (page 105)

Day 3 Try Alkaline Green Juice (page 105)

30–60 minutes after dinner

Mix 1 Tbsp greens powder with 4 cups of filtered, alkaline water and sip it throughout the evening.

Day 2 repeat **Day 3** repeat

5 pm

Drink 16–20 oz of green juice with 1 Tbsp healthy oil.

Day 2 Try Blender Greens (page 106)
Day 3 Try Raw Green Soup (page 182)

* Remember, if you don't have alkaline water you can drink a teaspoon of the salt sole in a glass of water once a day, right when you get up in the morning. You can also get alkaline drops to add to your water throughout the day.

TRY THIS: Ease Your Feasting Experience or Enhance It

If you're finding the cleanse tough, consider that your detoxifying process is linked to the state of your health when you began to cleanse. The more acids and toxins you need to get rid of, the more you may feel the effects. Here are some strategies to help you get the most from your cleanse—no matter where you're at.

1. **Do the veggie feast with your spouse, a friend, or a family member.** Supporting each other and sharing their ups and downs helps you both succeed.

2. **Dry-brush your body**. Improve your body's ability to detoxify by increasing the circulation of your lymph and your blood. Using a natural-bristle brush, start at your feet and stroke upward, moving toward the heart. Finish with the arms and the shoulders, stroking downward toward the heart. Follow with a warm shower or a bath.

3. **Take hot and cold showers.** When you alternate your body's exposure to hot and cold water, your lymph vessels dilate and contract to "pump" fluid that may have stagnated in the system, which increases circulation, releases the toxins from your lymphatic system, and energizes you! Stand in a hot shower for 2 minutes, then follow with a 30-second cold shower. Repeat 5 times.

4. **Enjoy some good exercise (page 74).** Yoga helps to move acids from your tissues, rebounding helps the lymph to release acids, and walking helps to release acids and clear your head (take tissues for that drippy nose!).

5. **Rest your body and your mind.** This is just the excuse you've needed! Take a nap, listen to some calming music, meditate, or curl up and enjoy your favorite book. You deserve this and your body needs it!

6. **Sweat deeply in an infrared sauna to release more acids and toxins.** And just keep drinking that alkaline water!

7. **Join an online alkaline cleanse group** (see Resources) that offers daily support and education by conference call to keep you engaged and allow you to ask questions and receive guidance. (Note: this is not a substitute for supervision from a health professional, which is essential, especially if you are not well.)

8. **Give yourself permission to back off**. Sometimes you're just not ready to embark on something difficult and the overwhelm is greater than the benefit. Acknowledge where you're at, and return to Inspire or head to Aspire. You can come back to the veggie feast when you're ready.

To transition from drinking only juices after even just 1 day, gently introduce texture with lightly cooked vegetables. Your digestive tract will have had a vacation, so go easy and listen to your body. If it wants warm soup all day, that's perfect—try the Healing Seasonal Vegetable Soup (page 188). Then move to some lightly steamed vegetables before you add salads and raw whole veggies. Chew really well to liquefy your foods and avoid a stomachache as your system readjusts. Thereafter, go ahead and enjoy solid food recipes that are purely alkaline, and then ease into alkaline-balanced recipes. If you can, continue to start every day with a green juice. You'll develop an amazingly beneficial habit. I certainly miss my green juice if I ever skip a day!

Master Green Juice

Play with these ingredients for a variety of flavors

ADD — **CHOOSE FROM THESE:** — **HOW MUCH?**

ADD	CHOOSE FROM THESE:	HOW MUCH?
citrus	lemons or limes	1 large or two small peeled
hearty greens	kale, collards, Swiss chard, beet greens	4–6 leaves + stalks
mild greens	spinach, lettuces	a large handful
sprouts	sunflower, soy, pea, buckwheat	a large handful
cruciferous	cabbage, broccoli, bok choy	1 small wedge, a small floret + stalk, or a couple of leaves and stems
cucumber	long English or field	1 large or 2 small
veggies & green tops	celery, carrots, beets (tops as well if you have them)	2 stalks celery or 1 carrot
herbs	parsley, mint, cilantro	6 sprigs
roots	ginger, turmeric or burdock	1/2–1" piece of any one

sweetener — 1–3 drops liquid stevia or 1/4–1/2 tsp green stevia–leaf powder, just to taste

BENEFITS:

* Oxygenates the blood, alkalizes to buffer acids

* Provides chlorophyll, to build healthy new blood cells

* Provides chlorophyll to build healthy new blood cells, alkaline minerals to buffer acids, and electrons for energy

* Transfer their life energy to your body

* Supplies phytonutrients that detoxify the liver and help eliminate carcinogens

* Provides water and alkaline minerals to buffer acids

* Celery provides water and stimulates the liver, carrots and beets are high in sugar (limit to 1 per day, or none when cleansing)

* Parsley cleanses the blood, mint promotes digestion, cilantro detoxifies

* Ginger is anti-inflammatory and soothes digestion, turmeric heals the bowels and improves liver function, burdock helps to purify the blood function

* Sugar-free to avoid feeding yeast and prevent blood sugar spikes; use in moderation

Master Blender Greens

ADD	CHOOSE FROM THESE:	HOW MUCH?
liquid	Coconut water, unsweetened coconut mylk, unsweetened almond mylk, water, or a combination of the above * Coconut water hydrates and provides electrolytes, mylks supply healthy fats	8–10 oz or to combine
greens	chard, kale, spinach, romaine, dandelion greens * Provides chlorophyll	3–4 cups
juicy tasty veggies	fennel, broccoli (go easy– it is strong–and drink immediately), celery, cucumber, bell peppers * Provides water and alkaline minerals and vitamins	1/2–1 cup
herbs	fresh mint, parsley, ginger * Detoxifies and aids digestion	small handful
citrus	fresh juice from lemon, lime, white grapefruit * Alkalizes, cleanses the liver, cuts the strong taste of the greens	3–5 Tbsp
optionall	raw coconut butter or raw young coconut meat * Provides lauric and caprylic acid to combat yeast imbalance	1/4 cup

Yields 12–16 oz

Play with these ingredients for a variety of flavors!

sweetener 1–3 drops liquid stevia or 1/4–1/2 tsp green stevia–leaf powder, just to taste
* Sugar-free to avoid feeding yeast and prevent blood sugar spikes, use in moderation

Master Green Smoothie

Yields 12-16 oz

Play with these ingredients for a variety of flavors!

ADD	CHOOSE FROM THESE:	HOW MUCH?
liquid	coconut water, alkaline water, unsweetened almond mylk	1 cup
hearty greens	kale, Swiss chard, beet greens	4-6 leaves + stalks
mild greens	spinach, green lettuces (except iceberg!)	a large handful
sprouts	sunflower, soy, pea, buckwheat	1/2 cup
cucumber	long English or field	6" piece
healthy fat #1	avocado, young coconut meat	1 whole avocado or 1/4 cup coconut
herbs	mint, cilantro	6 sprigs
roots	ginger, burdock	1/2-1" piece of either
citrus	lemon, lime, white grapefruit	3-5 Tbsp
healthy fat #2	flax oil, coconut oil, fish oil	1-2 Tbsp
protein	hemp hearts, sprouted brown rice protein (add last and blend just until creamed)	1-2 Tbsp

sweetener

1-3 drops liquid stevia or 1/4-1/2 tsp green stevia leaf powder, just to taste

* Sugar-free to avoid feeding yeast and prevent blood sugar spikes, use in moderation

BENEFITS:

* Oxygenates the blood, alkalizes to buffer acids

* Provides chlorophyll, to build healthy new blood cells

* Chlorophyll-rich, high in alkaline minerals, electron-rich

* Transfer their life energy to your body, contain chlorophyll

* Very alkalizing and high water content

* Fats bind to acids to assist in releasing them from tissues

* Mint promotes digestion, cilantro detoxifies

* Ginger is anti-inflammatory and soothes digestion, burdock helps to purify the blood

* Oxygenates the blood, alkalizes the body

* Rich in lauric and caprylic acid to combat yeast imbalance

* Fiber helps to cleanse the colon, fats help release acids, proteins build healthy blood and tissues

6. EMBRACE THE BENEFITS OF YOUR EFFORTS!

Congratulate yourself! Once you have released a good portion of those nasty acids and toxins you are well on your way to reaching optimal health. You will likely be feeling the benefits of the veggie feast with increased energy and alertness. I'll bet your taste buds will notice the more subtle flavors of vegetables that you may have missed before. You probably feel pretty clean inside and may no longer have the same desire for the many acidic foods that brought you to the cleanse in the first place. You've set yourself a goal, achieved it—way to go!—and are now ready to embrace the bigger challenge of sticking with a more alkaline diet and making changes to your lifestyle.

Your Desire stage doesn't have to end when you return to eating solid foods. As long as you are choosing 100% alkaline-forming foods, your body will continue to release acids. Along with your morning juice or a smoothie each day, enjoy steamed and raw veggies for lunch, dinner, and snacks. Chew your food well, drink your 12–16 cups of water daily, and continue to support the release of acids from your body with the 4 key alkaline supplements (page 41).

7. WHAT'S NEXT?

To continue veggie feasting, adhere to the purely alkaline juices and smoothies. If you have a medical condition and are not completely well, you may want to continue longer than a week or 2. If excess weight is part of your condition, an extended juice cleanse can help you to safely and naturally lose weight and improve your overall health. However, be sure to consult your health-care provider and an alkaline coach before you extend your cleanse. They will help monitor, support, and optimize your efforts.

If you have feasted on juices and/or blended veggies all you can, you are now ready to move on to the Aspire stage and begin to adjust your balance of alkaline foods from 100% to 85% over a period of 4–12 weeks by continuing with some juiced and/or blended meals and adding solid foods. Remember, this is your journey. Feel free to come back to this stage whenever you like, especially once you've healed yourself and found balance in your lifestyle.

TRY THESE 3 RECIPES
to nourish and cleanse
during your feast!!

Alkaline Green Juice (page 105)

Alkaline Green Smoothie (page 111)
(Day 3 and beyond)

Creamy Dill and Spinach Detox Soup (page 184)
(Day 3 and beyond)

ASPIRE

Releasing Deep-Tissue Acids and Toxins

Transitioning from the veggie feast to whole
alkaline foods with a huge focus on the high-
alkaline veggies will work wonders if you are
excavating deep tissue acids, reducing symptoms of
ill health, and helping to shed excess weight.

Start here if:

- you have successfully completed the Inspire and/or the Desire stage(s) and are ready to move on to dumping your stored toxins and beginning to heal

- you are keen to move quickly to a fully alkaline diet but cannot or do not want to drink only juices and blended drinks

- you are living an alkaline lifestyle but have done a bit too much zigging and zagging and need to regain your alkaline balance

Aim for:

- 90–100% alkaline foods at every meal. Choose purely alkaline recipes (marked ***) to start, then add a few alkaline-balanced ones (marked **) served with a salad. (See pages 98–99 for a key to which recipes are which.)

Plan on:

- 1–4 weeks, or up to 3 months

You can do it!

Think of the Aspire stage as a renovation. Maybe it's time to redesign and redecorate your old lifestyle which is so out of date! You've started to toss out the old stuff and now it's time to start designing, creating, and building the new you. If you did the veggie feast, that stage was like stripping off nasty old wallpaper. This stage is about finding what's underneath the paper, removing the next and the next, and the next layers, or just scrubbing off the glue. The cleaner you can get the walls the better, because you'll get longer-lasting results with your pretty new paint color.

Maybe you are lucky and the paper peeled right off. Or perhaps you lucked out and found vintage bead-board underneath, which you just adore! What I'm saying is that if you just completed the transition (the Inspire stage) or the veggie feast (the Desire stage) and are feeling great but don't plan to deep-cleanse any further right now, you can go straight to the Acquire stage and start living the alkaline lifestyle in your newly decorated interior. Ideally though, it's a good idea to maintain a high-alkaline diet for as long as you can to release those built-up acids and toxins before you move on. The best decorating jobs are thorough, detailed, and well thought out—and rarely happen without at least a few surprises.

I started the Aspire stage after 3 days on my first juice feast. It felt good to chew again! And I discovered that my taste buds were much more awake after the cleanse; many veggies I had grown tired of tasted vibrant and new. And many I had never tasted before quickly became favorites. What also got me hooked on alkaline foods was how good I felt after my tasty meals, both physically and mentally.

I'm not going to promise that your medical condition will disappear as soon as you start to eat 100% alkaline foods and that you won't feel any side effects.

Excavating those deep-seated toxins is a slow, gradual process. You allowed them to thrive over many years, and it will take some time to release them from your colon, liver, pancreas, heart, joints, and even fatty tissue such as your breasts. But gradually you'll see the whites of your eyes become whiter, your skin become more supple, your weight stabilize, and your inflammatory symptoms start to diminish and go away. Your digestive tract and your organs will be getting cleaner and will have begun to heal.

The idea of this stage is not to banish acid foods forever, but the longer you stick with a high-alkaline diet the more benefits you will reap. I ate 100% alkaline for more than 1 month before I gradually started to add 10–15% acid foods. Depending on your medical condition, your journey through this stage—and the length of time before you start to add a few acidic foods—may be shorter or longer. By the end of 3½ months, I was eating 85% alkaline and I was finally pain-free! So even if it feels like a long haul, stick with it and know that there's no right or wrong amount of time. You will feel healthier and stronger every. single. day.

1. EDUCATE YOURSELF: CLEANSING DEEP-ROOTED TOXINS

The Aspire stage is a continuation of the veggie feast, but with foods you can really sink your teeth into. In addition to juices and blended drinks, you can now eat lots of alkaline foods in solid form, which means exploring a whole new world of recipes that can transform your weekly menus forever. If you haven't already transitioned from drinking pure juices to blended drinks and soups, you'll want to do that before you start the Aspire stage. Reintroducing soft, easily digestible foods rather than skipping straight to solids will help your body ease back into its regular work of digesting denser foods.

The Aspire stage can seem confusing. You're increasing your quantity of alkaline foods, and yet sometimes you're not going to feel so great. In fact, it's not unusual for your current symptoms to initially seem as if they're getting worse! Or maybe you'll develop new ones! So why would you want to continue? Everyone is different, and every body deals differently with its acid overload. Those skin rashes or headaches or the diarrhea or

lightheadedness that you may feel will certainly improve. Have faith. You are providing your body with good, nutritious food, and it is doing its best to heal itself. It can help to know what is happening in your body during the Aspire stage: how the body is escorting the toxins out and how it is starting to heal. But remember, if at any time your symptoms are unbearable or something doesn't seem right, ease up, flush with water, and take a visit to your holistic health-care provider for support right away.

THE FACTS: Demystifying Detoxification

As you continue to alkalize, you continue to detoxify your body in a deeper way. Remember that when the blood gets overwhelmed with toxins it starts to tuck them away in the tissues, particularly your fatty tissues, so they don't damage your vital organs. Releasing acids and toxins from these deep-rooted tissues involves a battle with mycotoxins, the toxic waste from micro-forms such as fungus, mold, and yeast. Yeasts thrive on sugar, which means there are lots of them in an acidic body. The most common yeast in the body is *Candida albicans*, which exists in two forms: a round yeast that remains in the colon and reproduces, and a fungal yeast that eats through the intestinal wall, leaks into the bloodstream, and spreads throughout the body (a condition often called leaky gut).

If your body is acidic, you most likely have an imbalance of this fungal yeast to some degree. As you start to cleanse, you also start to get rid of the sugars that the yeast needs to survive. You'd think that's a good thing—and it is!—but as the fungal yeasts die, they release 70–80 different types of endotoxins. The strongest of those endotoxins are aldehydes, ethanol, and ammonia, and they are at the root of most of the symptoms you experience as you detoxify your body.

Ethanol and ammonia are the tools that *Candida* uses to change the environment in the intestine so that it can survive and reproduce there. Unfortunately, what's good for *Candida* is not good for our intestinal lining; ethanol and ammonia damage our digestive health and compromise our immune system. Ethanol also interferes with our ability to properly metabolize the nutrients necessary to produce energy, which leads to hypoglycemia, B12 deficiencies, and ulcers, among other ailments.

Acetaldehyde toxins can dilate brain cells (causing severe headaches), and damage the endocrine system (causing hormone imbalances), the adrenals (causing heart palpitations), the immune system, and the respiratory system. We know that they also damage blood cells, which lessens our oxygen supply. All these disruptions become the symptoms you experience as you chase the yeastie beasties and their acidic waste away.

Your symptoms may come and go as the yeast dies and then releases its toxins, a condition called the Herxheimer reaction. If you are diligent with your cleansing and don't cave in to your sugar cravings, you will win! Once you get through this tricky war zone and conquer the yeast beast, your foggy brain will clear and your tired body will become energized. Be sure to enlist professional support if you are struggling, as yeast overgrowths can be very stubborn and discouraging (see Resources).

In my case, I was quite amazed at how my body responded, especially since I wasn't completely convinced that my food choices could affect me so profoundly. Because I went cold turkey on my old diet by doing the veggie feast and my diet changes were so dramatic, I noticed changes quite quickly in the Desire stage. I experienced some headaches, hypoglycemic highs and lows, cravings, skin breakouts, and a foggy brain and coated tongue, but I embraced them for the sake of healing my pain and because I also began to see improvements. I slowly gained more energy, my digestion improved, my skin and my mind grew clearer, and I began to shed excess weight daily.

If your discomfort is too much, eat more solid and lightly cooked alkaline foods with fiber. You will see much more gradual but consistent changes. Reduce your supplement doses if necessary until you feel you are managing. Whether you go fast or slow, your body will continue to detox through your skin, breath, urine, and feces, and as there are fewer acids and toxins present in your body, your detox symptoms will slowly subside. But remember, it's not a race.

COMMON SIDE EFFECTS WHILE DETOXIFYING

UNCOMFORTABLE	NOT TOO BAD	PRETTY DARN GOOD
❏ Flu-like symptoms	❏ Nasal discharge	❏ Increased energy
❏ Diarrhea	❏ Fatigue	❏ Clearer mind
❏ Skin rash/eczema	❏ Foggy brain	❏ Clearer, glowing skin
❏ Headache	❏ Lightheadedness	❏ Weight loss
❏ Emotional swings	❏ Bad breath	❏ Improved sleep
❏ Nausea	❏ Weakness	❏ Good digestion
❏ Cravings	❏ Skin breakouts	❏ Improved vision
❏ Hypoglycemic swings	❏ Coated tongue	❏ Brighter whites of eyes
❏ Inflammation	❏ Flatulence	❏ Increased stamina
❏ Loss of sleep	❏ Sweating	❏ Positive attitude
❏ Anger/depression	❏ Sore throat	❏ Reduced pain and inflammation

2. SET YOUR INTENTION

If you have completed the Inspire and/or the Desire stages, congratulations: you have already started to nourish and heal your body. Keep it up! If you're starting with the Aspire stage, welcome. The changes you are about to start making to your lifestyle won't always be easy, but I guarantee that they will make a difference to your well-being.

Your goal in this stage is to make alkaline foods the largest part of your diet and form a habit for life. Remember I said this wasn't a diet? Well, this is where you want to make "alkalizing" your new routine. You might be tempted to give in to your old habits, but don't. If you're serious about getting rid of your medical condition, reducing your weight, and improving your overall feeling of well-being, it's time to make some permanent changes. So, start by aiming for 100% alkaline foods (at the very least 90%) at every meal and try to stick with them for as long as you can. When you're ready, start to add a few low-acid foods to a meal a couple of times a week.

You probably have some alkaline meals in your repertoire, or old recipes that you can easily modify: vegetable salads, soups, and stews are all good places to start. If this is a real change from your old way of eating, have a look through the recipe section of this book. I've developed lots of tasty recipes for you to try, from porridges and salads to soups and puddings, and, of course, juices, smoothies, and blended drinks. Experiment with any of the recipes marked as purely alkaline. And when you begin to introduce a few low-acid foods into your diet, try some of the recipes designated as alkaline balanced. Any of these recipes will support your body as it continues to cleanse and release built-up acids and toxins deep in the tissues while still balancing your pH.

Keeping a journal is an effective way to record your intention and keep notes on what's happening along the way. You can note your pH levels here from time to time, how you're feeling, the recipes you love, and so on. Once you are balanced, those notes can serve as a reminder and a motivator to stay on track!

What Does It Look Like?

Lots of water throughout the day and alkaline supplements.

A plate that is 100% alkaline foods is all veggies (at least half of these enjoyed raw; the balance may be lightly steamed). You can gradually move to 90% alkaline and 10% acidic by adding small amounts of low-acid fruits, sprouted legumes, and sprouted grains. Save organic animal protein for the next stage.

An alkaline smoothie, green juice, or blended greens drink for breakfast.

An abundance of cruciferous veggies (broccoli, cabbage, Brussels sprouts, kale, cauliflower, bok choy) for their cancer-fighting property, indole-3-carbinol.

That's it! With plenty of these purely alkaline foods, your body's pH levels will start to tip in the right direction and you'll soon feel the positive effects too.

3. SET UP YOUR ALKALINE KITCHEN

You may already have bought a juicer (page 45), stocked your fridge with veggies, and purchased a few supplements during the Inspire and/or Desire stage(s). Now it's time to get serious about alkalizing your kitchen. That means having a look at your equipment, your fridge, and your pantry to be sure you've got the tools and alkaline foods you need … and that you've got rid of all those tempting acid-forming foods that aren't going to serve you well. Out of sight, out of mind, right? Enlist supportive family members or friends to help you alkalize your kitchen.

TRY THIS: Turn Your Kitchen into an Alkaline Zone!

1. Turn to pages 88–91 to see what's in my kitchen, my fridge, and my pantry. These are the foods I eat most often and the tools I find handy for preparing them. Use those pages as a starting point for alkalizing your own kitchen—but be sure to include all or most of the top 10 alkaline foods (page 60).

2. Think about how to ensure you've got a regular supply of veggies on hand. Do you grow your own in the summer or sprout indoors in winter? Or regularly visit a farmers' market? Or shop at a local greengrocer or produce market? Are you a member of a community-supported agriculture (CSA) co-operative or do you take advantage of a veggie home-delivery service? Whatever method you choose, stock up on lots of fresh, local, organic, mostly raw green veggies.

3. To save time and waste less food, plan your menu for the week before you go to the grocery store. Then wash, cut, and pack several days' worth of veggies in reusable green vegetable bags when you get home.

4. Go through your fridge and your cupboards and give away all your high-acid foods. Not sure which ones those are? Have a look at the Alkaline Food Chart (page 8–9), but start with all highly processed foods; animal products, including deli meats, eggs, and milk and milk products; sweets, including chocolate; and condiments, including soy sauce and vinegar.

5. Stock up on fresh herbs and organic dried spices. Try parsley, mint, basil, and dill as well as cinnamon, ginger, and cayenne.

6. Set aside ½ day to make a batch of Spring Pea and Edamame Spread (page 278), Creamy Herb Dip (page 278), or Hemp Chipotle Kale Chips (page 246) for snacks and quick lunches. And keep one of the salad dressings (pages 284–285) handy too.

TRY THIS: 3 Ways to Prepare Your Mind and Body

1. Assess your current alkalinity by measuring the pH of your urine and saliva. Record the results in your notebook.
2. Affirm your commitment to alkalizing your diet and enlist the support of friends and family. Write your intention in your notebook.
3. Begin to introduce solid alkaline foods, such as steamed veggies, massaged kale, and delicious raw vegetable salads. Continue to drink 12–16 cups of water a day.

Finding your groove means preparing plant-based meals that make you excited to eat. If this lifestyle is new to you, a little planning will go a long way in helping you to stay on track.

TOP 10 ALKALINE FOODS

Try to eat these every day, or every other day, especially broccoli and avocado! I can. not. get. enough! These are always on our shopping list and in our fridge. We just continuously load up!

avocado: Considered nature's perfect food, avocados are rich in chlorophyll and 77% of an avocado's calories come from healthy fats. One avocado provides 40% of the daily requirement of fiber, and helps us to absorb nutrients from vegetables. I eat 2–3 every day!

garlic: Full of the alkaline minerals calcium, magnesium, phosphorus, and especially potassium, garlic also contains allicin, a sulfur compound that helps maintain blood pressure. It is anti-inflammatory and can help improve iron metabolism.

bell peppers: One of the highest sources of the antioxidant vitamins A, C, and E, bell peppers reduce the risk of type II diabetes, macular degeneration, cancer, and cardiovascular disease as well as inflammation.

kale: Super high in chlorophyll and antioxidants, 1 cup of kale has 1327% of the recommended daily allowance of vitamin K. It is a detoxifying superfood that can dramatically affect your health journey when consumed often.

broccoli: This cruciferous veggie is rich in protein, highly anti-cancer and anti-inflammatory, and very supportive of the immune system, metabolism, and digestive system. It helps detox the body. Eat it every day!

lemon: Lemon helps to detoxify the liver and kidneys as it is full of alkaline minerals. It is very high in antioxidant vitamins A and especially C. I add it to everything I possibly can!

celery: Being a high-water-content veggie, celery is very alkalizing. It is high in natural sodium and vitamin C, which helps reduce inflammation and supports immune function.

spinach: This leafy green ranks as the most nutrient-rich vegetable; it is extremely high in vitamins, minerals, and chlorophyll. Spinach builds strong blood and helps kick acids!

cucumber: The #1 alkaline vegetable, cucumber has the highest water content (a whopping 95%) of any veggie, which assists with detox! It is chock-full of vitamins and alkaline minerals that make up most of the vitamins the body needs in a day. Juice or blend daily!

tomato: High in water content, tomatoes are most alkalizing when eaten raw with lots of vitamin C to protect from heart disease. When cooked, tomatoes become mildly acidic but release loads of lycopene to protect your immune system.

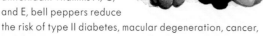

4. SUPPORT YOUR BODY WITH SUPPLEMENTS

When I began my alkaline journey, I found supplements vital to my recovery. They deliver more concentrated nutrients than whole foods alone, at a time when your body is incredibly depleted. They can also help to alleviate the symptoms of detoxification and work toward healing the gut.

I will always consume the 4 key alkaline supplements (page 41), and like many people, I sometimes supplement with vitamins and minerals if I have been overly stressed or am traveling, cleansing or just feeling a little low-energy. Because I choose to eat a vegan diet, I include vitamin B12, which is more difficult to get from plant foods alone.

This is simply an overview of some of the key supplements. Consult your holistic health practitioner who can assess your individual needs and make recommendations.

SUPPLEMENTS TO SUPPORT DIGESTION

- **Aloe vera:** This plant is packed with vitamins, minerals, fatty acids, and amino acids. Three to 4 spoonfuls of this gel soothe and cleanse the digestive tract by breaking down undigested animal proteins. It provides alkaline nourishment to heal the intestines and reduces the number of "bad" bacteria, which can be helpful in treating colon disorders. It is not recommended for prolonged use, and is best taken 15–30 minutes before meals, alone or with water.

- **Digestive enzymes:** Our bodies naturally produce their own digestive enzymes to break down carbohydrates, fats, proteins, and fiber, but sometimes you need a little extra help. Enzyme supplements are produced from beneficial plants, fungi, bacteria, or animal sources and usually come as a pill, which you take with your meal. If you are

eating a diet rich in predominantly raw alkaline foods and your digestive tract has healed, you probably won't need enzymes. (They are most certainly beneficial for proper digestion if you are consuming meat and dairy and overly cooked foods or if you are not soaking your nuts, seeds, grains, and legumes/beans.)

- **Hydrochloric acid (HCL):** Betaine hydrochloride is derived from beets and increases the concentration of hydrochloric acid in the stomach when taken at the very start of a meal, helping to re-train your stomach to produce enough on its own. It is sold in pill form and is recommended only for weak digestion, and usually only if you are consuming animal products or eating poorly combined foods. If any burning feeling occurs after you take this supplement, do not continue with it as you are over-producing HCL and can damage the stomach lining. Caution and supervision are required especially if you are taking anti-inflammatory medications.

- **L-glutamine:** This essential amino acid is anti-inflammatory, coats and protects the cell walls, repels irritants, and is used to support the repair and healing of the intestinal lining, which is critical if you are experiencing leaky gut. It is sold as a powder and is usually taken twice daily away from meals.

- **Probiotics:** Just 1 capsule contains billions of beneficial microscopic live bacteria. These live microorganisms are considered to be the "good" bacteria in the gut that assist in maintaining a healthy flora, or environment, for optimal digestion. These can be used effectively to correct an imbalance of yeast due to a highly acidic diet or after taking an antibiotic (if you absolutely must have a prescription). They can work beautifully to rebuild the beneficial gut flora and help to heal your digestive system.

They should only be used for a short time in consultation with a holistic nutritionist and as per directed on the packaging. That said, by doing a veggie feast for 10–14 days and then continuing with a high-alkaline diet (85% or more) for a few months, it *is* possible to dramatically reduce the yeasts in your system without using probiotics. I know, because I have done it!

4 KEY ALKALINE ESSENTIALS—AGAIN

- CHLOROPHYLL: 1 tsp of greens powder per 4 cups of water, 4–6 times per day

- WATER: 12–16 cups every day

- HEALTHY OILS: 2–3 Tbsp of a combination of healthy flax, hemp, coconut, fish, or krill oils every day

- ALKALINE MINERAL SALTS: 1 tsp powdered mineral salts in 1 cup of water, twice a day.

SUPPLEMENTS TO SUPPORT THE FUNCTIONING OF THE BODY

Choose whole food supplements that are extracted from plants as they are much easier for the body to absorb and use.

- **Multi-vitamin:** This dietary supplement is a combination of 3 or more vitamins that comes in a variety of forms and is generally taken once or twice a day with meals. It is beneficial because it ensures you get the full range of nutrients. When your digestion is impaired, I recommend liquid colloidal vitamins, which are absorbed in the mouth rather than in your gut.

- **Multi-mineral:** This dietary supplement ensures your body has all the minerals necessary for you to properly absorb vitamins and buffer acids. Unfortunately, you can't rely solely upon foods for these, no matter how well you eat. When your digestion is impaired, I recommend liquid colloidal vitamins, which are absorbed in the mouth rather than in your gut.

- **Vitamin B12:** This vitamin is produced in small amounts in the gut and is found in larger quantities in animal flesh and sprouted seeds. It is a vital nutrient that supports blood and nerve cells and helps to make DNA and break down fatty acids. As you adapt to a plant-based diet, monitor your B12 levels and use a supplement, if necessary. Take as per the directions on the package, either in pill or liquid form.

- **Vitamin B complex:** This vitamin is a balanced combination of all 8 B vitamins (thiamine (vitamin B1), riboflavin (vitamin B2), niacin (vitamin B3), pantothenic acid (vitamin B5), pyridoxine (vitamin B6), biotin, folic acid, and the cobalamins (vitamin B12)) that extract the energy from your food; build new cells and repair existing ones, including blood cells; strengthen muscles; and provide antioxidants, to name but a few of its functions. If you have low energy, taking a vitamin B complex supplement can help to support all these functions. Take as per the directions on the package, in pill form.

- **Vitamin D:** The body synthesizes this vitamin through exposure to sunlight, but you can give yourself a little extra with the occasional piece of wild salmon. Vitamin D affects our mood and helps facilitate the absorption of calcium and phosphorus to maintain a healthy immune system. If you don't get a lot of sun where you live, monitor your vitamin D levels and take a supplement if necessary. Take as per the directions on the package, either in pill or liquid form.

- **Magnesium:** This mineral is found naturally in the body and in many fiber-rich foods such as broccoli, squash, green leafy vegetables, nuts (especially almonds), seeds, and legumes. It is responsible for over 300 chemical reactions that keep the body working properly. Even if you take alkaline mineral salts, it is highly beneficial to supplement further. I don't go a day without it. Anyone with a kidney or heart condition must consult with their health-care provider first.

- **R-lipoic acid:** This powerful antioxidant is in every cell in the body and naturally protects us from damage by harmful molecules. It strengthens our immune system, increases cellular energy, and protects the brain while escorting heavy metals like mercury from the body. Supplementing regularly with this acid gently and safely releases these toxins from the body, as does consuming plant sources like broccoli, spinach, collard greens, and chard. Take as per the directions on the package, either in pill or liquid form.

- **Coenzyme Q10 (CoQ10):** This coenzyme is found in every cell in the body and is a powerful antioxidant that especially protects the brain and the cardiovascular system. It has also been shown to dramatically reduce glucose levels. Since the best food sources of CoQ10 are organ meats, sardines, mackerel, peanuts, and soy oil, it is worth considering a supplement, especially if your medical condition includes diabetes or pancreatic concerns. Take as per the directions on the package, in pill form.

- **N-acetylcysteine:** This antioxidant is derived from amino acids. Taking this supplement helps support your liver at a time when it is working extra hard to help eliminate toxins from the body. Take as per the directions on the package, in pill form.

- **Milk thistle:** This flowering herb helps to keep the liver healthy and protect it from the effects of toxins, especially during a cleanse. Take as per the directions on the product, in pill form.

These are just a few of the supplements that are beneficial as you regain your alkaline balance. Again, consult your alkaline coach, a holistic nutritionist, or your health-care provider to help you choose the right supplements and doses.

YOU *CAN* ENJOY A RESTAURANT MEAL!

You can still be sociable even when you are in this high-alkaline stage. Just be more creative and don't be shy to ask for what you need.

- **Salads and side dishes are often great options.** Order a couple of yummy seasonal steamed or sautéed veggies. Don't be afraid to deconstruct a salad to remove the cheeses, candied nuts, sugary cranberries, etc. Ask for an undressed salad with some lemon and olive oil, and maybe a little garlic and herbs on the side. And add avocado, if possible.

- **Try Greek, Mediterranean, or Lebanese restaurants.** Greek salad (hold the cheese), hummus, tabbouleh, falafel (baked not fried), and crudités are excellent alkaline options. Avoid Italian, which will trigger carbohydrate and bread cravings; Thai, which contains lots of sugar in its dishes; and Asian, which is often laden with monosodium glutamate (MSG), soy sauce, and salt. A simple veggie stir-fry is fine.

- **Find a self-serve deli.** Choose a wrap, or better yet, a large kale or chard leaf, and fill it with your ideal fillings. Lettuce, tomatoes, sprouts, avocados, cucumbers, hummus—mmm!

- In a pinch, **choose a small piece of poached salmon and a salad or veggie side.** This is a good option if you are at the end of the Aspire stage.

- Whatever you do, **skip the fried foods**. If you really have to have fries, look for baked ones. Or a baked sweet potato. Or why not wait and try a healthier, alkaline option at home like the Green Bean Fries (page 244) instead?

- **Ask for fresh lemon in your water.** Many restaurants now offer filtered or bottled water, but if not, lemon juice helps to alkalize and purify your water. I always carry alkaline drops in my purse.

- **Avoid alcohol for now.** This may be tricky if you are inclined to have a glass of *vino* with your meal. Ask the bartender to pour you a sparkling water with freshly squeezed lime, lemon, or grapefruit and fresh mint. You'll feel and look like you are having a cocktail!

- **After dinner, ask for a mint tea.** Tea made with fresh or dried mint leaves is the perfect way to help the digestion of your meal. A small square of 90% or higher dark chocolate with your tea can be a real treat if you are nearing the end of this stage. Be mindful, though, because it can become addictive if you enjoy it too often.

5. PREPARE FOR THE UNEXPECTED!

Pay attention to your hunger. You most likely are accustomed, as many people are, to having 3 meals a day and nothing in between. When your digestive tract is sluggish and bogged down with heavy, low-water-content foods and poor food combinations, you will feel satiated but may not actually be getting all the nutrients you need. With an efficient digestive tract and alkaline foods, your body is quickly taking in all the vital nutrients you need to be healthy, which is exactly what you want. Provided you are nourishing yourself with wholesome, predominantly alkaline foods, it's perfectly fine to eat (or better yet, drink a green juice) if you are hungry—even if it is soon after you last ate. There's no need to count calories or weigh your food, but be prepared for those surprise moments so you can make good food choices. I keep greens powders handy in my purse to add to water between meals and this curbs my hunger within minutes. I also never leave the house without some soaked nuts or veggie sticks to snack on when needed.

GET CHARGED ON WATER!

In nature, water maintains its electrical charge because it is always moving. Most tap and bottled water lies static in reservoirs and containers that can cause it to lose its electrical charge, reducing its surface area and making it harder for the body to absorb. Restructure your water with an ionizing filter or a non-electric portable unit (see Resources). Remember, hydrate with 12–16 cups of filtered alkaline water (page 43) per day.

Keep in mind that sometimes the body's cry for food is actually a cry for water. So always try to hydrate first and then have a healthy snack or juice if you still feel hungry. Just be sure not to ignore your body's requests.

As your body dumps its deep-seated acids, you may experience some discomfort. If you have already begun to cleanse your body in the Inspire and/or Desire stages, these side effects will usually be less pronounced. However, if you are responding severely, or maintaining a 100% alkaline diet feels too taxing, simply step back, pat yourself on the back for how far you've come and the toxins you've let go thus far, and then, if need be, adjust your course. Review your intention and recommit to the Aspire stage, or perhaps return to the flexibility of the Inspire stage until you feel ready to dive in to 100% alkaline eating again.

Sometimes the hardest part about being in the Aspire stage is not the physical stuff but the social and emotional effects. It can be hard to make a big change to your lifestyle when your friends and family members are questioning your choices or you are unsure about how to fit in restaurant dinners and meals out with friends. Here are a few strategies to consider: invite or challenge friends, family, or co-workers to try a day or 2 with you by choosing, prepping, and eating some yummy recipes together; call ahead to the restaurant and ask the chef to create something delicious for you; carry digestive enzymes with you in case your options are limited in a restaurant. Avoid getting stressed over being different or eating something too acidic, as that actually creates acids within the body. You may not win over everyone or eat perfectly, but that's okay. Stay true to your intention and do the best you can so that you will continue to see your health improve. Remember, this stage won't last forever! Once you are alkaline balanced, you will have much more flexibility with your meals.

6. EMBRACE THE BENEFITS OF YOUR EFFORTS!

Yay, you're doing it! By sticking with a high-water-content, high-alkaline diet, you are dumping toxins, squeaky-cleaning your body, and developing a healthy new lifestyle. You are surely inspiring other people with your commitment and vitality—even though they may not be telling you this. And best of all, you are resolving your medical condition, your weight issues, your feelings of sluggishness gradually, sustainably, and, if you continue to choose predominantly alkaline foods, for life.

By the time I reached the end of this stage after 3½ months, I was truly in seventh heaven. My pain was virtually gone! I was consuming a small amount of acidic food—10–15%—and had gotten into a real rhythm with this lifestyle. I had lost over 40 pounds of excess weight, which just fell off. Of course I was just ecstatic about this! My energy levels had soared, and I can honestly say that my mental health and positivity had improved. Part of that feeling was certainly the relief from chronic pain, but it was more than that. I felt on top of the world!

THE BRAIN-GUT CONNECTION

If you have never experienced the "feel-good" factor that comes with regular bowel movements, you will experience it here. The sense of satisfaction, relief, and overall wellness are real—a number of neurotransmitters in your gut with at least 7 kinds of serotonin receptors are directly connected to your brain. Paying attention to your bowel function and your emotions is all part of a new awareness for your healthy body.

What you experience will be unique to you, but I can say you will most certainly get more than you bargained for—in a good way. The effects are not only physical, but also mental, emotional, and spiritual. Maintain an alkaline balance, and these benefits will be long-lasting too.

7. WHAT'S NEXT?

By now you will have established an alkaline balance for your body and will know what feels right and healthy for you. Until you experience this feeling of optimal wellness, it's impossible to know where to return to when you tip the acidic scale and it's hard to be truly inspired to continuously make the choices that will keep you feeling great. Now, however, you *can* zig and zag as you like with the confidence of knowing you have a home base you can always return to.

Your symptoms most likely have subsided, your energy is dramatically improved, and your pH is near 7.0–7.2, or higher, which means you are ready to move on to the Acquire stage. There you can increase the amount of acidic foods in your diet, including some mildly acidic recipes. You will be aiming for a balance of 75% alkaline-forming foods to 25% acidic foods, or even an optimal 80/20 balance, for each of your meals or, at the very least, for the day. With your digestion working well and your body cleaned up, you'll add the last pieces of your lifestyle change: exercise and mental and emotional balance. Congratulations! You've come a long way! Now carry on!

TRY THESE 3 RECIPES
as you Aspire to solid alkaline foods

Creamy Lemon Chia Porridge (page 135)

Kale Caesar (page 246)

Steamed Asparagus and Snow Peas with Lemon Parsley Gremolata (page 208)

ACQUIRE

Maintaining an Alkaline-balanced Lifestyle

Your alkaline choices will give you control
of your well-being and provide confidence that
you will have the energy you require to live a
full and ambitious, long, happy life,
free from sickness and disease.

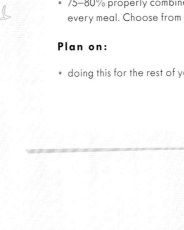

Start here if:

- you have successfully completed the Inspire and/or the Desire and/or the Aspire stage(s) and are ready to move on to making alkaline foods, exercise, and positivity a permanent part of your life

- you already eat a high-alkaline diet, your body is mostly free of toxins and your digestive tract is clean, and you are ready to optimize your well-being with exercise and positivity

- you just want to jump right into an alkaline lifestyle and balance all your meals

Aim for:

- 75–80% properly combined (page 25) alkaline foods at every meal. Choose from any of the recipes in this book.

Plan on:

- doing this for the rest of your life!

Think of the Acquire stage as a permanent life-style choice. Once you reach this point, you will have made it through the storm, love how you feel, and want to share your abundant energy and vibrancy with the world! You will be glowing! Way to go! While you are here, right now, make a note of how it feels. Just really feel it, take a mental snapshot, and lock it in your memory for the days when you fall off track. And why not record it in your journal or with a selfie too? This feeling of wellness and vibrant energy will keep you loving your lifestyle.

I feel amazing when I eat in an alkaline way, balancing my meals every day and consuming lots of water in between. It's a way of living now that keeps me completely free of back pain, and when I stray, I am quick to recover my regime as my body gives me the signs to get me back on track. Often I might do a short veggie feast (Desire), then eat lots of purely alkaline meals (Aspire), and, yay, it's all good again (I'm back at Acquire).

Changing what I eat was the biggest piece of alkalizing my lifestyle, but notice that I said "lifestyle" and not "diet." An alkaline lifestyle also means taking a look at your exercise program and at your emotional, mental, and spiritual health and making changes to support your return to optimal wellness.

 ## 1. SET YOUR INTENTION

Making a life-long commitment to nourish and nurture your body by eating well, getting regular exercise, and taking care of your mental, emotional, and spiritual health is an awesome and inspiring declaration. (Quick, get that journal out!) Look at the journey that's brought you to this place and congratulate yourself! Your body is now in a good position to be able to manage a wider variety of foods. Your alkaline buffers are strong and your body has the capability to release acids and toxins effectively. But let me remind you that it probably took a bit of hard work to get here, right? Your body is nice and tidy now, so do your best to keep it this way. When you choose to zig or zag, pull out your alkaline tricks and get back on track so that you don't find yourself with a body that is sick and tired all over again.

Make a commitment to add 30–35 minutes of exercise to your day to help your body move out its daily accumulation of acids and prevent a recurring buildup. Try 15 minutes of yoga and 15 minutes of brisk walking—mixing it up makes the exercise more fun and doable. Also make time each day for enough rest and for 1 activity that will provide you with a positive mental, emotional, or spiritual experience. Try journaling what you are grateful for, enjoying quality time with loved ones, meditating, listening to calming music, or if necessary, meeting with a professional to work toward emotional, psychological, or spiritual healing. Pay attention to this part of your life: acids result from stress and negative emotions, so your alkaline success depends on a healthy emotional, spiritual, and mental state.

2. MAINTAIN YOUR ALKALINE DIET

Balance your daily intake, meal by meal, with alkaline foods, aiming for an overall balance of 75% alkaline to 25% acidic foods, and drink 12–16 cups of water throughout the day. By combining your foods properly at each meal and eating and drinking separately (see sidebar, page 72), you will be able to maintain good digestion. By preventing foods from fermenting inside you, you will have a healthy, balanced gut flora. Avoid yeasts and fungi (vinegar, pickles, mushrooms, algae, spirulina, etc.). Limit your consumption of beer and wine (save them for special occasions) and fish and meats (eat them 1–3 times a week at most, as no more than 20–25% of your meal, and only the best sources you can find and afford), all of which cause the body to form acids that bog down your digestion and can lead to inflammation and disease. If you are experiencing a serious medical condition, refrain from all animal products until you are balanced and well.

With any lengthy deviation from the alkaline diet, you will feel the difference in your body—your early warning sign that you are veering off track. But you can still indulge in highly acidic and mucus-forming foods, such as dairy cheese, sweets, and alcohol, as long as you consume them no more than a few times a week and in small portions. Make or buy the best-quality, indulgent organic acidic foods you can and enjoy them without beating yourself up. Ideally use low heat and carefully steam-fry (in broth or water), braise, poach, or bake your animal proteins and soft-boil your eggs to minimize denaturing the proteins and help retain the nutrient value of the protein. If you overindulge, just bump your diet back up to 90–100% alkaline foods, boost your alkaline supplements a little until your pH levels rise, and move on.

What Does It Look Like?

Lots of alkaline water throughout the day.

A plate that is 75% veggies (of which half should be raw, the balance may be steamed) and 25% acid foods, like nuts, seeds, legumes, or healthy plant or organic animal protein now and then.

An alkaline smoothie, a green juice, or a blended green drink with or for breakfast.

A smaller selection of soaked nuts & seeds alongside legumes, whole grains, or plant and/or animal proteins.

An abundance of cruciferous veggies, such as broccoli, cabbage, Brussels sprouts, kale, cauliflower, and bok choy (their phytonutrients increase the production of alkaline buffers to help eliminate acids).

That's it! With plenty of these purely alkaline foods and the 4 alkaline essentials (page 35), you will be able to maintain your body's balanced alkaline pH level.

EAT AND DRINK SEPARATELY

Break the habit of drinking during mealtimes.

- Drink alkaline beverages, including water, up to 30 minutes *before* you eat.

- Drink nothing *while* you eat.

- Drink more alkaline beverages, including water, 60 minutes *after* you eat.

Why? Liquids, including water, dilute your digestive juices right when they will be going into high gear to break down your food into usable nutrients. Allowing your body to fully digest foods without interference prevents fermentation in the gut.

If you really have to drink something during a meal, enjoy up to 1 cup of alkaline green vegetable juice or alkaline lemon water with a completely raw salad (that you chew well). The vegetables have a high water content and plenty of live enzymes and will require less effort from your digestive system to process, thus a drink during your meal won't interfere.

Drinking wine/alcohol with a meal, especially if it contains meat or grains, is particularly tricky for your digestive system. If you indulge, take a digestive enzyme with your meal and always add a nice big leafy salad.

THE PROTEIN QUESTION

Does a plant-based diet provide enough protein? The answer is, yes! An alkaline diet provides exactly what the body needs.

- A diet rich in a wide variety of plant-based foods provides the body with plenty of the most easily assimilated forms of protein.

- Experts now say that consuming 20–35 grams of protein per day is better for your health than previous recommendations. Most folks are consuming much more. Too much protein has been shown to increase the risk of cancer, particularly animal protein, which is highly acidic.

- A single meal of ½ cup of lentils (9 grams), 1 cup cooked kale (2.5 grams), ½ cup peas (4 grams), and ¼ cup almonds (7 grams) gives you 22.5 grams of protein

Of the 20 amino acids that form the building blocks of protein, 9 are termed essential. Foods that contain all 9 essential amino acids are called complete proteins, but you can get complete proteins by eating a wide variety of plant-based foods throughout the day that together contain all 9 essential amino acids, especially greens and grasses.

Athletes as well as pregnant or breastfeeding women may require more protein. If necessary, supplement with isolated plant proteins such as hemp or sprouted brown rice. Consult your holistic health-care provider who can assist with your individual needs.

3. GET ACTIVE THE ALKALINE WAY

Exercising in an alkaline way helps release acids and toxins from the body, increases your breathing capacity, ups your production of red blood cells, improves your digestion, and stimulates your metabolism, to name just a handful of the benefits. You don't need to run marathons; in fact, please don't until you consult an alkaline coach to help you combat all the lactic acid you create with intense exercise. But do find a way to bring balance to the active part of your life.

THE FACTS: How Exercise Helps Alkalize the Body

Engaging in physical exercise is a great natural way to elevate your mood, reduce stress, and regain calmness and clarity of mind. Exercising moderately for 30–35 minutes releases "feel-good" chemicals, such as endorphins, adrenaline, serotonin, and dopamine, in the brain. And these chemicals can reduce stress hormones like cortisol to produce feelings of well-being and even euphoria (a "runner's high"). Even doing gentle exercise, such as yoga or a handful of good stretches for just 10–15 minutes, can improve your mood and decrease fatigue. Move your body in some way every. single. day. and you *will* feel the benefits.

Alkalizing your exercise routine means choosing an aerobic (with oxygen) activity to improve your body's use of oxygen. You need to sweat so the lymphatic system will release acids and toxins through your largest elimination organ, your skin, and by respiration. Increase your heart rate enough that you can still carry on a conversation while exercising without being in pain or gasping for air. Once you push it to a state of exhaustion, you are exercising in an anaerobic (without oxygen) manner that produces lactic acid. Remember, an alkaline lifestyle is about reducing acids, not creating them. Extreme athletes should be aware of recharging with electron-rich alkaline foods, which will buffer the acids and restore the electrical charge to sore, tired, and depleted cells in the muscles. Rich greens powder combined with alkaline water can be a great pick-me-up in the middle of a workout and afterward to help buffer and release the lactic acid.

New research shows that healthy fat provides more than twice as much potential energy as protein or carbohydrates. Ultra runner Stu Mittleman is living proof that a diet rich in healthy fats and electrons from alkaline plant-based foods provides enough energy to successfully fuel intense exercise—and with far less lactic acid production. He ran across America from coast to coast! More and more athletes are skipping the carb-loading and finding tremendous results and optimal wellness with an alkaline lifestyle.

TRY THIS: Alkalize Your Exercise

1. Assess your current level of activity. Record in your notebook what gets you moving and how often. Is it indoors? Outdoors? With a friend?

2. Review your current exercise program with your health-care provider or a personal trainer, especially if it is intense or you have a health condition. Work together to choose the exercise(s) you like best and develop a program that's right for you.

3. Make a commitment to follow a program that includes at least 30–35 minutes of moderate exercise every day. If your fitness program is extreme and contributing to your ill health, commit to reducing it until you are healthy and balanced again.

4. If you are an athlete, work with an alkaline coach to balance your lactic acid and train your body to burn fats instead of carbs/sugars for optimal energy.

Once you make one change, you'll start to see other things shift—for the better. Move your body in some way every day, and your mind will become clearer, your energy will improve, and your body will heal faster. It's proof that everything is connected and that you never can tell where that first step will lead.

Move your body

These activities are great for anyone, anytime, especially when you're healing from a medical condition or when you've been inactive for a while. According to Dr. Brian Clement of the Hippocrates Institute, exercise can speed up healing significantly. Do 1 of these or combine them for a total of 30—35 minutes of daily exercise.

- **Rebounding.** Never heard of it? It's just bouncing on a mini trampoline, like when you were a kid. All you do is bounce *without allowing your feet to leave the tramp*. It's gentle on your joints and helps to improve digestion and elimination. Your calves get a really good workout, as do your heart, blood, and lymphatic system, which regulates the immune system and helps to clean up debris and release acids and toxins from the body. The pumping action of your calves triggers the movement of lymphatic fluid, so rebounding for up to 30 minutes (all at once or in two 15-minute sessions) jump-starts the lymph, is simple to fit into your day, and will greatly enhance your alkaline lifestyle. Start with 2—3 times per week and gradually increase your frequency.

- **Whole Body Vibrating.** A vibration template is a simple platform that you stand on. It vibrates at varying degrees. Ten minutes on the vibe is like a 60-minute walk, and it can move and stimulate nearly every muscle in your body. These machines have also been proven to assist in rebuilding bone density. Who knew? I used this machine every single day as I healed my herniated disk because I was unable to bounce and couldn't walk for more than a few minutes at a time. I still use my vibration plate,

sometimes doing stretches to increase its effectiveness. It's great exercise on its own, and makes a great warm-up or recovery for another activity since it reduces any fatigue or pain you may feel as you begin a new exercise regime.

- **Walking.** This is a simple exercise that needs no special equipment. Try for 30 minutes or more, but don't beat yourself up if you only fit in 10. Even just 10—15 minutes a day at a brisk pace is better than no walking at all. And breathe . . . breathe in the fresh air, and take nice deep breaths of oxygen to nourish and alkalize your cells. Allow your mind to wander or be quiet, or connect with a companion along the way. Walking does a body good!

- **Yoga.** This combination of meditation and stretches calms the mind and encourages circulation, which helps to release toxins from the body. It's like multi-tasking! After a class, my mind feels rejuvenated and my body feels like a stretchy rubber band. Even though I no longer suffer from back pain, I am still cautious with some poses. Tell your instructor if you have any physical limitations; they can help you modify your practice so you don't overdo it. Once you're familiar with the poses, using a yoga video (see Resources) at home can make it easier to fit exercise into your day.

4. ADOPT A HEALTHY SLEEP ROUTINE

According to the National Sleep Foundation, most adults should be sleeping 8 hours per night, but the national average is just 6.7 hours. Not only do you feel cranky and groggy when you're sleep-deprived, but your body doesn't have the chance to do all the digesting and cleansing and detoxing and repair work that happen while you're at rest. Healthy eating and exercise aren't enough to maintain optimal health if your body doesn't get the chance to use the nutrients and take out the garbage.

TRY THIS: Cultivate Good Sleep Hygiene

1. Commit to sleeping 8 hours per night. Record in your notebook what prevents you from getting enough rest. Is it not going to bed early enough? Difficulty falling asleep? Or staying asleep?

2. Review your sleep hygiene with your health-care provider, especially if you are chronically undersleeping. Work together to implement changes that will allow you to get enough consistent rest.

3. Take naps if you need to, but don't let these be a substitute for a good night's sleep.

5. EDUCATE YOURSELF

The Mind-Body Connection

By now, if you've cleaned up your diet and introduced regular exercise, you are probably noticing that all the good things you're feeding your body are helping you think clearly and positively. It can be enormously empowering to realize you've just moved your acidic body to a healthier, alkaline state and that you have the means to control your health and well-being. (I still feel euphoric when I think about how lucky I was to discover this way of living.) However, this positive outlook needs nurturing so that negative thoughts and feelings don't creep in, take over, and adversely affect your physical health. Learning to cultivate a balanced mental, emotional, and spiritual outlook is critical to your overall success with an alkaline lifestyle.

This was a huge piece of learning for me. I honestly couldn't see how a whole bunch of vegetables, green juice, and water could possibly change the tough cartilage of my herniated disk. Like the doctors and neurosurgeons who were treating me, I really thought I would require serious surgical intervention to repair or replace the disk. But since I absolutely did not want the highly invasive surgery and since nothing else was working and I was still in agony, I was willing to give alkalizing a try. In addition to changing my diet, I learned how to use visualization and the power of belief. I practiced picturing my disk as perfect. I hung images of a healthy spine with perfect disks around the house to remind me to see my disk as already healed. After just 3½ months of alkalizing and daily visualization, I was completely free of pain (and I still am)! It felt like a miracle. I can honestly say that my beliefs helped to shape my physical reality.

Bruce Lipton, author of *The Biology of Belief,* describes your mind as the computer for your body. If you tell your body it can't, it can't. If you tell your body it can, it can. This same thinking is at the root of many mind-body therapies, and practicing one or a combination of these activities regularly is a great way to increase your mental strength as well as your emotional and spiritual vitality. Try meditation, prayer, yoga, tai chi, hypnosis, guided imagery, cognitive-behavioral therapy, creative art therapies, and simple relaxation. Regardless of what you choose, a regular practice will help you become more conscious of your mental state and adjust your course as necessary to manage stress, build and maintain a positive attitude, and create meaningful relationships in your life. This is whole-body healing, the optimal well-being that I want for you!

TRY THIS: 3 Ways to Prepare Your Mind and Body

1. Assess your current alkalinity by measuring the pH of your urine and saliva. Record the results in your notebook.
2. Affirm your commitment to alkalizing your lifestyle, from your diet to your exercise program to your emotional and spiritual happiness. Write your intention in your notebook.
3. Begin to identify areas where your life still feels out of balance. Record these in your notebook. On your own or with someone else, brainstorm strategies for finding and working toward balance that feels right for you. (Need some ideas? Gabrielle Bernstein's book *May Cause Miracles* might help.)

Achieving optimal balance all the time can be difficult. We get busy, we get injured, our relationships get stressed, our mood fluctuates. That's life. But the alkaline lifestyle gives you the tools to get back on track. If your diet is out of balance, return to the Desire or Aspire stages to clean up your digestive tract. If your exercise routine has gone haywire, see if you can bike to work or fit in a yoga class at lunchtime. Or meet a friend for a walk rather than tea—and make it a regular date. If you feel lethargic or burned out, it can be hard to get out of the rut. Try some of these strategies to achieve a fresh, new balance in your life:

*   Discover your zest for life by giving yourself permission to follow your passion! Let go of your negative thoughts or limiting beliefs.
*   Work on expressing your emotions openly, respectfully, and constructively.
*   Make time to listen to your inner dialogue and resolve any outstanding grievances.
*   Seek help if you need to journey through trauma and loss so you can heal.
*   Identify your stressors and then monitor and reduce the stress from your day job, your home life, and your relationships. (This was huge for me: I thought I was busy, not stressed!)
*   Make your home and work environments joyful places.
*   Surround yourself with positivity by first embracing it yourself. Be kind.
*   Discover your connection with the energy fields that surround you and are within you.
*   Be conscious of the everyday personal and household chemicals/cleaners you use; switch to healthy alternatives, if necessary.
*   Choose to live sustainably and empower yourself and others by buying fairly traded, organic, sustainable goods; taking care of the Earth; and acting ethically.
*   Be gracious. Do your best to do, be, and live well without harboring feelings of regret or guilt when you fall off track.

As overwhelming as this list may seem, if you slowly wake up and do one small thing each day, you will find your world becoming much calmer, cleaner, and far less toxic and you will begin to heal and feel vibrant for years to come. Just knowing you have choices is an important step in managing stress and alkalizing your lifestyle for optimal health.

ALKALINE LIFESTYLE
Daily Snapshot

upon WAKING

1. Drink 1–2 glasses of lemon water (juice of 1/4–1/2 lemon in 1 cup of warm or room-temperature water).
2. Take 1 tsp of mineral salts dissolved in 1 cup of water.

Tip for exercise:
gentle 30–35 mins workout— *yoga *walking *stretching *rebounding *light jogging

15-20 mins later

Drink a green juice and eat a breakfast porridge, yeast-free bread, or salad, or just have an alkaline smoothie.

BEDTIME
Take 1 tsp of mineral salts dissolved in 1 cup water.

—sleep well—

throughout the MORNING
Drink at least 4–5 cups of water. Add some greens powder to nourish and energize you and to release toxins.

journaling

exercise

meditation

reading

pampering

throughout the EVENING

Drink at least 4–5 cups of water. Add some greens powder to nourish and energize and to release toxins.

DINNER
Load up your plate with 75% veggies (half steamed veggies, the balance a raw salad) and 25% low-acid foods.

throughout the AFTERNOON

1. Drink at least 4–5 cups of water. Add some greens powder to nourish and energize and to release toxins.
2. Nibble on some soaked nuts, veggie sticks, and hummus, or have a green drink, if you're hungry. (But don't nibble while you drink your water.)

LUNCH
Fill your plate with at least 75% alkaline foods (with at least half of them raw alkaline veggies) and 25% or less of low-acid foods.

Tips for spiritual, emotional, & mental wellness:
* take a long bath *enjoy quiet time *sip herbal tea *eat mindfully *connect with friends & family *buy yourself flowers

6. OPTIMIZE YOUR LIFE AND YOUR LIFESTYLE

An alkaline lifestyle, in my eyes, is a perspective. It is a choice and a feeling of well-being. It is desired by many and achievable by everyone. It is the lifestyle nature designed us to follow. The key to the Acquire stage is making your alkaline lifestyle sustainable: balancing your diet, your exercise, and your mental and emotional well-being in a way that works for you in the long term. Remember, your goal is to make at least 75% of your diet alkaline vegetables (with at least half of these enjoyed raw and the balance lightly steamed) and the remaining 25% or less cooked or raw healthy, minimally processed (but ideally unprocessed) acidic foods; to exercise moderately for 30–35 minutes per day; and to build in time for at least one activity that brings you joy and mental/emotional strength. The Daily Snapshot (page 78) shows what a typical day in my life looks like.

Follow all the dietary guidelines, get in your exercise, and find your emotional balance in a way that works for you. The key is to always find the joy in life: enjoy simple pleasures and live the meaningful life you were meant to lead. One of the daily reminders in my digital calendar is this quote from Maya Angelou: "Be *present* in all things and thankful for all things." Enjoy the company of those you love, often, in gatherings, connecting and sharing with nutritious, hearty meals and good conversation. This is a vital part of every culture and a healthy, precious part of life. Adapt and create food rituals that fit with your new lifestyle and respect the choices of the people around you; introduce others to your favorite dishes by sharing them—but don't force others to follow your lead. Even if we can be successful in extending our life through an alkaline lifestyle, we will only experience true health when we are living authentically and joyfully and in harmony with others.

Be willing to share the knowledge that you have gained and inspire others with your words, wisdom, and experience. This doesn't mean pushing the information on those who are not interested, but being generous and open with those who are. Help them on their way to their own journey toward health. Remember, people who are happy and optimistic and living a joyful life live far longer and attract others who also live this way!

TRY THIS: Bring joy to your own life and the life of others

1. In your notebook, make a list of the things that make you happy.
2. Make a second list of all the things you could do to bring joy to others.
3. Make a commitment to embrace positivity and share that outlook with your family, your friends, and the world.

7. PREPARE FOR THE UNEXPECTED!

> "Healing is a matter of time, but it is sometimes also
> a matter of opportunity." —Hippocrates

The longer you consistently follow the alkaline life-style, the more it will feel like second nature. If pain or chronic illness motivated you to change your diet, then thinking back to those days is a good way to stay on track (because you never want to wind up *there* again). If your journey wasn't so dramatic, then building a support network can be a good way to stay motivated. When you continue to be conscious of your choices, your fallbacks won't be as damaging. But you can still lose your way. Here are some ways to stay accountable for your own well-being:

PAY ATTENTION TO YOUR MUCUS

I know, I know, this is supposed to be a cookbook, but a clear annoying nasal drip is my early warning sign that my kids or I have indulged in acidic toxins. Mucus naturally assists in buffering these acids and releasing them safely from the body. Too much mucus, of course, means a lower pH, which creates an environment that breeds bacteria and leads to inflammation. So, at the first sign of a drippy nose, out comes the chlorophyll (I use liquid chlorophyll) and super greens powder. We also start to consume 90% alkaline foods or more and extra doses of green juice, alkaline water, good oils, and mineral salts. We make sure we get some alkalizing exercise and lots of rest, and we avoid every speck of sugar. I keep the tissue box handy!

Be sure to avoid decongestants and other over-the-counter medicines—let the mucus flow and do its job so bacteria and viruses cannot set up camp! If you are very acidic, that mucus may be accumulating to prevent them from damaging the blood and tissues. Instead of a drippy nose, you may develop sticky mucus—a thicker nasal or lung congestion— asthma, poor digestion, or lightheadedness. Alkalizing your lifestyle, boosting your alkaline supplements, and hydrating your body will gradually get rid of the mucus and clear up these symptoms.

- **Check your pH levels** on the 1st of each month to see if you are maintaining your alkaline balance.

- **Review your week every Sunday night.** If it was a pretty balanced week, give yourself a pat on the back and carry on. If you veered off course, just make a commitment (write it down with specifics) to increase your intake of alkaline foods and sup-plements, maintain your exercise program, and balance your emotional life. Need to create the habit of checking in with yourself regularly? Place a sticky note on your bathroom mirror that says "Is it Sunday today?"

- **Keep a journal,** and record your successes, your favorite recipes, and your zigs and zags from the lifestyle. This information will help to reinforce the positive, motivate you to stay on track, and help you anticipate when you're likely to lose your way so you can strategize ways to avoid it. When life gets busy or you're traveling, use your journal to plan dinner, what foods to soak, or when and where to find a yoga class!

- **Reward yourself** by celebrating milestones with a treat like a relaxing massage, a pedicure, a cozy new sweater, or even just a candlelit bubble bath. Positive reinforcement only breeds more positive behavior.

- **Commit to a veggie feast twice a year,** or however often feels right for you, and mark it in your calendar. Feast on your own or find a partner to join in, even if it's just for 1 day. Join an online group (see Resources) for added support, if necessary.

- **Ignore the naysayers** and take pride in your achievements. Change always involves resistance, which can make you—and others—doubt your choices. Those inner gremlins are your fears—and the fears of others who are afraid they'll need to change too—so acknowledge them and then stand strong. You know you're making positive changes, so make another green smoothie and toast the goddess of kale or your Alkaline Sister!

- **Develop a support network** of cheerleaders, like-minded folks, and professionals who can teach, guide, and support you along the way. If you use food as an emotional comfort in times of stress, seek out a good counselor who can help you get to the root of your issues and solve them so they don't get in the way of your alkaline journey. If you tend to get sidetracked while on vacation or around the holidays, work with an alkaline coach or an online support group to help you get back on track if you need help.

Remember, no one is perfect, so most of all, don't be down on yourself. Set a goal to begin again and then just go for it! Go back to that mental snapshot (or selfie) you took when you were feeling healthy and vibrant. Open your journal and reread just how clean and alive you felt after completing the veggie feast. Work your way back to your alkalizing commitment with whatever support it takes, 'cuz you deserve to feel great!

TRICKY FOODS

How is it that some foods always seem to send us way off track? Be especially careful with:

- wine (remember, it takes 8 glasses of alkaline water to neutralize 1 glass of wine)

- dark chocolate (choose 90% cacao, without refined sugar)

- caffeine (1–2 times a week at most)

- sugar (this one is the worst!)

- wheat (choose spelt if you can)

- dairy (especially cheese!)

These tend to creep back into our diet as a social thing, not just once but often. If you find yourself consuming these regularly, embrace a cleansing regime to regain balance. Commit to a veggie feast 1 day a week or 1 day every 2 weeks, or at least stick to juices until lunchtime a few days a month and have a big salad for dinner. This way you'll maintain the fruits (umm, I should say "veggies") of your labor!

8. EMBRACE THE BENEFITS

By choosing to alkalize your lifestyle, you have taken on responsibility for your own health. This is the most empowering step you can take to improve your quality of life, for good. You now have the necessary tools to choose optimal well-being at any time.

If you have followed the 4 steps of the alkalizing program—or even if you've just jumped in at the Aspire stage—you have learned more about your body, from its strengths and weaknesses to how best to work with these to improve digestion, reduce cravings, and overcome yeast overgrowths. You have a clearer picture of what it means to alkalize your meals and what foods generate acidity in the body as well as how to balance them with alkaline mineral supplements, mindful meals, and alkaline thoughts. You have likely improved your diet and digestion, even if you've just begun to make small changes. And you are reaping the benefits of vibrant energy and diminishing ill-health.

Perhaps you have reached out or have a plan to connect with new communities that align with your alkaline journey, or maybe you have deepened your personal relationships. Perhaps you have evaluated your work-life balance and consciously minimized your stress load. If you have expanded your healthier choices to include all areas of your life—from alkalizing your exercise to buying organic or switching to less toxic cleaning products in your home—you will be rewarded with greater peace of mind and a healthier You. Congratulations! You are well on your way to optimal wellness.

9. WHAT'S NEXT?

This is when the alkaline party begins! Woo hoo! Hip, hip, hooray! Make yourself a beautiful celebratory Pancake Cake (page 268) and share it with your loved ones, or simply make time for your very favorite activity and bask in the feeling of vibrant health that you have created for yourself. Look in the mirror, acknowledge yourself for regaining control of your health, and give thanks.

Your journey doesn't end here. I have been alkalizing my lifestyle for many years, but I continue to learn about my body, about how it responds to different situations, and about how to enhance my well-being with complementary practices. Many natural health-care providers and holistic practitioners can help you to fine-tune your health through thyroid and adrenal hormone testing, hair analysis, and metabolic typing, and to deep-clean specific parts of your body through lymphatic massage, liver cleansing, colon hydrotherapy, infrared sauna, and even chiropractic. Look for workshops offered by specialists in your own community; they are often found advertised on bulletin boards at your local health food store. The resource section at the back of this book includes links to websites and recommended books that provide more information about many of the topics I've covered. Whatever you do, continue this magnificent journey to living well!

The Aries in me encourages you to gently share your journey with others, particularly those who are curious about the changes you've been making. (Sharing with people who are not interested is not only discouraging but also puts doubt in your mind—trust me, I've been there!) Just be the example and live the life. People will see how you glow, notice your boundless energy, and want to know what your secret is. **You can be part of the movement toward global optimal wellness just by taking care of you!**

And please stay in touch!

I blog at www.alkalinesister.com, where you'll find articles about alkalizing your lifestyle and many more recipes (and pretty pictures, of course!). If you create any yummy ones, share them in the comments. You can also follow me on Instagram (@alkalinesister), where I share even more recipes and pretty pictures, or on Pinterest (alkalinesister), where I am constantly compiling a wealth of alkaline information for you. Wherever you connect with me, be sure to say hello and let me know how you are doing. I am incredibly inspired by You! As your Alkaline Sister, I truly care about you and your journey and your well-being, and I'll do my best to answer your comments and questions.

Jiddu Krishnamurti said, "It is no measure of health to be well adjusted to a profoundly sick society," and my true hope is that you find your way and live the wildly vibrant life you were meant to, free from sickness and disease.

Another green smoothie cheer to you! Now let's eat some yummy alkalizing food!

TRY THESE 3 RECIPES
for your new lifestyle

Rhubarb Almond Scones (page 144)

Thai Spaghetti Squash Noodles with Sweet Chili Sauce (page 222)

Raw Ravioli with Pesto and Macadamia Cheeze (page 168)

The
Recipes

GETTING STARTED

There are no real rules about how to prepare for alkalizing your life. If you are anything like me, you'll just dive right into your favorite-looking recipe, gathering the necessary ingredients and tools to get started, and then testing your skills as you go.

However, there's no denying that a well-stocked and organized kitchen helps make meal prep easier. In the following pages, you'll find information about the tools and foods I like to have on hand, and some tips for soaking and sprouting beans, grains, and nuts—in case doing this is new for you.

When you get to the recipes, don't get too hung up on measurements, ingredients, or equipment, because a little tweak here or there won't spoil any recipe in this book. Many of these dishes are designed to go together with others, so mix and match as you please.

Lastly, be sure to note that there are 3 different kinds of recipes—purely alkaline, alkaline balanced, and mildly acidic (see pages 98-99)—select the ones that are appropriate for where you're at in your alkalizing journey. Alrighty, off you go . . .

What's in My Alkaline Kitchen?

The tools I love and use most often! I have a penchant for nifty gadgets and appliances, and these have become my favorites because they make my everyday food prep easier and faster. I hardly put them away before I need them again.

rasp * high-speed blender (page 45) * lemon squeezer (my all-time fave)

* lettuce spinner * sharp knives * food grater * wooden spoons * mason jars for storage

baking sheets, tart pans, muffin tins

ice cream maker (optional)

rice cooker

spiral cutter for veggies

dehydrator (optional)

nut mylk machine or nut mylk bags

steamer pots and pans

colander

food processor

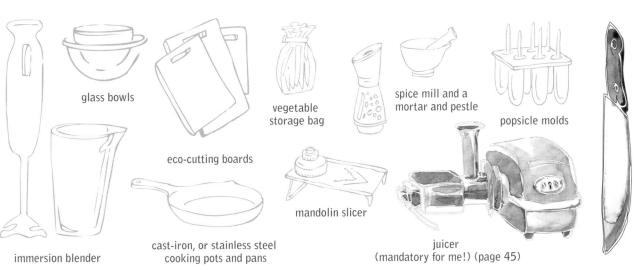

glass bowls

vegetable storage bag

spice mill and a mortar and pestle

popsicle molds

eco-cutting boards

mandolin slicer

immersion blender

cast-iron, or stainless steel cooking pots and pans

juicer (mandatory for me!) (page 45)

fresh!

What's in My Alkaline Fridge and Freezer?

I am addicted to veggies and usually try to cram all those listed below in my fridge at once, but buy the foods you love the most in quantities you'll use. Choose the freshest local, organic groceries you can find and pop the veggies into green produce bags to maximize their freshness.

Greens: arugula, baby greens, butter lettuce, chard, dandelion greens, kale, mâche, romaine, curly or leaf lettuce, spinach, wheatgrass (now and then or when veggie feasting) Vegetables: beets (all colors, keep the tops); bell peppers: red, orange, yellow; bok choy; broccoli; cabbage: red, napa, savoy; carrots (keep the tops for juicing); cauliflower; celery (organic only); lots of cucumbers; jicama; kohlrabi; zucchini; and seasonally, winter squash, sweet potatoes, radishes, Jerusalem artichokes, artichokes, asparagus, Brussels sprouts, green beans Sprouts: garlic, mung, onion, pea, radish, soybean, sunflower Fresh herbs: basil, cilantro, dill, mint, parsley, and seasonally, rosemary, thyme, chives, and sage grow outside my door Alkalizing fruits: avocados, fresh young coconuts, white grapefruit, lemons, limes, tomatoes Other fruits: cantaloupe, watermelon (in season, in moderation), organic berries (in season), green pears, green apples, mangoes (all in extreme moderation) Roots: fresh ginger, fresh turmeric, and burdock roots Healthy oils: Udo's 3-6-9 oil, flax oil, hemp oil, fish oil, grapeseed, hazelnut, almond, and sesame oils Mylks: organic almond mylk, coconut mylk (and pure coconut water) Staples: homemade salad dressings (pages 284-85), pesto (page 280), hummus (page 277), savory nut sprinkle (page 281) Raw nuts, seeds, and flours: almonds, Brazil nuts, cashews (the freshest raw cashews I can find), hazelnuts, pecans, pine nuts, raw pistachios, walnuts, flax seeds, hemp hearts, pumpkin seeds (pepitas), sesame seeds, sunflower seeds, almond flour, coconut flour Seed and nut butters: raw almond and sunflower butters, tahini (raw sesame butter) Freezer: fresh local fish (usually Pacific salmon); organic edamame; organic berries; Veggie Bouillon Cubes (page 277); pesto (page 280); sprouted grain unleavened bread (i.e., Manna bread); sprouted grain, spelt, or brown rice; extra flours, nuts, or seeds to maintain freshness

What's in My Alkaline Pantry?

The dry goods that round out this lifestyle! I luuuv to eat veggies on their own, but with just a few organic spices, other flavorings, and low-alkaline nuts, grains, or seeds I can turn them into many different and really tasty meals. Ask the staff in your local organic market for a tour if some of these goodies are new to you.

Spices: allspice, black pepper, cardamom, cayenne pepper, chipotle, cinnamon, cumin, Madras curry, dried mustard, nutmeg, onion powder, oregano, paprika, smoked paprika; freeze-dried or dried herbs (organic, non-radiated) as in basil, dill, oregano, thyme.

Flavorings: pure vanilla (ground or beans or alcohol-free pure liquid extract); salts (Celtic, Himalayan, Maldon, real unrefined sea salt); fresh garlic, onions (sweet, white, or purple, or shallots), Bragg Liquid Aminos (a non-fermented soy sauce), kombu, dulse; raw cacao, carob powder, lucuma; sun-dried tomatoes.

Grains: brown rice, wild rice, black and red rice, whole kamut, whole and flaked spelt **Seeds:** buckwheat, quinoa, quinoa flakes, chia (black or white), millet, kaniwa, amaranth, teff **Flours:** almond, amaranth, brown rice, buckwheat, chickpea, kamut, quinoa, sprouted spelt

Legumes: dried organic chickpeas, white beans, pinto beans, split green peas, mung beans, lentils (red, black, green)

Oils: cold-pressed, extra-virgin raw oils, including olive, coconut, avocado **Olives:** cured, dehydrated, and vinegar-free

Pasta: buckwheat soba, quinoa, kamut, brown rice, spelt **Herbal teas and coffee replacement:** organic mint, rooibos, herbal chai, pau d'arco, ginger, chamomile, licorice, roasted chicory, or roasted dandelion root

Crackers: organic rice (plain or seasoned with seaweed), raw vegetable crackers **Sweeteners:** chicory root (inulin), coconut nectar, lucuma, maple syrup (pure, organic, in extreme moderation, best kept in fridge once opened), stevia, yacón syrup **Thickening agents:** agar, arrowroot, tapioca starch **Coconut products:** thick, full-fat organic coconut mylk; coconut manna/cream; dried, flaked, or shredded, organic coconut **Mylks:** storebought organic unsweetened almond, hazelnut, or hemp mylks, for when you don't have your own nut/seed milk on hand **Dried unsulfured organic fruit:** goji berries, sour cherries, golden berries, figs, dates (all in extreme moderation)

SOAKING, COOKING, AND SPROUTING BEANS, LEGUMES, GRAINS, NUTS, AND SEEDS

In a perfect world, all of us would soak our grains, seeds, nuts, legumes, and beans. Soaking removes bitterness and improves the body's ability to digest these foods, and it is what earlier generations did until modern food processing took over. Sprouting makes these foods even more digestible by allowing them to go from acid-forming to more alkaline, and sprouts are biogenetic, which means they can transfer their life force to your body.

All grains, seeds, nuts, and legumes/beans contain phytic acid and enzyme inhibitors, and some contain oligosaccharides. Collectively, these are known as anti-nutrients. *Phytic acid* protects the seed of a plant from germinating too early, but if it is not released before cooking and eating, it can bind with calcium, zinc, magnesium, iron, and copper in the food, preventing your body from absorbing these beneficial minerals. *Enzyme inhibitors* are proteins created by a plant to protect itself from predators. They block the proper functioning of the digestive enzymes in plant-eating animals, including humans, which means we can't properly metabolize and absorb nutrients from our food. For example, when trypsin, our enzyme responsible for digesting protein, cannot do its job properly, the body compensates by secreting too many enzymes in the pancreas—where trypsin is created—which is very taxing on the body. Mineral deficiencies are also a common result of enzyme inhibitors. Not good! *Oligosaccharides* are complex sugars that a plant uses to send signals that help it grow, develop, and respond to changes in its environment. However, humans have a hard time digesting these sugars as we don't have the enzyme to do so.

Soaking these foods long enough to allow them to germinate—typically about 24 hours—activates an enzyme called phytase that breaks down and neutralizes most of the phytic acid. Adding a good squeeze of

> ### FRESH VERSUS CANNED
>
> One 15-ounce tin of beans will give you: 1½–1⅔ cups of cooked beans
>
> One cup of dried beans will give you: 2–3 cups of cooked beans
>
> One pound of dried beans will give you: 5–6 cups of cooked beans

lemon juice to the water when soaking your grains can help neutralize the phytic acid too. Germination also neutralizes most of the enzyme inhibitors. Soaking harder beans such as kidney, black, and navy beans in water with a piece of kombu seaweed alkalizes the soaking liquid and helps to minimize the oligosaccharides. If you don't have kombu, substitute 1 teaspoon of baking soda. Nuts and seeds can benefit from a pinch of Himalayan salt in the soaking water.

The good news is that with an alkaline-balanced diet, you will probably be eating less of these foods since most grains, seeds, nuts, legumes, and beans are acidic, unless they have sprouted (page 96). Soak them if you can or, in a pinch, choose tinned beans and legumes from companies like Eden Organics that soak their products overnight, add kombu to the soaking water, and use BPA-free tins. Look for soaked/sprouted flours and nut butters if you can find them. If you can't, you *can* make your own. Your next best bet is to take a digestive enzyme with your meal to help your body break down the food more effectively while minimizing the negative effects of the anti-nutrients.

Do your best and minimize the things that you now know are not optimal, but don't fret. Worrying will just cause more acidity, and we don't want that! So, you see, soaking and sprouting are kind of worth it, even if they take some getting used to.

Soaking Your Beans, Legumes, Grains, and Nuts

1. Place the grains, seeds, nuts, beans, or legumes in a bowl and discard any that are discolored or broken. Rinse 2–3 times until the water runs clear.

2. Cover with 3 inches of filtered water (unless otherwise noted as in seeds). Add the suggested alkalizing agent, cover with a plate or a lid, and consult the table on pages 94–95 for soaking times. For longer soaks, 12–24 hours, rinse the half-soaked food partway through and continue to soak.

3. Drain and rinse well. (Save the soaking water for your houseplants; they love it!)

4. Sprout your food, eat it raw as in chia, or go ahead and cook it.

Cooking Beans, Legumes, Grains, and Seeds

Cooking times may vary according to the age of the dried goods, how they've been stored, and your own personal preference.

1. Place the soaked, rinsed, and drained food in a large pot filled with filtered water and add kombu or lemon juice (or add salt only in the last ½ of the cooking time) and any seasonings as per the directions in the chart on pages 94–95 or the recipe. Bring to a boil, uncovered, skim off any foam that accumulates on top, and then turn down the heat to low.

2. For beans and legumes, simmer, uncovered, checking periodically to be sure there is enough water in the pot, until the food is soft but not mushy. For grains and seeds, simmer, covered, checking periodically to be sure the pot is not boiling dry, until the liquid is absorbed and the food is soft but not mushy. (See the chart on pages 94–95 for cooking times.)

3. Remove the pot from the heat. Drain the beans and legumes and add to your recipe. Allow grains and seeds to stand, covered, for 5–10 minutes and fluff with a fork before using.

6 REASONS TO SOAK YOUR FOODS

1. **Soaking improves digestibility** by removing phytic acid, enzyme inhibitors, and some oligosaccharides.

2. **Soaking your own foods is healthier** than buying tinned. You get less salt, no BPA, and more varieties of heirloom beans and legumes, and you can cook them to your preferred texture.

3. **Soaking nuts and seeds gives them more flavor and a richer, creamier texture.**

4. **Soaking can reduce your cooking time by up to ½,** especially for large dried beans.

5. **Soaking costs less and yields more.** Dry goods cost about ⅕ the price of tinned or processed equivalents, and 1 cup of dried beans yields nearly double what you get in a typical tin. Because it's no extra effort, you'll be inclined to soak double or triple batches to use in other recipes or freeze.

6. **Soaking reduces your carbon footprint** by reducing packaging waste, especially if you grow, harvest, and dry your own or buy in bulk and store in reusable glass jars.

SPROUT FOR HEALTH!

When we eat plants in sprouted form, not only are they easier to digest, they are dramatically higher in nutrients:

- vitamin B6 increases by 500%
- folic acid increases by 600%
- riboflavin increases by 1300%

And their life force is transferred to your body, which provides energy.

SOAKING AND COOKING CHART FOR BEANS/LEGUMES, GRAINS, NUTS, AND SEEDS

DRIED FOOD (1 CUP)	SOAKING TIME	WATER TEMP.	VOLUME OF COOKING WATER	ALKALIZING AGENT	COOKING TIME*	APPROX. YIELD
BEANS/LEGUMES						
Cannellini (white kidney beans) **or navy** (great northern beans)	8–12 hrs	warm	3½ cups	3-inch piece of kombu	60–100 mins	2½ cups
Chickpeas (garbanzo beans) **or black beans**	8–12 hrs	warm	4 cups	3-inch piece of kombu	60–90 mins	2¼ cups
Kidney beans or pinto beans	8–10 hrs	warm	3 cups	3-inch piece of kombu	60–90 mins	2¼ cups
Lentils, brown, green, or black	7–8 hrs	warm	2 cups	3-inch piece of kombu	20–30 mins	2¼ cups
Lentils, red	7–8 hrs	warm	2 cups	3-inch piece of kombu	10–20 mins	2½ cups
Mung beans	4–8 hrs	warm	2½ cups	3-inch piece of kombu	50–70 mins	2 cups
GRAINS						
Amaranth	7–8 hrs	warm	2 cups	1 Tbsp of lemon juice	12–15 mins	2½ cups
Buckwheat groats	7–8 hrs	warm	¼–½ cup	1 Tbsp of lemon juice	3–5 minutes	2½ cups
Kaniwa	7–8 hrs	warm	2 cups	1 Tbsp of lemon juice	10–15 mins	2 cups
Millet, hulled	12–24 hrs	warm	3–4 cups	1 Tbsp of lemon juice	10–15 mins	3½ cups
Quinoa	8–24 hrs	warm	1¾ cups	1 Tbsp of lemon juice	15–20 mins	3½ cups
Rice, black or brown	7–8 hrs	hot	2½ cups	1 Tbsp of lemon juice	30–40 mins	3 cups
Spelt and kamut berries	12–24 hrs	hot	2–3 cups	1 Tbsp of lemon juice	30–45 mins	2½ cups
Teff	7–8 hrs	warm	2–3 cups	1 Tbsp of lemon juice	5–20 minutes	3½ cups

DRIED FOOD (1 CUP)	SOAKING TIME	WATER TEMP.	VOLUME OF COOKING WATER	ALKALIZING AGENT	COOKING TIME*	APPROX. YIELD
Activated NUTS and SEEDS (up to 1 cup)						
Almonds	8-12 hrs**	room temperature	3 cups	½ tsp Himalayan salt	n/a	2 cups
Cashews and macadamias	2 hrs**	room temperature	3 cups	½ tsp Himalayan salt	n/a	2 cups
Hazelnuts, brazil nuts, and pistachios	8 hrs**	room temperature	3 cups	½ tsp Himalayan salt	n/a	2 cups
Pecans and walnuts	4 hrs**	room temperature	3 cups	½ tsp Himalayan salt	n/a	2 cups
Pine nuts	6 hrs**	room temperature	3 cups	½ tsp Himalayan salt	n/a	2 cups
Walnuts	4 hrs**	room temperature	3 cups	½ tsp Himalayan salt	n/a	2 cups
Buckwheat groats	30 mins–8 hrs**	room temperature	1½–2 cups	½ tsp Himalayan salt	10 mins if cooking, can be eaten raw after soaking	3 cups when cooked (2 cups when soaked)
Chia seeds (1 Tbsp)	20–30 mins	room temperature	3 Tbsp soaking water	n/a	n/a	3 Tbsp soaked
Flax seeds (1 Tbsp)	15–30 mins	room temperature	3 Tbsp soaking water	n/a	n/a	3 Tbsp soaked
Pumpkin/sesame/sunflower seeds	6–8 hrs	room temperature	3 cups soaking water	½ tsp Himalayan salt	n/a	1½ cups soaked

*Note: Cooking times especially for beans and legumes are very approximate as the age of dried foods is tough to determine and typically older dried foods will take longer to rehydrate.

**Refrigerate nuts while soaking.

DON'T SKIP THE SOAK!

Any amount of soaking is better than no soaking at all. If you're short on time, a quick soak won't eliminate as many anti-nutrients, but it will decrease the cooking time of dry goods. And just cooking your food helps to reduce its anti-nutrients.

- For a quick soak, cover the sorted dried beans or legumes with 4 inches of filtered water. Bring to a full boil, uncovered, for 1 minute, remove from the heat, cover, and allow to sit for 1–4 hours at room temperature. Drain and rinse well. Then cook as directed.

Sprout Your Beans, Legumes, Grains, and Nuts

1. Place ¼ cup (if sprouting for greens, e.g., alfalfa sprouts) or up to 1 cup (if sprouting for tails only, e.g., mung beans) of your soaked but uncooked food in each sprouting tray (see Resources) or place in a 1-quart mason jar. Cover the trays (or jar—sprout with the jar inverted to ensure good drainage) tightly with 2–3 layers of cheesecloth, and place them in a warm, dark spot.

2. Two to 3 times per day, rinse the seeds under running water (tap water is fine) for a few minutes and drain them well.

3. Allow the sprouts to grow until they reach the desired length. If they are slimy or taste sour, start again. Your seeds could be poor. Or maybe you soaked them too long, or didn't rinse them enough, or drain them properly. (Rancid sprouts can make you very ill, so use caution.)

4. Use the sprouts, both raw and lightly cooked, in wraps, salads, stir-fries, soups, and just on their own. My daughter munches on sprouted mung beans as an after-school snack! Transfer leftovers to a container or produce storage bag and refrigerate nuts and seeds for up to 2 days, rinsing daily, or sprouted beans or grains for up 5 days.

5. You can also dehydrate any of your sprouted foods. Spread them on dehydrator trays and allow them to dry at 115°F (or place them in a 150°F oven) for up to 24 hours. Eat out of your hand (nuts or seeds) or grind into flour (nuts, seeds, grains, beans, and legumes).

* Note: The only nut that will sprout a wee bud of a tail is almonds, as most nuts are pasteurized and will no longer germinate, but you must purchase non-pasteurized almonds.

SPROUTING CHART FOR BEANS, LEGUMES, GRAINS, NUTS, AND SEEDS

FOOD	QUANTITY	SOAKING TIME	NO. OF RINSES/DAY	DAYS UNTIL HARVEST	OPTIMAL HEIGHT	APPROX. YIELD
Alfalfa	2 Tbsp	6–8 hrs	2–3	3–6	1–2 inches	1½ cups
Almonds, unpasteurized	1 cup	8–12 hrs	2–3	1–3	⅛ inch	1½–2 cups
Broccoli	1½ Tbsp	4–8 hrs	2–3	3–6	1–2 inches	1½ cups
Buckwheat	1 cup	1 hr	3 (rinse well)	1–2	¼–4 inches	2–3 cups
Chickpeas (garbanzo beans)	1 cup	8–12 hrs	2–3	3–6	½–1 inch	3 cups
Lentils	1 cup	8–12 hrs	2–3	2–4	½–1 inch	3 cups
Mung	1 cup	8–12 hrs	2–3	1–2	½–1 inch	3 cups
Peas	1 cup	8–12 hrs	2–3	2–3	½–1 inch	2 cups
Pumpkin seeds, hulled	1 cup	8–10 hrs	2	3–6	up to ¼ inch	2 cups
Radish	1½ Tbsp	6–8 hrs	2–3	3–6	1–2 inches	1½ cups
Soybean	1 cup	16 hrs	3	3–5	½–1 inch	3 cups
Sunflower, hulled	1 cup	6–8 hrs	2	1–2	up to ¼ inch	1½ cups
Sunflower, unhulled	1 cup	8 hrs	2	2-4	2–3 inches	3 cups

FINDING YOUR ROUTINE

Anything you can do to simplify your meals is going to make it easier to embrace this lifestyle. Here are a few tricks I use.

1. **Aim for 2 grocery shops each week** so you have vegetables on hand at all times for snacks, meals, and juices. I go to the farmers' market once a week, then supplement with produce and fresh pantry items from an organic grocer.

2. **Join a local community-supported agriculture (CSA) co-op** and have a box of farm-fresh vegetables delivered weekly or pick them up at the farm. This is a great way to push your boundaries with lovely vegetables you might not ordinarily select.

3. **Plant your own garden**—even just a pot of fresh herbs or tomatoes—on your balcony, in your backyard, or in a local community plot.

4. **Make double batches of your favorite recipes** and enjoy the leftovers for lunches or another dinner. This includes salads, to pair with cooked foods like rice or quinoa, and to load up wraps in a jiffy.

5. **Buy lots of lemons and avocados** at various stages of ripeness to make quick toppings and tasty dressings.

6. **Keep healthy homemade dips and spreads at hand** to serve with raw veggies, roll into a wrap, or eat with a salad. Make a double batch of hummus (page 277) or a pesto (page 280) and freeze half. Over time, you'll build a reserve to draw from.

7. **Use your slow cooker and your rice maker to prepare meals ahead of time.** Pop on a pot of brown rice or millet in the morning and you'll have the start of a simple porridge or rice dish. Top with a bit of broth or dressing, a good handful of greens, some grated veggies, and a sliced avocado.

8. **Soak something every other day**, either lentils, nuts, seeds, or a grain, and then either cook it or continue to sprout it. Nuts make great snacks on the go, but be sure to date the jars when soaking and rinse the contents daily to ensure freshness.

9. **Grow a batch of sprouts or micro greens once a week or more.** Use them to dress your salads and dishes, and be sure to include your kids in the process.

* purely alkaline variant
** alkaline-balanced variant

MILDLY ACIDIC RECIPES

These recipes are the acid part of your diet, so eat small portions, pair them with lots of purely alkaline and alkaline-balanced foods, and take a digestive enzyme if necessary. Avoid these recipes when you are cleansing (Desire and Aspire stages).

JUICES, SMOOTHIES, AND NOURISHING DRINKS

Green juices, smoothies, and blended drinks are the keys to replenishing your alkaline energy bank because live green plants are rich in electrons that directly influence chemical reactions within the body and invigorate you with their life force. Once you become accustomed to drinking your greens every day you may never look back! Drink these easier-to-digest foods until noon if you like and then hydrate throughout the rest of the day with flavored waters, creamy nut mylks, and soothing herbal teas. Adjust the alkalinity and consistency of your drinks by adding more or less filtered, alkaline water.

FAMILY GREEN JUICE

MAKES ABOUT 30 OZ (DEPENDING ON THE SIZE OF YOUR VEGGIES)

6 leaves + stalks kale or chard (or a combination)

1 good handful spinach leaves

2 large English cucumbers, scrubbed

2 stalks celery

2 carrots, scrubbed (optional)

6–10 sprigs parsley

6 sprigs mint

1 lemon, peeled

½-inch piece ginger, scrubbed

1 green apple, peel on (optional)

1 cup filtered water

I credit this juice recipe, which has evolved over time, with transforming my family's health. Since making a commitment to serve it every. single. day. we've avoided all illnesses, save for an occasional drippy nose. It took some time for my kids to acquire a taste for veggies in the morning, but now they totally crave their green juice.

This version is our go-to recipe, though we do switch up the greens with lettuces and collards to vary the nutrients. You can add more cucumber to increase the volume, if you wish, and if you're not used to drinking veggie juice, go ahead and add the apple. Be sure to leave it out if you are going sugar-free or doing a juice feast. This recipe makes a lot, so halve the recipe if you're on your own, or do like me . . . and drink the entire pitcher!

Working in batches if necessary, feed the ingredients through your juicer one at a time, alternating between leafy and hard veggies. Pour the water through the juicer spout or stir into juice. Stir, pour into your favorite glasses, season to taste, and drink up your morning cocktail!

HOW TO GET IN THE JUICING GROOVE

1. **Cut and pack 4 or 5 days' worth of veggies** so you can pull a bag out of the fridge, toss the ingredients in the juicer, and whip up a drink. (Juice greens and herbs with veggies such as cucumber or celery that have a high water content.)

2. **Follow the same recipe for a few days** so you don't have to fumble about for ingredients or new combinations. Try Family Green Juice (above) to get started.

3. **Make your juices tasty!** Lemon, lime, and cucumber help to cut the strong chlorophyll taste of greens, so add generous amounts.

4. **Prepare a double batch and save some for later**—but only if you have a slow or masticating machine that makes juices with a good shelf life (page 45). To store juice for longer than 20–30 minutes, chill, add ½ tsp of vitamin C crystals dissolved in a couple of ounces of filtered, alkaline water, and stir.

5. **Use 1 part fruit to 4 parts greens** to start, then work toward 100% green veggies.

6. **Boost your electrolytes by adding unsweetened coconut water:** use 4–8 ounces of water from fresh young coconuts or buy it.

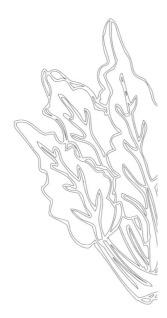

FRESH JUICES

The ingredients may vary, but the method is always the same. Feed all the ingredients 1 by 1 through your juicer, alternating between leafy and hard veggies, and process, in batches if necessary. Stir, pour into your favorite glass(es), dilute to taste with up to 25% alkaline water and drink up your morning cocktail! Yum!!

SWEET GARLICKY VEG JUICE

PURELY ALKALINE

I luuuv this nourishing, sweet anti-bacterial juice. To mini-mize the sugars, phase out the beet and carrots as you juice-feast. I tend to sweeten with stevia (with or in place of car-rots and beets), as I enjoy the sweet-garlic combination, but it's your choice.

MAKES 12–16 OZ

3 cups spinach leaves

2 large English cucumbers, scrubbed

2 carrots, scrubbed

8 sprigs parsley (about ⅓ cup)

2 large cloves garlic, peel on

1-inch piece ginger, scrubbed

1 small beet (optional)

2–3 drops liquid stevia (optional)

8-VEG JUICE AND BROTH

PURELY ALKALINE

Drink the juice straight up, use the broth as a soup base, or save the dry pulp (juice the tomatoes separately) to make crackers (page 282). Add the salt and olive oil after juicing the vegetables.

MAKES 24 OZ

2 cups spinach leaves

3 stalks celery

3 tomatoes

2 carrots, scrubbed

1 large English cucumber, scrubbed

1 small broccoli, crown and stem

¼ small sweet onion

2 cloves garlic, peel on

4–6 sprigs parsley

Himalayan salt

drizzle of extra-virgin olive oil

TUSCAN SUNSHINE WITH TURMERIC

PURELY ALKALINE

Fight inflammation, gas, and infection with this insanely yummy glass of sunshine packed with essential vitamins and minerals.

MAKES 12–16 OZ

2 cups spinach leaves

2 stalks celery

2 tomatoes

2 green onions

1 English cucumber, scrubbed

½ large red, orange, or yellow bell pepper

½ lemon, peeled

2 sprigs basil

1 sprig oregano (optional)

1 small clove garlic (optional)

1-inch piece turmeric root

GREEN DANDELION LEMONADE

ALKALINE BALANCED

Bitter greens make me want to hide, but they are sooo incredi-bly good for healing that I've found a way past my fear: just add a dose of lemon and pear!

MAKES 12–16 OZ

2½ cups dandelion greens (or spinach leaves)

1½ lemons, peeled

1 English cucumber, scrubbed

½–1 green pear or green apple, peel on

1-inch piece ginger, scrubbed

2 drops liquid stevia (optional)

PINK JUICE WITH BURDOCK ROOT

ALKALINE BALANCED
(use white grapefruit and skip the carrot for PURELY ALKALINE)

Packed with cleansing carotenoids (carrots and zucchini) and indoles (red cabbage) plus burdock root to purify the blood. Go easy on the burdock, which acts as a laxative!

MAKES 12–16 OZ

6 romaine leaves

¼ small red cabbage

6-inch yellow zucchini

2 small carrots, scrubbed

1-inch piece burdock root

1 pink grapefruit, peeled and quartered

1-inch piece ginger, scrubbed

3 drops liquid stevia (optional)

GINGERED BEET AND/OR CARROT LIVER TONIC

MILDLY ACIDIC

This sweet juice cleanses the liver, but avoid it if you're juice feasting and go easy if you're not. Serve with a straw to prevent a colorful mustache!

MAKES 8–10 OZ

6-inch piece English cucumber, scrubbed

1 medium yellow (or purple) beet with leaves and/or 3–4 carrots, scrubbed, ends trimmed

1 lemon, peeled

1-inch piece ginger, scrubbed

ALKALINE GREEN JUICE

PURELY ALKALINE

Add greens powder and a wee bit of cayenne to get your blood circulating and your metabolism moving.

MAKES 12–16 OZ

1½ cups spinach leaves

3–4 leaves + stalks bok choy

3 leaves + stalks kale or Swiss chard

3–4 florets + stalks broccoli

1½ English cucumbers, scrubbed

½ medium bulb fennel

1½ stalks celery

1½ lemons, peeled

1 tsp greens powder (optional but awesome)

pinch cayenne pepper (optional)

Minted Yellow Watermelon Cooler

LEAN INTO GREEN JUICE

PURELY ALKALINE

A mild juice for getting accustomed to this green juice thing! If you aren't a fan of cilantro, try fresh mint or fennel greens.

MAKES 12–16 OZ

8 romaine lettuce leaves (or better yet, spinach)

3 stalks celery

½ English cucumber, scrubbed

1 large handful pea shoots

1 large handful cilantro (about 24 sprigs)

½ lime, peeled

MINTED YELLOW WATERMELON COOLER

ALKALINE BALANCED

Summer days at the cottage call for organic watermelon and its cousin the cucumber. Drink this cooler on a hot day or freeze it in molds with popsicle sticks for an icy treat.

MAKES ABOUT 32 OZ (OR 8 POPSICLES)

6-inch piece English cucumber, peeled

½ small yellow or red watermelon, rind on if organic, chilled, and diced (about 4 cups)

6 sprigs mint + more for garnish

MAKES 16–20 OZ BLENDER **GREENS**

2 cups spinach leaves

2 leaves + stalks kale

2 leaves + stalks Swiss chard

8–10 oz filtered, alkaline water or coconut water

juice of 1 lemon

1 stalk celery

½ small romaine or leaf lettuce

½ English cucumber, scrubbed

6 sprigs parsley

6 sprigs mint

1-inch piece ginger, scrubbed

1–2 Tbsp omega-3 oil

If you don't have a juicer yet, this recipe is for you! And if you find that juices leave you feeling hungry, the fiber in this drink should fill you more. Pack the blender chock-full of whatever greens you have handy, but if you toss in lots of kale, use lemon generously to cut the bitter taste. Switch up the herbs with cilantro, lemon thyme and mint.

Blend the spinach, kale, and Swiss chard with the alkaline water (or coconut water) and lemon juice until smooth. Add the celery, lettuce, cucumber, herbs, and ginger and blend again until smooth. Stir in the omega-3 oil and pulse lightly to combine. Pour into glasses and sip with a straw to avoid the foam.

BLENDED DRINKS AND SMOOTHIES

Most of these recipes are deliberately generous to keep you full. Store the leftovers for up to 8 hours if you can't finish it all.

LEMON-LIME
GREEN GOODNESS

MAKES 32 OZ (1 LARGE OR 2 MEDIUM SERVINGS)

1 large English cucumber, scrubbed, 1-inch pieces

juice of 1 lemon

juice of 1 lime

½ cup coconut water, or more as needed for consistency

1 cup spinach leaves

2 stalks celery, roughly chopped

1 large kale leaf, rib removed (save for juicing)

1 large handful parsley

1 large handful mint

1-inch piece ginger, scrubbed

1 avocado (optional)

2 Tbsp hemp hearts

1–2 Tbsp Brazil nut, brown rice, or hemp protein powder

1–2 Tbsp omega oil

2–3 drops liquid stevia (optional)

You might be surprised by how neutral all these veggies taste together, especially if you were never really a big veggie fan. Give it a try, 'cuz this drink is packed with alkalizing minerals to scare those acids out of your body! Added protein and healthy fat make this a great post-workout drink in the morning.

Blend the cucumber with the lemon and lime juices and coconut water to liquefy. Add the spinach, blend, and then add the celery, kale, parsley, mint, ginger, and avocado (if using) and blend again. Add a splash of coconut water, if needed. Pour in the hemp hearts, protein powder, omega oil, and stevia (if using) and blend until well combined.

CREAMY AVOCADO
BREAKFAST JUICE BLEND

MAKES 16–20 OZ

2 stalks celery

1 firm green pear, scrubbed, and/or 3–5 drops liquid stevia (optional)

1 English cucumber, scrubbed

1 lemon, peeled

2-inch piece ginger or more, scrubbed

10–12 spinach leaves

½ small crown broccoli

1 avocado

Break. the. fast. If you need super-charging in the morning, this yummy drink will do it! Because this recipe is part juice and part blended veggies, your body quickly assimilates the concentrated vitamins and minerals. The blended fiber keeps you feeling satisfied for a little longer. Healthy avocado fats facilitate nutrient absorption from the greens and are great for "super brain power" on exam day, or add a good splash of omega-3 oil for even more of a boost. Share it or refrigerate the leftovers for the day, consuming them over 1–2 meals.

Juice the celery, pear, cucumber, lemon, and ginger and pour the mixture into a high-speed blender. Add the spinach, broccoli, and avocado and blend until creamy and smooth.

AVOCADO, PEAR,
AND MINT SMOOTHIE

MAKES 16 OZ

2 medium kale leaves + stalks, tough ribs removed

1 cup unsweetened coconut water or filtered, alkaline water

juice of ½ lemon

6-inch piece English cucumber, scrubbed

1 small firm pear, scrubbed, cored, and seeded

2 large sprigs mint

½–1 whole avocado

2 Tbsp hemp hearts

1 softened dried date, pitted and roughly chopped (optional) or 2–3 drops liquid stevia

This smoothie is a treat. The pear gently rounds out the other flavors, the date is a little indulgent, and the avocado and hemp hearts keep you satiated for 2–3 hours. If you are accustomed to adding banana to your smoothies, switching to an avocado—or using ½ banana and ½ avocado to start—is a great way to maintain the creaminess while benefiting from nature's perfect food: avocados provide good fat, protein, and optimal nutrients for alkalizing your body. Go, avocados, go!

Blend the kale with the coconut water and lemon juice until smooth. Add the cucumber, pear, mint, avocado, hemp hearts, and the date (or stevia) and blend again until smooth and well combined. Pour into a glass and serve.

Avocado, Pear, and Mint Smoothie

Creamy Avocado Breakfast Juice Blend

SAVORY GREEN

MAKES 8–10 OZ ## JUICE SHAKE

3 leaves + stalks bok choy

1 large leaf + stalk curly kale

¾ cup white cabbage or sui choy

6-inch piece zucchini or English cucumber, scrubbed

2 stalks celery

6 sprigs parsley

3–4 florets + stalks broccoli (optional)

1 parsnip, scrubbed (optional)

1 avocado

1 clove garlic, minced if adding once the soup has been blended

2 Tbsp fresh dill weed or basil leaves, roughly chopped

1 Tbsp hemp hearts

2 tsp Bragg Liquid Aminos (optional)

1 Tbsp extra-virgin olive oil

Himalayan salt

1–2 Tbsp Brazil nut, brown rice, or hemp protein powder

1–2 Tbsp omega oil

2–3 drops liquid stevia (optional)

This super-deluxe combination of ingredients is one of my favorites. I save it for lunch or dinner during a cleanse, sometimes serving it as a soup just gently warmed in a Vitamix or over low, low heat. Stir in a spoonful of your favorite healthy oil once the shake has been blended, if you wish.

Juice the bok choy, kale, cabbage, zucchini, celery, and parsley (and broccoli and parsnip if using) first and pour them into a high-speed blender. Add the avocado, garlic (unless serving as soup), dill, hemp hearts, and Bragg, and blend until smooth and creamy. Now add the olive oil, blend briefly, and season with salt. To serve it as a soup, hold off on the garlic until after you have blended the other ingredients in a Vitamix for 1–2 minutes or gently warmed them in a saucepan on the stove. Stir in the minced garlic, drizzle with the olive oil and a sprinkle of salt, then look out, world!

ALKALINE GREEN SMOOTHIE

MAKES 16–18 OZ

3 medium leaves kale, torn

⅓ cup thick coconut mylk or meat of ½ young coconut

juice of 1 lime

6-inch piece English cucumber, scrubbed

5 sprigs mint

3 sprigs parsley

1-inch piece ginger, scrubbed

1 avocado

1 cup coconut water, or more as needed

2–3 drops liquid stevia

1–2 Tbsp hemp hearts

1–2 tsp Udo's 3-6-9 omega oil

Not all green smoothies are created equal! Most are made with tons of fruit and just a token fistful of spinach to turn it greenish. This version contains no fruit, although I occasionally add ½ cup of frozen blueberries, raspberries, or strawberries. A ratio of 4:1 alkaline-forming ingredients to fruit will maintain a fine balance. Look for a fresh young coconut in the market from which to extract the juice and the meat. Otherwise, buy bottled unsweetened, unflavored coconut water, or you might get lucky and find fresh frozen, un-pasteurized coconut water. This is my go-to smoothie!

Blend the kale with the coconut water and lime juice until smooth. Add the cucumber, herbs, ginger, avocado, coconut mylk (or coconut meat), stevia, and hemp hearts and blend again. Stir in the Udo's 3-6-9 oil and pulse lightly to combine. Pour into a glass, pretty it up with a sprig of mint or a wedge of lime, and drink your greens.

CREAMY **MELON AND ROMAINE SMOOTHIE**

MAKES 16 OZ

6 large romaine
lettuce leaves

8 oz fresh or bottled
coconut water

1 cup chopped cantaloupe
+ more for garnish

1 avocado

1-inch piece ginger,
scrubbed

2 drops liquid stevia

This smoothie flouts the food-combining rule for eating melons solo, so enjoy it only when your digestion is strong (in the Acquire stage). Melons are low-sugar, thus less acidic than most fruits, which makes this smoothie a nice treat. Choose local, organic, and fairly firm fruit with little give on the non-stem end. Scrub the melon well with a brush and veggie wash, then peel and slice it. Use it right away or refrigerate it in an airtight container and consume it within 1–2 days.

Blend the lettuce with the coconut water until smooth. Add the cantaloupe, avocado, ginger, and stevia and blend again until smooth and well combined. Pour into a glass, garnish with cantaloupe, and serve with a leaf of romaine lettuce.

Creamy Chai
Hemp Smoothie

Chia Mint Smoothie

CHIA MINT **SMOOTHIE**

MAKES 20 OZ

* 2 cups coconut water + 2 Tbsp chia seeds

4-inch piece English cucumber, scrubbed

10 sprigs mint

juice of 1½ lemons

juice of 1 lime

1 Tbsp extra-virgin coconut oil

4–6 drops liquid stevia

Himalayan sea salt

Chia is good brain food! It contains the essential omega-3 fatty acid (EFA) called alpha-linolenic acid (ALA), which our body doesn't produce but which we need in our diet to create other omega-3 fats, EPA and DHA, which are vital to our health. EFAs improve our mood, our memory, and our overall brain function. So you can't go wrong with this smoothie, especially if you are feeling a slump in the afternoon. It will perk you up and completely alkalize your body at the same time. Hydrating the chia seeds wakes up their life force.

* DO AHEAD: Soak 2 Tbsp chia seeds in 2 cups coconut water for 15–20 minutes before using.

Blend all of the ingredients until smooth. Pour into glasses, garnish with mint, sip, and feel your brain come to life!

PURELY ALKALINE
(WITH ALMONDS)
ALKALINE BALANCED
(WITH CASHEWS)

MAKES ABOUT 16 OZ

* ⅓–½ cup soaked almonds or cashews, drained and rinsed

1½ cups filtered, alkaline water

½ large avocado

1-inch piece ginger, scrubbed

2 tsp chicory root powder (optional)

¼ tsp ground cinnamon

¼ tsp ground allspice

pinch ground cardamom

pinch ground cloves

2–3 drops liquid stevia

sea salt

freshly ground black pepper

¼ cup hemp hearts

2–3 ice cubes (optional)

CREAMY **CHAI HEMP SMOOTHIE**

In the afternoon I sometimes have a hankering for something creamy and smooth, sweet and spicy. This smoothie is packed with protein and good fats to fuel a sluggish brain and is easy to whip up if you have some almonds already soaking. Consume this drink within 1 hour, before the hemp hearts can fully oxidize and alter the flavor.

* DO AHEAD: Soak ⅓–½ cup almonds in 1 cup filtered, alkaline water overnight or ⅓–½ cup cashews in 1 cup filtered, alkaline water for 1 hour.

Blend the almonds (or cashews) and water until creamy. Add the avocado, ginger, ground spices, stevia, salt, pepper, and hemp hearts and blend until smooth and well combined. Drop in the ice cubes (if using) and process. Pour into glasses, sprinkle with extra hemp seeds, and serve.

GREEN DRINKS

MAKES 32 OZ

32 oz filtered, alkaline water

1 scoop or tsp of
greens powder

Optional additions

juice of ½ lemon

2 sprigs mint, leaves rubbed

¼ tsp green stevia-leaf
powder or 2 drops
liquid stevia

juice of ½ lime

4 verbena leaves, rubbed

juice of ¼ grapefruit

pinch ground cinnamon

If you've ever been to an Anthony Robbins 3-day event or read Dr. Robert O. Young's book *The pH Miracle*, you may already be in the habit of drinking green drinks before and between meals. I've been a green drink gal now for over 5 years, and it gives me constant energy and helps to maintain my optimal alkaline balance.

Look for a greens powder with lots of chlorophyll-rich green grasses, including wheatgrass, and green veggies, such as broccoli, but *without* algae, spirulina, or chlorella, as these thrive in very acidic conditions and may contain toxins (see Resources.) The plainer your drink, the easier it is for your body to assimilate but jazzing it up a little won't hurt if that's what it takes to love your greens powder! Keep your drink as fresh as possible by adding the greens powder only when you are ready to drink it.

Pour the water into your favorite glass or pitcher. Stir in the greens powder and any additions, and shake well. Shake the greens as you drink them or stir them with a straw so you don't leave any of the goodness behind.

POWER-PACKED WATERS

Drink your water! You've heard me say it over and over in this book. You might say, "I don't like water!" or "How can I possibly drink 3–4 quarts a day?" Well, let me tell you, when you make the effort to green it, infuse it, or power-pack it, it's a cinch!

FLAVORED **WATERS**

MAKES 16 OZ PER FLAVOR

Add these flavors to a 16-ounce glass or pitcher of alkaline water, allow them to infuse for at least 30 minutes (leaving them in as you sip if you like), *et voilà*, you have a delicious, hydrating drink. If you are cleansing or still working to balance your pH, skip the first 3 variations, which contain low acidic fruit. I especially like the version with star anise because when sweetened with a pinch of stevia, it's like having a licorice chew! Feel free to add a spoonful of chia seeds, or a few drops of liquid stevia, or a pinch of green stevia-leaf powder to sweeten this drink and bring out the flavors.

1. RASPBERRY, ROSE, AND MINT:

Add 3 or 4 raspberries, diced or gently squeezed to release their juices; ½ tsp rosewater or to taste; and a sprig of fresh mint, rubbed between your fingers.

4. LEMON, LIME LEMON THYME, AND SAGE:

Add 2–3 lemon slices and 2–3 lime slices (peels on), squeezing them as you add them to the water, and 1 sprig of fresh lemon thyme and 1 fresh sage leaf, both rubbed between your fingers. Try a few lemon grass slices if you don't have lemon thyme.

2. BLACKBERRY, LAVENDER, AND VANILLA:

Infuse a vanilla pod (I save my scraped pods for infusing) in 16 oz of water overnight. Remove and discard the pod, then add a couple of halved blackberries and 1 sprig of fresh lavender or ¼ tsp dried lavender petals, rubbed between your fingers.

5. CINNAMON AND GRAPEFRUIT:

Infuse a cinnamon stick in 16 oz of filtered, alkaline water overnight. Remove and discard the stick, then add a few slices of grapefruit (peel on), gently squeezing them.

3. CUCUMBER, PEAR, AND ROSEMARY:

Add 3–4 slices of English cucumber; 1 Tbsp diced pear; and 1 sprig of fresh rosemary, rubbed well between your fingers.

6. STAR ANISE, SLICED FENNEL, AND FENNEL GREENS:

Infuse 4 star anise pods in 16 oz of water overnight. Remove and discard the pods, then add a few slices of fresh fennel. Rub some fennel greens between your fingers and add them too.

LEMON-LIME CHIA FRESCA

MAKES 32 OZ

32 oz filtered, alkaline water

juice of ½ lemon

juice of ½ lime

3–5 drops liquid stevia

¼ cup chia seeds

lemon and lime slices, peel on

3–4 mint leaves, rubbed between your fingers (optional)

I can. not. get. enough. chia. These seeds release energy slowly to fuel the body and were used by the Aztec Indians to protect and heal joints, as the omega oils in the seeds are anti-inflammatory. The seeds can absorb 12 times their weight in water to provide excellent hydration and are also great for distance runners to prevent muscle cramping and reduce fatigue. I take this drink with me while doing errands or attending my yoga class, as it seems to make me drink more water and keep me satiated. The floating seeds may look funny in my water bottle but the more people I tell about them the more I see hooked on chia!

Pour the water into a carafe or water bottle, then add the lemon and lime juices, stevia, and chia seeds and shake or stir immediately for about 30 seconds. Wait for 20 seconds, then stir again to stop the chia seeds from sticking together. Set this mixture aside to thicken for 20–30 minutes, stirring occasionally. Add the citrus slices and mint, if using, and serve or take it with you for the day. This keeps well for 4–6 hours at room temperature.

"SQUEEZE" LEMONS IN WHEREVER YOU CAN

Lemons are an alkaline power food! They contain more of the 4 key minerals—calcium, sodium, potassium and magnesium—than any other fruit, and they cleanse and stimulate your liver, dissolve uric acid, and help your colon eliminate waste more efficiently. Drinking lemon water twice a day can help relieve belching, sore throats, heartburn, and bloating, and control diarrhea and constipation. And get this: lemons are the only food with more negative ions than positive ones, which means they're a great energy-giving food!

CHAI-SPICED HEMP MYLK

MAKES 24 OZ

½ cup hemp hearts

2½ cups filtered,
alkaline water

½ tsp ground cinnamon

2 cardamom pods

2–3 grinds fresh pepper or 2
whole peppercorns

8 star anise seeds or ¼ tsp
ground star anise

pinch ground cloves or 1 bud
from a whole clove stem

½ tsp freshly grated ginger
or ⅛ tsp ground ginger

✱ 2 dates, soaked, pitted, and
roughly chopped

6 drops liquid stevia (or more
if you skip the dates)

½ tsp pure vanilla extract or
seeds from ½ vanilla pod

Don't let the long list of ingredients scare you off, 'cuz you'll be missing out BIG TIME. Even my kids think that drinking this mylk is heaven. I like it over Breakfast Seednola with Coconut, Lime, and Ginger (page 140) and Lavender and Almond Chia Pudding (page 135). Hemp is the best plant-based source of omega-3 oils, and the seeds don't require any soaking or straining. If you don't have a high-speed blender to process the spices, grind them ahead of time in a spice mill or with a mortar and pestle (or use a packaged chai spice mix). If necessary, strain the mylk through a fine-mesh sieve before you serve it.

> **✱ DO AHEAD:** Soak 2 dates in ½ cup filtered, alkaline water for 10 minutes.

Blend all ingredients until smooth. Pour into mylk bottles and serve.

MYLKS

Make soaking nuts a part of your routine, in part so you are ready to make these delicious non-dairy mylks. If you already buy storebought mylks, give these homemade versions a try; they're creamy, satisfying, versatile, and free from additives. I like a glass of mylk as an afternoon treat, and I stir it into juices or soups, and pour it over my porridge. For a richer mylk, cut back the water in these recipes by ¼–⅓.

LAVENDER **ALMOND MYLK**

MAKES 24 OZ

3 cups filtered, alkaline water

✱ 1 cup soaked almonds, drained and rinsed

2 soaked dates, pitted and diced or 3–4 drops liquid stevia

1½ tsp fresh lavender petals or 1 tsp dried lavender

1 tsp pure vanilla extract

Storebought almond mylk is unbeatably convenient but it just doesn't come close to the incredible flavor and creaminess of homemade. It's delicious plain or with lavender, which is known to help alleviate headaches, insomnia, depression, digestive discomfort, and stress. For best results, use raw, organic, unpasteurized Marcona almonds (or other raw nuts) and have on hand a sheer fabric nut mylk bag (or clean pantyhose) or use a nut mylk machine (see Resources).

Set a nut mylk bag in a large bowl or an 8-cup measuring glass. Set aside.

Place all the ingredients in a high-speed blender and process for a good minute until you see very fine granules in the mix. Pour the mixture into the nut mylk bag and allow the liquid to run through it into the bowl. Pull the drawstring on the bag closed and gently wring it between your hands to squeeze out as much liquid as possible into the bowl. Work your way along the length of the bag until you can no longer extract any liquid. (You'll find numerous recipes online and one on my blog for using up this almond pulp.)

Pour the mylk into a pretty bottle and refrigerate it for up to 5 days—if you don't slurp it all down before then!

> ✱ DO AHEAD: Soak 1 cup almonds (or other nuts) in 3 cups filtered, alkaline water for 8–12 hours, or overnight. Soak 2 dates in ½ cup filtered, alkaline water for 30 minutes.

CREAMY ALMOND
MYLK GREENS

MAKES 16–20 OZ

3 leaves + stalks kale

2 leaves + stalks Swiss chard

1 cup spinach leaves

1 large English cucumber, scrubbed

1 lemon, peeled

6 sprigs mint

3–5 drops liquid stevia or 1 small green apple, peel on (optional)

10 oz almond mylk (page 122)

½ tsp pure vanilla extract

Green mylk is not just for St. Paddy's day! The first time I made this creamy business, well . . . I drank the whole jug (while hiding in the closet). It's hard to share, really, especially when made with homemade almond mylk (page 122). I often add almond mylk to my juice recipes—carrot is especially delicious—but this is one of my all-time faves! Serve it alongside any breakfast porridge or as an afternoon snack. Substitute unsweetened storebought almond mylk if you don't have time to make your own.

Juice the kale, chard, spinach, cucumber, lemon, and mint (plus the apple if using). Pour the juice into a pitcher and stir in the almond mylk, stevia (if using), and vanilla.

CHIA BUBBLE TEA

MAKES 8 OZ

1–2 tsp of your favorite herbal tea (I love berry or rooibos teas)

1 cup filtered, alkaline water

3–4 drops liquid stevia (optional)

1 Tbsp chia seeds

Drinking bubble tea has become a real novelty; however, most storebought versions are loaded with sticky tapioca balls and flavored syrups that are full of refined sugar. If you like the textural appeal of bubble tea—and not everyone likes bits floating in their drink—try this one made with herbal tea, steeped nice and long, and then jazzed up with some chia superfood seeds! It's a perfect opportunity to sneak a dose of omega-3s, fiber, protein, and antioxidants into your diet while helping to cleanse your colon and hydrate at the same time. Take this tea to yoga class or anywhere else you need to energize!

Steep your favorite herbal tea in the water according to the package instructions, then let it cool so it's gently warm or at room temperature. Stir in the stevia (if using) and the chia seeds for 10 seconds to prevent them from clumping. Wait for 30 seconds and then stir again. Allow the tea to stand for 10–15 minutes, then stir occasionally while drinking to redistribute the seeds.

WARM DRINKS

A warm, nutritious drink is nourishing in so many ways: the ritual of preparing it, the comfort of its warmth, and the knowledge that it is alkalizing the body instead of depleting it like the typical cup of joe. I often double or triple the recipes to make a pot of tea or nog to share, adding even more joy!

DIGESTION TEA
TWO DELICIOUS WAYS

**MAKES 4 CUPS OR
1 BIG TEAPOT FOR 4**

These teas are absolute bliss for me because I sooo love the flavors! They are perfect for soothing a funny tummy, curbing cravings in between meals, and igniting your spirit with their life energy force. Drink them daily for best results!

1. FRESH MINT TEA

I fell in love with this recipe while in Morocco, where fresh mint is sold in heaping wheelbarrows in the souks!! Mint is thought to improve the flow of bile through the stomach to speed and ease digestion, and this tea is excellent while veggie-feasting or after any meal. I love it as an afternoon tea. Two cups a day is plenty. Use caution if you are taking any medications or experiencing GERD (gastroesophageal reflux disease). For a change of pace, try licorice tea, which is also excellent for digestion: use 8 tsp roughly chopped licorice root in place of the mint.

10 sprigs mint

4 cups filtered, alkaline water, boiled

4 drops liquid stevia (optional)

Place the mint in a teapot and add the boiling water. Replace the lid, cover the pot with a tea cozy, and allow the tea to steep for 5–10 minutes. Pour the tea through a strainer into cups, adding 1 drop of stevia per cup, if desired.

2. SPICY GINGER AND LEMON TEA

Lemon and ginger root are full of antioxidants that inhibit inflammation and they stimulate bile, which aids in digestion. Lemon also promotes saliva, the production of gastric juices, and the release of toxins from the body. Drink it first thing in the morning. To stimulate your circulation for more effective detoxification, add the cayenne. Avoid the pear if you are juice-feasting.

2-inch piece ginger, scrubbed, grated on a rasp or very finely minced (about 1 generous Tbsp)

4 cups filtered, alkaline water, boiled

juice of 1 large lemon

1 small firm green pear, juiced (optional)

1 whole cinnamon stick or ½ tsp ground cinnamon

10–12 drops liquid stevia or ½–1 tsp green stevia-leaf powder

pinch cayenne pepper (optional)

Place the ginger in a teapot, cover with the boiling water, and allow the tea to steep for 10 minutes.

Add the remaining ingredients, stirring well, then pour the tea through a strainer into cups. Serve warm or cooled.

COCONUT ALMOND NOG

MAKES 11 OZ

⅔ cup thick, organic coconut mylk

⅔ cup almond mylk (page 122), leaving out the lavender

½ tsp lucuma + more for garnish

¼ tsp pure vanilla extract

⅛ tsp pure almond extract

1–3 drops liquid stevia (optional)

This creamy mylk will warm your insides and nourish your body with healthy fats and an overall feeling of happiness no matter which stage of the program you are doing. Lucuma is the key to the body and sweet caramel flavor of this nog, so look for it in your health food store. If you can't find it, you will still have great flavor but it won't be as thick.

Place all the ingredients in a small saucepan and slowly warm the mixture, whisking well, over medium-low heat. Heat until it is warm to the touch but not hot. Pour into a mug and sprinkle with extra lucuma. Enjoy.

THE HEALTHY LATTE

MAKES 8 OZ

⅔ cup almond mylk (page 122), leaving out the lavender

⅓ cup full-fat coconut mylk

1 Tbsp coffee replacement or 1½ tsp each roasted chicory and roasted dandelion root combined in a tea ball

1 tsp raw cacao powder (optional)

⅛ tsp ground cinnamon + more for garnish

2–3 drops liquid stevia

I was a latte girl and I always thought I'd really miss coffee while I was transitioning my diet. I've come to much prefer the other nourishing warm drinks in this section, but I do find this chicory "coffee" quite enjoyable. Roasted ground chicory root, often called coffee replacement, is available at health food stores or in bulk. It is sometimes sold as a blend with roasted dandelion root, and while chicory on its own is a little more like coffee, blending the two is quite pleasing. Add cacao powder if you prefer a mocha now and then. Adjust the ratio as you like.

Warm the 2 mylks in a small saucepan over medium-low heat until they steam, 3–5 minutes. Stir in the coffee replacement and dissolve (or turn down the heat to low, add the tea ball, and allow to steep for 7–10 minutes). Remove the tea ball, if necessary. Whisk in the cacao powder (if using), cinnamon, and stevia until frothy, then pour into a mug, sprinkle with more cinnamon, and serve.

SIMMERED QUINOA *with* SPICED ALMOND MYLK *and* SWEET POTATOES

SERVES 4–6

1 large sweet potato, peeled, cut into ¼-inch dice

 1 cup soaked white quinoa, rinsed well

3 cups unsweetened almond mylk + more for serving (page 122) (substitute coconut mylk for a yummy change)

1 tsp ground cinnamon

¼ tsp ground allspice

½ tsp pure vanilla extract

1–2 drops liquid stevia or a drizzle of pure maple syrup

½ cup walnuts, chopped + a few whole ones for garnish

hemp hearts for garnish (optional)

calendula flower petals for garnish (optional)

I never tire of quinoa, especially when it's on the sweet side for breakfast, and it satiates me for hours. If quinoa bothers your belly or nauseates you, you could be low on protein-digesting enzymes. Quinoa is very high in proteins as well as saponins, which can increase the permeability of the gut and cause you to absorb undigested nutrients in your food. Abstain from quinoa until you improve your digestion or try eating it with a digestive enzyme containing protease, but be sure to soak and sprout it before cooking it to reduce the saponins.

Place the sweet potatoes in a steaming basket over a pot of boiling water and cook until fork-tender, 12–15 minutes. Remove from the heat and keep warm.

In a medium saucepan, combine the quinoa with the almond mylk, cinnamon, allspice, and vanilla and bring to a boil, uncovered, over medium-high heat. Turn down the heat to low, cover, and simmer for 5 minutes. Stir and simmer for 5–7 minutes more, still covered. If most of the liquid has been absorbed, remove from the heat and allow to rest, covered, for another 5 minutes. If there is still lots of liquid in the pot, allow it to simmer for 3–5 minutes longer, but keep a close eye on the pot so the quinoa does not boil dry and burn. Remove from the heat and allow it to rest, covered, for 5 minutes.

Season to taste with stevia (or maple syrup or a combination) and stir in the chopped walnuts. Gently fold in the steamed sweet potato, reserving a few cubes for garnish. Top each serving with a few whole walnuts, a sprinkle of hemp hearts, and even a few flower petals. Serve with a little extra almond mylk if desired.

✳ DO AHEAD: Soak 1 cup quinoa in 3 cups filtered, alkaline water overnight or for up to 24 hours to allow it to sprout (page 94). Rinse well.

CHIA SEED
BREAKFAST PORRIDGES

**EACH RECIPE SERVES
1 (LARGE BOWL) OR
2 (SMALL BOWLS)**

Chia porridge has to be my most favorite breakfast ever! Its creamy yet tapioca-like texture is total comfort for me. You can even whip it up in a hotel room while traveling. You can also make any one of these recipes the night before (without the toppings) and place it in the fridge overnight. In the morning, add a little more almond mylk and allow it to come to room temperature (which is nicer than eating it cold) while you get ready or warm it gently and very briefly on the stove and then add the toppings.

The basic method for each of the 3 variations is the same. Pour the mylk into a medium bowl. Add the chia seeds and stir for 30 seconds to prevent them from clumping. Stir again after 1 minute, and set the mixture aside to thicken for 15–20 minutes, stirring occasionally to avoid clumping. If it becomes too thick, thin with a little extra mylk.

Creamy Lemon Chia Porridge

Cinnamon-spiced Chia with
Seeds, Nuts, and Berries

CINNAMON-SPICED CHIA WITH SEEDS, NUTS, AND BERRIES

1 cup almond mylk (page 122)

3 Tbsp chia seeds

1 Tbsp dried unsulfured cherries (optional)

½–1 tsp ground cinnamon

¼ tsp ground allspice

⅛ tsp ground cardamom

½ tsp pure vanilla extract

2–3 drops liquid stevia

1–2 Tbsp hemp hearts (optional)

small handful of fresh raspberries, strawberries, and or blueberries for garnish (optional)

soaked almonds, cashews, and sunflower seeds (optional)

mint leaves for garnish (optional)

To the soaking chia (page 134), add the cinnamon, allspice, cardamom, vanilla, and stevia and stir well. Pour into a serving bowl and top with your favorite seeds, berries, and nuts and garnish with a sprig of mint. Yummy!

CREAMY LEMON CHIA PORRIDGE

1 cup almond mylk (page 122)

¼ cup full-fat organic coconut mylk

¼ cup young coconut meat or coconut mylk

juice of 1 lemon

1½ Tbsp raw almond butter

½ tsp pure vanilla extract

4–6 drops liquid stevia

3 Tbsp chia seeds

unsweetened shredded coconut for garnish

lemon zest for garnish

In a blender, combine the almond mylk, coconut mylk, coconut meat, lemon juice, almond butter, vanilla, and stevia until nice and creamy. Pour the mixture into a small bowl, reserving ¼ cup. Stir in the chia and soak (page 134). Top with the shredded coconut and lemon zest, and serve with the reserved mylk.

LAVENDER AND ALMOND CHIA PUDDING

1 cup Lavender Almond Mylk (page 122) or Chai-spiced Hemp Mylk (page 121)

3 Tbsp chia seeds

soaked and/or dried almonds or pumpkin or sunflower seeds for garnish (optional)

Add the nuts or seeds to the soaking chia (see page 134) and stir well before serving. Bliss.

Lavender and Almond Chia Pudding

Creamy Lemon Chia Pudding

MAKING HEALTHIER BREAKFAST CHOICES ON THE RUN (PART ONE)

1. **Take your green juice and/or porridge to go.** Prepare your green juice before you leave the house, possibly the night before. In a pinch, pack your green juice in a travel mug and sip it on the way to or at work. Or pour your porridge into a glass jar to eat mid-morning.

2. **Create an emergency juice kit.** Keep a Magic Bullet blender and a stock of hemp hearts at the office for days when you're running late and pack fresh greens to go. Even simpler, buy a quality vegan green smoothie mix and a shaker cup. Just add water or coconut water et *voilà*—instant alkaline breakfast! Perfect for travel too.

3. **Ask for what you want.** If you have to buy something along the way, don't be shy about asking for:

   - a simple green salad from the lunch menu with avocado and fresh berries (I sometimes carry an avocado in my purse—call me crazee!)
   - a smoothie made with avocado, greens, almond mylk or coconut water, and a few fresh berries
   - Avocado Tomato Toast (page 203) on gluten-free bread with sliced tomatoes
   - unsweetened oatmeal with cinnamon, nuts, seeds, and a few fresh berries

4. If all else fails, **eat from the regular menu and balance your day later.** Enjoy your breakfast and work in as many raw greens as possible at lunch and dinner. Take a digestive enzyme, if necessary.

5. **Keep an eye out for new, healthier restaurants.** Lots of clever folks are opening up juice bars, socially and environmentally conscious cafés, and food trucks with raw, vegan, and gluten-free options! Give them your business—it's a win-win!

WARM CARDAMOM BUCKWHEAT PORRIDGE

MAKES 3 CUPS (3–4 SERVINGS)

* 1 cup raw buckwheat groats, soaked and rinsed

1 cup full-fat organic coconut mylk

½ cup almond mylk (page 122) + a little for serving

¼ tsp ground cardamom

¼ tsp pure almond extract

¼ tsp pure vanilla extract

sea salt

6–8 drops liquid stevia

handful of soaked almonds for garnish (optional)

pomegranate seeds for garnish (optional)

I love this hearty porridge on cold wintry mornings and also on summer market mornings when I need a breakfast to hold me over for a while. Buckwheat is an alkaline seed rather than a grain and it's gluten-free and chock-full of soluble fiber, antioxidants, and essential minerals—including manganese, magnesium, zinc, and copper. It also has anti-inflammatory properties. Best of all it is slightly alkaline . . . Yay! Avoid this during the veggie feast, and always soak raw buckwheat (groats) to help break down the anti-nutrients so they're easier to digest and to help release highly beneficial nutrients.

Place the buckwheat, coconut and almond mylks, cardamom, almond extract, vanilla extract, and salt in a small saucepan over medium-high heat. Stir to combine, bring to a bubbling boil for 1 to 2 minutes, then cover and remove from the heat. Allow the buckwheat to absorb the coconut mylk for 10 minutes. No peeking! It should be tender but firm with a bit of a toothy texture. Stir in the stevia to taste. Top with almonds and/or pomegranate seeds and serve with a little almond mylk if desired.

* **DO AHEAD**: Soak 1 cup buckwheat groats in 3 cups filtered, alkaline water overnight. Soak a handful of almonds in 1 cup filtered, alkaline water overnight too (if using).

PURELY ALKALINE (WITH
WHITE GRAPEFRUIT)
ALKALINE BALANCED
(WITH PINK GRAPEFRUIT OR
STRAWBERRY OPTION)

RAW BUCKWHEAT MUESLI
with GINGER, GRAPEFRUIT, AND AVOCADO

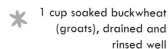

SERVES 3–4

* 1 cup soaked buckwheat
  (groats), drained and
  rinsed well

  juice of 1 lime

  ⅛ tsp lime zest

  1 generous tsp
  grated ginger

  4 drops liquid stevia

  1 pink or white grapefruit,
  peeled and diced

  1 avocado, diced

  mint leaves for garnish

Here's an alkaline breakfast that will make you feel as if you're at the spa! This wee breakfast parfait is refreshing, light, and sooo nourishing. With its raw soaked buckwheat groats (don't be misled by toasted buckwheat called kashi), this will provide ⅓ of your recommended daily allowance of manganese (which helps to balance blood sugars) as well as a fine dose of mood-enhancing tryptophan, blood-enhancing magnesium, and colon-cleansing fiber. To save time, soak enough buckwheat for a few mornings and refrigerate it in an airtight container for up to 3 days. Rinse well before serving to remove the gel-like film.

Save this for the Aspire stage if you're doing the veggie feast, even though it's purely alkaline.

In a large bowl, combine the buckwheat, lime juice and zest, ginger, and stevia. Spoon the mixture into individual bowls and top with the diced grapefruit and avocado. Garnish with mint and serve immediately.

* **DO AHEAD**: Soak 1 cup buckwheat in 3 cups filtered, alkaline water overnight.

Strawberry and Cucumber
Raw Buckwheat Muesli

VARIATION:
STRAWBERRY AND CUCUMBER RAW BUCKWHEAT MUESLI

For a summery version, replace the grapefruit and avocado topping with 1 cup finely diced English cucumber, 1 cup finely diced fresh organic strawberries, and ¼ cup finely chopped mint leaves. Stir to combine with the muesli and allow to stand for 5–10 minutes so the flavors can mingle. Garnish with mint and a slice each of strawberry and cucumber and serve immediately.

Breakfast Seednola
(page 140)

Raw Buckwheat Muesli
(page 138)

BREAKFAST SEEDNOLA
with COCONUT, LIME, AND GINGER

SERVES 6–8

 1 cup sprouted, dehydrated buckwheat groats

¾ cup large-flaked, dried, unsweetened coconut

½ cup soaked, dehydrated sunflower seeds

½ cup soaked, dehydrated pumpkin seeds

¼ cup soaked, dehydrated sesame seeds

¼ cup hemp hearts

1½ Tbsp grated ginger

1 tsp lime zest

2 Tbsp lucuma

½ tsp ground cardamom

¼ tsp ground cinnamon

⅛ tsp ground allspice

fine Himalayan salt

10–12 drops liquid stevia

1 tsp pure vanilla extract

¼ cup chia seeds

If you love granola, give this recipe a shot. Traditional granola is full of commercial additives and sugar and it's usually topped with sweet yogurt. This alkaline version is packed with sprouted buckwheat—also called buckinis—along with 4 different activated seeds rich in vital nutrients, including omega fatty acids, minerals, vitamins, protein, and fiber. Serve this Seednola with some homemade Chai-spiced Hemp Mylk (page 121), Almond Mylk (page 122), Vanilla Almond Lemon Cream (page 257), or my very favorite, the Non-fermented Vegan Vanilla Bean Yogurt (page 286).

Preheat the oven to its lowest temperature, preferably not higher than 150–160°F. Line 2 baking sheets with parchment paper.

In a medium bowl, combine all of the ingredients except the chia seeds. Toss extremely well, arrange the mixture evenly between the baking sheets, and bake for 20–30 minutes. (If your oven temperature is higher than 150°F, leave the oven door open a crack.) Turn off the oven, open the door a crack, and allow the mixture to rest until the oven is cool. (Alternatively, if you have a dehydrator, set it to medium and dry for a couple hours until crisp.)

Pour the Seednola into an airtight container, then stir in the chia seeds. This will keep fresh at room temperature for 3–4 weeks.

> ❋ DO AHEAD: Soak and sprout 1 cup buckwheat (page 94). Activate all the seeds (except the hemp seeds) together for 8 hours in 3 cups filtered, alkaline water. Dry the buckwheat and seeds in a dehydrator for 8 hours. Or arrange them on a baking sheet and dry them in the oven on the lowest setting for 2–4 hours.

photo on previous page···

BROCCOLI AND ONION
BREAKFAST BITES

I definitely used to be a sugary muffin and latte girl. How times have changed! This nutritious and nummy savory breakfast bite hits the spot, especially with a green juice or a salad, or for lunch with a bowl of soup. Substitute cauliflower or asparagus for the broccoli, if you prefer, and serve these with the Healthy Vegan Butter (page 276).

To make a loaf rather than individual muffins, preheat the oven to 325°F and line a 4- × 9-inch loaf pan with parchment paper. Scoop the prepared mixture into the pan and bake for 45–60 minutes, or until a skewer inserted in the center comes out clean. Allow to cool briefly, lift the loaf from the pan using the parchment paper, and place on a wire rack to cool completely. Cut into slices or keep refrigerated in an airtight container for up to 3 days. This crumbly loaf is perfect for Avocado Tomato Toast (page 203); just toast it lightly to release its moisture.

MAKES 8 MUFFINS OR 1 LOAF

1 cup spelt flour (sprouted if possible)

1 cup chickpea flour

1 Tbsp baking powder

½ tsp baking soda

½ tsp sea salt

2 Tbsp fresh dill or 2 tsp freeze-dried dill weed

½ cup diced zucchini

½ cup + 2 Tbsp almond mylk (page 122)

1 Tbsp lemon juice

3 drops liquid stevia

¼ cup coconut oil, melted

1 cup diced red onion (reserve ¼ cup for topping)

1 cup broccoli florets, cut into tiny, bite-sized pieces

coarse sea salt for finishing

Preheat the oven to 350°F and line an 8-cup muffin tin with baking papers.

In a medium bowl, sift together the spelt and chickpea flours, baking powder, baking soda, and ½ tsp sea salt. Stir in the dill and set aside.

In a blender, combine the zucchini, almond mylk, lemon juice, and stevia until the zucchini is puréed. Pour in the coconut oil and blend the mixture briefly.

Gently stir the zucchini mixture into the dry ingredients until just moistened. If the batter is too dry, add 1–2 Tbsp more almond mylk. Fold in the onion and broccoli.

Divide the batter evenly among the muffin cups, filling them completely; top with the reserved red onion and sprinkle with a pinch of coarse sea salt. Bake for 18–22 minutes, or until a skewer inserted in the center comes out clean. They will not rise much. Allow to cool briefly on a wire rack. Serve warm or at room temperature. These will keep in an airtight container in the fridge for 5 days or in the freezer for up to 1 month. Heat them before serving.

photo on next page . . .

Broccoli and Onion
Breakfast Bites (page 141)

Good Morning Broccolini
and Beans

GOOD MORNING
BROCCOLINI AND BEANS

Fruit until noon used to be a health rule, but that was well before it became clear that most fruit acidifies the body and feeds yeast. This savory chlorophyll- and protein-rich breakfast maintains an alkaline balance and provides far more energy than sweet fruit. Be careful not to oversteam the broccolini, as too much heat harms its vitamins and minerals. And if broccolini's just not for you at breakfast, well . . . you can serve this tasty dish for lunch or dinner!

SERVES 2

½ cup unsoaked hazelnuts or almonds

1¼ tsp lemon zest

¾ tsp whole pink peppercorns

½ tsp sea salt

2 cups diced broccolini

1 cup diced green beans

2 Tbsp Healthy Vegan Butter (page 276) or extra-virgin olive oil and/or flax oil

broccolini or kale flowers for garnish

In a food processor, combine the hazelnuts, lemon zest, peppercorns, and sea salt until you have an even fine crumble (be careful not to overdo it, or it will become nut butter). This crumble will keep refrigerated for 7–10 days in a small airtight jar if you don't use it all.

Bring a medium pot of water to a boil on high heat. Put the broccolini and beans in a steaming basket and steam them for 2–3 minutes, or until crisp-tender. Transfer them to a medium bowl, toss them with the butter, and divide them among individual dishes.

Generously spoon some nut crumble over each serving and garnish with broccolini or kale flowers. Serve with more nut crumble on the side.

RHUBARB **ALMOND SCONES**

1 cup almond flour

1 cup sprouted spelt flour

2 tsp baking powder

½ tsp baking soda

½ tsp sea salt

¾ cup + 1½ Tbsp full-fat coconut mylk (½ can)

1 tsp pure vanilla extract

26 drops liquid stevia (or 2 tsp coconut nectar + 16 drops stevia)

1¾ cups sliced rhubarb, including ½ cup for garnish

1 tsp ground cinnamon

¼ cup dried, finely shredded, unsweetened coconut

A weekend favorite with our guests at the cottage after a glass of green juice, these delicious hearty scones are perfect with a cup of tea. By most definitions, rhubarb is a vegetable, which makes it a great alternative to berries and a good food combination with the nutrient-dense sprouted spelt flour. If your digestion is good and you prefer to use berries, go ahead, but add them in moderation. Unsprouted almond flour is made without the almond's skin, which is where most of the bothersome anti-nutrients are present. Sprouted almond flour is a rare find and pricey unless you make your own. (See sprouting guide on page 96.)

Preheat the oven to 350°F. Line a baking sheet with parchment paper.

In a medium bowl, combine the almond and spelt flours, baking powder, baking soda, and salt until well mixed.

In a glass measuring cup, whisk together the coconut mylk, vanilla, and 16 drops of the stevia (or 1 tsp coconut nectar and 8–10 drops stevia).

In a bowl, toss the rhubarb with the cinnamon and remaining 10 drops of stevia (or 1 tsp coconut nectar and 5–6 drops stevia).

Pour the coconut mylk mixture into the flour mixture and stir to just combine. Gently fold in the rhubarb. Spoon this puffy batter into 3-inch rounds on the baking sheet. Gently press 3 slices of rhubarb into the top of each scone. Sprinkle with the coconut and bake for 18–20 minutes, until a toothpick inserted in the center comes out clean. Allow to cool on the baking sheet for a few minutes, then transfer them to a wire rack to cool further. Serve warm. These will keep refrigerated in an airtight container for up to 3 days. Warm gently in the oven to refresh.

SPROUTED SPELT AND VANILLA PANCAKES *with* LEMON COCONUT CREAM

SERVES 4

This simple vegan recipe took a few tries to get right, but the combination of sprouted spelt and buckwheat flours makes for a tasty pancake that's easy to digest. You can also make a deelish, crunchy lemon-chia version by adding 2½ Tbsp whole chia seeds and the zest of 1 lemon to the dry pancake ingredients and ½ cup more almond mylk, 2 Tbsp lemon juice, and a couple of extra drops of stevia to the wet ones.

The rule in our house is still green juice first, pancakes second. This way, we have a pretty good balance even when serving the pancakes with a little maple syrup. I love them with raw almond butter.

✳ DO AHEAD: Refrigerate a 13½ oz tin of coconut mylk overnight. If using almonds, soak ¼ cup in 1 cup filtered, alkaline water overnight.

Lemon Coconut Cream

✳ 13½ oz chilled full-fat coconut mylk (1 can)

¼ cup cashews or soaked almonds

3 Tbsp hemp hearts

3 Tbsp lemon juice

1 tsp lemon zest

3–5 drops liquid stevia

1 tsp pure maple syrup (optional)

Sprouted Spelt and Vanilla Pancakes

1 Tbsp ground flax seeds

2½ Tbsp filtered, alkaline water

¾ cup sprouted spelt flour

½ cup sprouted buckwheat flour

2 Tbsp baking powder

½ tsp fine Himalayan salt

1 cup almond mylk (page 122)

2 Tbsp cold-pressed sunflower oil

1 Tbsp pure maple syrup or 5–6 drops liquid stevia

1½ tsp pure vanilla extract

¼ cup coconut oil

CREAM: Open the bottom of the tin and carefully pour the liquid coconut water into a small airtight jar (reserve it for smoothies). Scoop the coconut solids into a blender, add the cashews, hemp hearts, lemon juice and zest, stevia, and maple syrup (if using), and blend until creamy and smooth. Pour the mixture into a serving pitcher. Any leftovers will thicken further when chilled and can be used as a tasty spread. This will keep in the fridge for 3–5 days.

PANCAKES: Set a wire rack in the oven and preheat it to 300°F.

Place the flax seeds in a small bowl with the water, stir to combine, and allow to stand for 5–10 minutes.

In a large bowl, combine the spelt and buckwheat flours, baking powder, and salt until well mixed. In a separate bowl, stir together the almond mylk, sunflower oil, maple syrup, vanilla, and flax mixture. Pour the wet ingredients into the dry, stirring with a fork just until mixed. Set aside for 5 minutes to allow the batter to rise.

Place a frying pan or griddle over medium-low heat and add the coconut oil. When the pan is warm, gently spoon 3 Tbsp of batter into the pan for each pancake. Repeat until the pan is full. Cook for 2–3 minutes, or until bubbles appear on the surface and the pancakes are golden underneath. Flip the pancakes and cook for 2–3 minutes more. Transfer the cooked pancakes to the wire rack in the oven to keep warm. Repeat with the remaining batter.

Serve warm on individual plates with the coconut cream. The pancakes keep well in an airtight container in the freezer for 1 month, or refrigerated for up to 4 days.

SPROUTED BUCKWHEAT
SILVER DOLLAR PANCAKES
with ALMOND SYRUP

SERVES 6–8 (24 TWO-INCH PANCAKES)

Almond Syrup

3 Tbsp raw almond butter

3 Tbsp avocado oil or grapeseed oil or almond oil

¼ tsp ground cinnamon

3 Tbsp thick organic coconut mylk

6–8 drops liquid stevia or 1 tsp green stevia-leaf powder

¼ tsp pure vanilla extract

¼ tsp pure almond extract (optional)

Buckwheat Pancakes

coconut oil for grilling

 1 cup soaked buckwheat groats, drained and rinsed well

2 Tbsp ground chia seeds

¾ cup almond mylk (page 122)

¾ cup thick organic coconut mylk

1 tsp pure vanilla extract

¼ tsp pure almond extract (optional)

¼ tsp fine Himalayan salt

1 Tbsp lemon juice

2 tsp baking powder

I love concocting meals from the versatile buckwheat seed, using it raw, sprouted, and cooked, and in savory and sweet dishes! This gluten-free pancake recipe is great for lazy Sunday mornings: it's a hearty, filling, and nourishing breakfast that's easy to make in the blender and cleans up easily. Just remember to start soaking your buckwheat before you hop into bed. Enjoy it with a non-traditional coconut almond syrup, served warm or at room temperature, in place of the usual high-sugar maple syrup. Note that using the green stevia powder will give the syrup a greenish color.

SYRUP: Place the almond butter in a small bowl and pour the oil over top. Using a fork or a mini whisk, work the oil into the butter to thin it. Add the cinnamon then the coconut mylk, stevia, vanilla, and almond extract (if using) and stir until creamy. Transfer to a small saucepan and set aside.

PANCAKES: Preheat a pancake griddle to medium or lightly grease a frying pan with coconut oil and place it on medium heat.

✱ DO AHEAD: Soak 1 cup buckwheat in 3 cups filtered, alkaline water overnight.

In a blender, combine all the ingredients, except the lemon juice and baking powder, until you have a smooth batter. Add the lemon juice and blend just to combine. Pour into a medium bowl. Just before you are ready to cook the pancakes, quickly and gently stir in the baking powder, ensuring that you mix it in thoroughly.

Ladle enough batter onto the griddle to make a 2-inch pancake. Keep ladling and making pancakes until you run out of room. Cook the pancakes until bubbles form and the surface is pretty much dry, 3–5 minutes. Flip the pancakes and allow them to heat through for another minute or 2. Repeat until you have used up the batter. Transfer the cooked pancakes to the wire rack in the oven to keep warm.

Divide the pancakes among individual plates and drizzle with the almond coconut syrup. Store these in an airtight container for 2–3 days or freeze them for 1 month. I often reheat any leftovers in the toaster.

SALADS

It's called chop therapy! In our family,
making salad at least once a day is a ritual,
as is arranging a crudités (raw veggie) plate.
We keep our favorite paring knife and a bamboo
cutting board close by; we take them when we
travel, so we can snack on cucumber, carrots,
jicama, and bell peppers. What I put in my
salad depends on my mood, what's in the fridge,
and how simple or fancy I want to get!
Use these recipes as a springboard for
your own creative variations.

BABY GREENS
with FLOWER BLOSSOMS, MINT, AND CINNAMON CHICKPEA CROUTONS

SERVES 1

Lemon Dressing

⅓ cup extra-virgin olive oil

juice of 1 lemon

1½ tsp coconut nectar or
3–5 drops liquid stevia

sea salt

freshly ground
black pepper

Baby Greens and Blossom Salad

2 cups mixed baby lettuces

½ cup mixed sprouts (pea,
sunflower, buckwheat)

½ cup torn mint leaves

handful of edible blossoms
(rose, calendula, kale, nigella)

½–1 avocado, sliced

¼ recipe Macadamia Cheeze
(page 283)

¼ recipe roasted Sweet
Cinnamon Roasted Chickpeas
(page 248)

sprig of thyme for garnish
(optional)

Nothing is more enjoyable for me than pretty (and healthy!) food. This salad made with lovely edible flowers is just that. Enjoy it in the garden or on an outside patio for the full summer effect. You'll savor the memory during the colder, winter months.

DRESSING: Combine all the ingredients in a glass measuring cup, whisk well, and allow to stand while you prepare the salad. This will keep refrigerated in an airtight container for up to 3 days.

SALAD: In a medium bowl, combine the lettuce, sprouts, mint, and ⅔ of the blossoms. Pour in the dressing and toss gently until evenly coated. Arrange the salad on a serving plate and top with avocado, small curds of macadamia cheeze, and roasted chickpeas. Garnish with the remaining blossoms and a sprig of thyme.

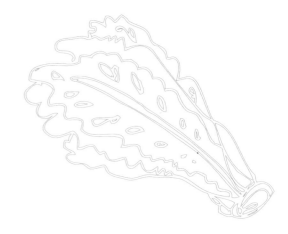

SUMMER BERRY SALAD

SERVES 1

This salad is delicious made with raspberries, strawberries, and blueberries but substitute whichever berries—alone or in combination—you have on hand. And be sure to add the mint—this is what makes it just perfect! Soak and dehydrate the nuts beforehand if you can (page 94).

Sweet Nut Crumble

* ¼ cup soaked almonds

¼ cup Brazil nuts

¼ tsp ground cinnamon

12 mint leaves

4–5 drops liquid stevia or ¼–½ tsp green stevia-leaf powder

2 Tbsp hemp hearts

CRUMBLE: In a food processor, combine the almonds, Brazil nuts, cinnamon, mint, and stevia until they form an even but rough crumble. Pour in the hemp hearts and pulse to just combine. Spoon the mixture into an airtight container and refrigerate for up to 5 days.

> **＊ DO AHEAD:** Soak ½ cup almonds in 1 cup filtered, alkaline water overnight. Or dehydrate in your dehydrator for 8 hours, or by heating in the oven on the lowest setting for 1–2 hours until dry and crunchy.

Raspberry Dressing

½ cup raspberries

10 mint leaves

1 Tbsp diced shallots

¼ cup extra-virgin olive oil

juice of 1 small lemon

8–10 drops liquid stevia

Himalayan salt

freshly ground black pepper

DRESSING: Combine all the ingredients in a blender and process until smooth and creamy. Pour into a serving jug. Any leftovers will keep for up to 2 days in the fridge.

Summer Berry Salad

2 cups mixed baby lettuces

½ cup mixed fresh raspberries, blueberries, and strawberries

1 avocado, diced

SALAD: Arrange the lettuce on a large plate, and then top with the berries and avocado. Drizzle with the dressing, sprinkle with the crumble, and dig right in!

BUTTER LETTUCE AND MINCED PEAR *with* FRENCH LIMONETTE DRESSING

SERVES 4

Butter lettuce makes me lose my mind! I love how tender the leaves are and how mild and sweet they taste. This is a salad I make often in the summer—almost too often—but the kids love it too. Make it fancy by keeping the lettuce leaves whole or easier to eat by tearing or chopping them into bite-sized pieces. Add sliced avocado if you want a more substantial salad. Use the pear in moderation and chop it just before you serve the salad so it doesn't oxidize. The dressing is reminiscent of my favorite old French vinaigrette, minus the vinegar. The added flax oil means you are getting a nice dose of omega-3s and you can vary the amount of mustard according to your preference.

French Limonette Dressing

⅓ cup extra-virgin olive oil

2 Tbsp flax oil

juice of 1 lemon

2–4 drops liquid stevia

2 Tbsp minced shallots

2 Tbsp finely sliced chives

¼ tsp dried mustard, or to taste

sea salt

freshly ground black pepper

DRESSING: Combine all the ingredients in a glass measuring cup, whisk well, and allow to stand while you prepare the salad. This will keep refrigerated in an airtight container for up to 3 days.

Lettuce and Pear Salad

1–2 heads butter lettuce, leaves washed and torn into bite-sized pieces, core discarded

1 fresh organic pear, peel on, cored and finely diced

finely chopped chives for garnish

SALAD: Divide the lettuce among 4 serving plates, arranging the larger leaves on the bottom and stacking the smaller ones on top. Sprinkle with pear and drizzle with the dressing. Garnish with chives and serve immediately.

KALE SALAD *with* AVOCADO AND MANGO AND KALE BLOSSOMS

SERVES 2

Zippy Lemon Dressing

½ cup extra-virgin olive oil

juice of 1 lemon

2 drops liquid stevia or coconut nectar (or 1 drop of each)

1 Tbsp chia seeds

1 clove garlic, grated on a rasp

½ tsp dried mustard

sea salt

freshly ground black pepper

Kale salad

8 leaves + stalks kale, tough ribs removed, finely chopped

1 avocado, finely diced

½ mango, finely diced

⅓ cup mint leaves, finely chopped

handful of kale blossoms (optional)

I love this refreshing salad, rich in chlorophyll and magnesium and flavored with fresh mint and lemon. And kale is an alkaline powerhouse. Cutting it into bite-sized pieces and massaging it makes it softer and easier to chew. A little bit of finely diced mango is perfect but not mandatory—but don't forget the avocado! You can scatter edible flowers over this to pretty it up, if you like.

DRESSING: Combine all the ingredients in a glass measuring cup, whisk well, and allow to stand while you prepare the salad. This will keep refrigerated in an airtight container for up to 3 days.

SALAD: Place the kale in a large bowl. Pour ½ of the lemon dressing over the kale leaves and add ½ of the diced avocado. Using your hands, massage the dressing and the avocado into the kale by kneading the leaves, ensuring that the folds and curls are really well coated and the avocado is creamed. Allow the salad to stand for 10 minutes to further tenderize the kale leaves.

Divide the greens evenly among individual plates and sprinkle with mango, mint, and the remaining avocado and kale blossoms (if using). Drizzle with more lemon dressing and toss gently to combine.

GREEK SALAD

SERVES 1 (MAIN COURSE) OR 2–3 (SIDE SALAD)

12 cherry tomatoes, halved

1 English cucumber, scrubbed, halved lengthwise, and sliced

1 orange, red, or yellow bell pepper, seeded and cut into small strips

¼ Maui or Walla Walla onion, diced

10–12 cured, dried black olives, or your favorite olives

juice of 1 lemon

¼ cup extra-virgin olive oil

2 drops liquid stevia (optional)

1 clove garlic, minced

1 tsp freeze-dried oregano or ½ tsp regular dried oregano

Himalayan salt

freshly ground black pepper

4–5 Tbsp Macadamia Cheeze (page 283)

This Greek salad is a keeper! I like it best with cherry tomatoes, but large tomatoes are fine. And to get your greens in, pile this salad on a bed of mixed lettuces. The kids love this salad in their lunch boxes, and if you make a double batch of the dressing, you'll have it handy to pack along with whatever veggies you've got around or to drizzle it over a side salad at any meal. The dressing is so delicious you won't even notice the vinegar is missing. I usually add the stevia as it balances the tart lemon. It will keep refrigerated in an airtight container for up to 4 days.

In a medium bowl, combine the tomatoes, cucumbers, bell peppers, onions, and olives and set aside.

In a glass measuring cup, whisk together the lemon juice, olive oil, stevia (if using), garlic, oregano, salt, and pepper and allow to stand for 5 minutes. Whisk again, pour the dressing over the veggies, and toss to combine. Top with the cheeze.

SERVES 8–10

Herb Dressing

4 cloves garlic, minced or grated

¼ cup minced fresh parsley

¼ cup minced cilantro

¼ cup minced fresh basil

¼ cup minced chives or green onions

1 cup extra-virgin olive oil

juice of 2 lemons

4–6 drops liquid stevia or coconut nectar (or 2–3 drops of each)

¼ tsp Himalayan salt

freshly ground black pepper

Layered Salad

6 medium carrots, scrubbed, sliced on the thinnest setting

2 large red bell peppers, halved and seeded, sliced on the 2nd-thinnest setting

12 cherry tomatoes, quartered

1 long English cucumber, scrubbed, sliced on the 2nd-thinnest setting

¼ red cabbage, sliced on the thinnest setting

4–6 radishes, sliced on the thinnest setting

sprig of parsley, cilantro, or basil for garnish (optional)

2 heads butter lettuce or your favorite lettuce, chopped into bite-sized pieces

2 cups radish or broccoli micro sprouts

2 cups sunflower sprouts

1 recipe Savory Nut Sprinkle (page 281)

1 recipe Macadamia Cheeze (page 283) (optional)

2–3 avocados, halved and cut into diamond shapes

SIMPLE SALAD
FOR A CROWD

A trusty ole mandolin will win you rave reviews for this gorgeous salad made with layers of brightly colored vegetables. It's fun to make and it will inspire even non-salad fans! You can save time by preparing the layers of veggies early in the day, chilling them until you are ready to impress your guests, and then tossing the salad with the herb dressing at the last minute. If any veggies become dry, just moisten them carefully with a spritz of cool water. For variety, replace ¼ of the olive oil with your favorite nut oil and try the sweet nut crumble (page 154) as a topping.

DRESSING: In a glass measuring cup, whisk together all the ingredients. Pour the dressing into a small serving pitcher and allow it to infuse while you slice the vegetables. It will keep refrigerated in an airtight container for up to 3 days.

SALAD: On a large serving platter, arrange the carrots, bell peppers, tomatoes, cucumber, and cabbage in dense rows. Add the radishes and garnish with a herb sprig. In a large bowl, toss together the lettuce and sprouts. Arrange them in a tall mound on a second serving platter.

To serve, place the platters in the middle of the table with the dressing, nut sprinkle, and macadamia cheeze. Scoop the avocado into a bowl just before serving. Allow guests to help themselves.

photo on next page · · ·

Simple
Salad for a
Crowd
(page 161)

Seriously Alkaline Salad

THE SERIOUSLY ALKALINE SALAD

¼ cup organic extra-virgin olive oil

juice of ½ lemon

1 drop liquid stevia or ½ tsp pure maple syrup (optional)

1 large clove garlic, finely minced, not pressed

Himalayan salt

freshly ground black pepper

½ head your favorite lettuce, torn

1 handful spinach

1 handful baby kale leaves, torn

10 sprigs parsley, chopped

10 sprigs cilantro, chopped

1 handful pea shoots

1 handful sprouts, such as broccoli, alfalfa, or radish

6 cherry tomatoes, halved

6 radishes, quartered

½ carrot, scrubbed, julienned or grated

½ cup thinly sliced red cabbage

½ stalk celery, sliced

½ avocado, sliced

½ watermelon radish, slivered

This combination of veggies came together after a successful winter visit to my local market, which sources incredible farm produce from surrounding growers. If these particular ingredients aren't available to you, just do your best to get the finest and most organic veggies you can and load 'em up on your plate! I love butter or red leaf lettuce for this salad, but any green will work well. Choose your favorite, or a combination, or change up the mix each time. Try the simple dressing in this recipe, or choose another yummy one on page 284.

DRESSING: In a measuring cup, whisk together the olive oil, lemon juice, stevia, garlic, salt, and pepper until well combined.

SALAD: Arrange the lettuce, spinach, kale, parsley, and cilantro in the bottom of a large salad bowl. For a nice presentation, arrange each of the veggies in its own little grouping around the perimeter, saving the watermelon radish for the center.

To serve, pour the dressing over the salad and toss well.

STACKED **BEET SALAD**

SERVES 2

2 large red beets or 4 small yellow beets, trimmed and scrubbed

2 large or 4 small yellow beets, trimmed and scrubbed

⅓ cup extra-virgin olive oil

juice of 1 lemon

1–3 drops liquid stevia or coconut nectar (or half of each)

sea salt

freshly ground black pepper

1–2 Tbsp Macadamia Cheeze (page 283)

1 cup fresh sprouts, such as sunflower, radish, micro greens

2 chive blossoms (optional)

I may have gotten a wee bit fancy on you with this recipe, but if you are having a friend to lunch, why not try it? If you're in a hurry, just dice the beets and toss them with the sprouts and top with the cheeze. Oh . . . and if you can't locate yellow beets, no worries . . . your liver will be just as happy to be detoxified with the red beets—and the salad will still look pretty!

Place the beets in a covered steamer over boiling water. Steam them whole until tender, 20–30 minutes depending on their size. Remove from the heat and allow to cool enough to handle. Carefully peel the beets, discarding the peels, and slice the flesh into rounds about ⅜ inch thick. Reserve ¼ cup of the red beet for the dressing.

Place the ¼ cup beets in a blender with the olive oil, lemon juice, stevia, and salt and pepper and pulse until smooth and well combined. Set aside.

To serve, alternately layer the colorful beet slices 4 high, with the cheeze gently placed in between the slices (to avoid staining the cheeze), finishing with a layer of cheeze. Surround the stack with sprouts and garnish with more sprouts and a chive blossom (if available). Drizzle with dressing and serve more on the side. Enjoy any leftover beets with more cheeze and dressing the next day. This will all keep refrigerated for up to 3 days, stored separately.

Homemade is best

ALKALINE SALAD DRESSINGS 101

If you're not used to eating a lot of salads and raw veggies, it can be tempting to smother them in a whole lot of dressing. Storebought dressings are loaded with vinegars, dairy products, sugars, and preservatives, which will quickly send your alkaline balance out of whack. Whipping up healthier options—and knowing how to modify your favorites—will have you eating your greens and luuuving them. Which is what we want. For more dressing recipes see page 284.

- Replace vinegars with lemon or lime juice.

- Make dressings creamy with blended raw zucchini, avocado, nuts, seeds, hemp hearts, and/or nut butters (and a little filtered, alkaline water).

- Flavor dressings with finely chopped fresh herbs (or pinches of dried ones) and fresh garlic and ginger grated on a rasp.

- Replace highly processed and GMO oils with raw, cold-pressed olive oils, nut and seed oils, avocado oil—or very occasionally, a drop or 2 of toasted sesame oil.

- Substitute Bragg Liquid Aminos for salt in Asian dressings, and stevia (or coconut nectar or yacón syrup if you're not feasting) for sugar in all dressings.

- And did I mention that avocado makes any salad—or any food, really—creamy and delicious?! I can't get enough of them.

VEGAN CRUNCHY THAI GREEN SALAD

SERVES 4 (AS A MAIN COURSE) OR 6 (AS A SIDE DISH)

Crunchy Green Salad

2 cups julienned jicama

2 small bok choy, chopped into bite-sized slices

6 leaves Napa cabbage or sui choy, chopped into bite-sized slices

4 radishes, thinly sliced

3 green onions, thinly sliced lengthwise and cut into 1-inch lengths

1 small bunch watercress, chopped

1 cup chopped cilantro

½ cup chopped fresh mint

½ cup chopped fresh basil

1 avocado, sliced (optional)

Spicy Lime Dressing

4½ Tbsp Bragg Liquid Aminos

juice of 1 large lime

2 Tbsp avocado or grapeseed oil

6–7 drops of liquid stevia or 1–2 Tbsp coconut nectar

4 cloves garlic, minced or crushed

1½ tsp finely minced jalapeño pepper

Garlicky Crumble

½ cup unsoaked almonds

1 clove garlic

½ tsp Himalayan salt

1–2 fresh chilies or a pinch of dried red chili flakes

Everywhere I look, from the market to the local paper, I find inspiration for creating healthy food. The idea for this salad came from GOOP, Gwyneth Paltrow's newsletter—I love her stuff! I adapted her version, to make it vegan, and it's earned rave reviews. The idea is to balance the sweet, salty, sour, and spicy, so make adjustments if you don't find that your dressing has an equal balance of all 4 flavors. The garlicky crumble is optional, but it adds a lovely crunch. This salad is chock-full of detoxifying herbs and chlorophyll, which will certainly tidy up those blood cells! Refrigerate the greens separately from the dressing if you make a double batch. The dressing will keep refrigerated in an airtight container for 2–3 days.

SALAD: Place all the veggies except the avocado in a large salad bowl. Toss well to combine.

DRESSING: In a measuring cup, whisk together all the ingredients until well combined. Allow to stand for 5–10 minutes until the flavors meld.

CRUMBLE: Place all the ingredients in a food processor and pulse continuously until a crumble forms.

To serve, pour the dressing over the salad and toss until just coated. Divide the salad into individual bowls, top with slices of avocado, and sprinkle with the crumble.

SERVES 4 GENEROUSLY

RAW VEGGIE NOODLE PASTA *with* SHELLING PEAS

Veggie Noodle Pasta

½ daikon radish, scrubbed, julienned or spiral-cut (2–3 cups)

2 small yellow zucchini or patty pan squash, scrubbed, julienned or spiral-cut (about 2 cups)

2 orange carrots, scrubbed, julienned (about 1 cup)

1 red carrot, scrubbed, thinly sliced (orange carrots are fine too)

1 white carrot, scrubbed, thinly sliced (orange carrots are fine too)

1 cup thinly slivered snowpeas

½ cup shelled fresh peas

2 cups arugula

½ bunch cilantro, chopped, plus 4 whole sprigs for garnish

6–8 chives, slivered

1 mango, thinly slivered (about ½ cup), for garnish (optional)

sesame seeds, for garnish (optional)

Tahini-almond Sauce

¼ cup tahini

¼ cup smooth almond butter

juice of 1 lemon

3 Tbsp filtered, alkalized water

2½ Tbsp Bragg Liquid Aminos

1 tsp grated ginger

Himalayan salt

Changing the way you chop, slice, and dice your veggies transforms their flavor and makes them endlessly versatile. If you haven't tried spiralizing your veggies, here's your chance. A spiralizer is a really cool gizmo, essentially a vegetable slicer that produces spirals instead of strips (see Resources). You can also use a regular veggie peeler and make wide fettuccine noodles instead. When you taste the noodles tossed with this creamy tahini-almond sauce, I know you'll be squeezing in a second helping! Note that both the noodles and the sauce keep well separately, so this recipe can be made ahead and assembled quickly and easily the next day.

PASTA: Place the radish, squash, carrots, snowpeas, and peas in a large, pretty bowl. Add the arugula, cilantro, and chives and toss until well combined.

SAUCE: In a measuring cup, whisk the sauce ingredients until smooth and creamy.

To serve, divide the pasta evenly among individual bowls. Pour the sauce into a small pitcher and pass it around or serve it in a small bowl on the side so everyone can help themselves. Toss with the sauce and garnish with slivered mango, sesame seeds, and a sprig of cilantro.

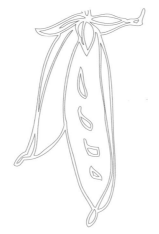

photo on next page...

Raw Veggie
Noodle Pasta
(page 169)

Angel Hair
Zucchini Pesto

ANGEL HAIR ZUCCHINI PESTO *with* ROASTED CHERRY TOMATOES

SERVES 4

Zucchini Pesto with Roasted Tomatoes

24 cherry tomatoes, halved

1 Tbsp grapeseed oil

½ tsp sea salt + more for dusting the tomatoes

½ cup + 1 Tbsp extra-virgin olive oil

2 cups basil leaves

¼ cup walnuts and/or pine nuts or almonds

3 Tbsp hemp hearts

3 cloves garlic, roughly chopped

6 six-inch zucchinis, spiral-cut, julienned, or angel hair–cut with a slicer

Garlic Cheeze Crumble

½ cup walnuts or almonds

1 clove garlic

½ tsp sea salt

½ tsp dried oregano

freshly ground black pepper

I found this dandy noodle gizmo (see Resources) that makes it super easy to cut the zucchini in this recipe into the thinnest noodles ever! Mixed with the pesto, these zucchini noodles are pretty dreamy. Add sweet roasted tomatoes and the whole dish becomes a slice of heaven. If you don't have time to roast the tomatoes, by all means enjoy them raw on top; it'll still be divine. Zucchini is wonderfully full of water—just what we want—but it will get soggy if you toss it with the pesto and tomatoes and allow it to stand too long. So, toss and then enjoy right away. For a quicker preparation, the noodles can be cut and chilled separately from the pesto, and then assembled at the last minute for the quickest alkaline meal ever!

PESTO: Preheat the oven to 325°F. Line a baking sheet with parchment paper. Arrange the tomatoes, cut side up, on the baking sheet and drizzle with grapeseed oil. Sprinkle with some sea salt, then bake for 1 hour. Remove the tomatoes from the oven, allow to cool, and drizzle with 1 Tbsp of the olive oil. Set aside.

In a blender or food processor, process the basil, walnuts, hemp hearts, garlic, ½ cup of olive oil, and ½ tsp of sea salt until well combined. Scrape down the sides of the bowl and process until the pesto has an even consistency. Add a wee bit of extra olive oil, if necessary. Set aside.

CRUMBLE: Place all the ingredients in a food processor and pulse continuously until a crumble forms. Spoon the mixture into a small bowl and set aside.

TO SERVE: Place the zucchini noodles in a large bowl with the pesto and toss well. Divide the noodles between 4 bowls and top each one with ¼ of the roasted tomatoes. Sprinkle with a spoonful of the garlic cheeze crumble. Toss again and serve immediately while the zucchini is still crisp and crunchy.

SERVES 6–8

SPANISH BEAN SALAD

Spanish Dressing

½ cup extra-virgin olive oil

2 Tbsp flax oil (optional)

1 Tbsp hemp oil (optional)

juice of 1 lime

juice of 1 small lemon

2 Tbsp pure maple syrup or
5–6 drops liquid stevia (or
½ of each)

1–2 cloves garlic, minced

¼ cup chopped cilantro

1½ tsp ground cumin

1½ tsp Celtic salt or sea salt

1 tsp freshly ground
black pepper

1 tsp chili powder

Bean Salad

2 cups cooked pinto beans
or 1 can (15 oz) pinto
beans, rinsed and drained

2 cups cooked chickpeas or
1 can (15 oz) chickpeas,
rinsed and drained

2 cups cooked cannellini
beans or 1 can (15 oz)
cannellini beans, drained
and rinsed

2 carrots, peeled
and chopped

2 stalks celery, chopped

2 green onions, chopped
(optional)

1 red bell pepper, chopped

6–8 cups fresh baby
lettuce greens

cayenne pepper

Canned beans make this yummy salad especially quick and easy. My brand of choice is Eden because the beans are soaked with kombu (to help minimize anti-nutrients, improve digestibility, and add precious minerals and flavor) and the cans are BPA-free. So, when life gets crazy, buy cans of beans if that makes things more doable. However, I do find that there's just somethin' yummier about beans you soak and cook yourself, so, if you can, spend the time to start from scratch!

> **✳ DO AHEAD:** Soak ⅔ cup each dried pinto beans, cannellini beans, and chickpeas in 3 cups filtered, alkaline water overnight. Drain and cook them as per the chart on page 94. Cooking times will vary, thus cooking them together might be tricky.

DRESSING: Place all the ingredients in a medium bowl and whisk until well combined. Set aside.

SALAD: In a large salad bowl, gently combine the beans, carrots, celery, green onions, and bell pepper. Pour the dressing over the vegetables and gently combine without mashing the beans.

To serve: Arrange the fresh greens on individual plates. Spoon some of the bean mixture over top and allow guests to season with cayenne pepper to their liking.

SPROUTED MUNG BEANS
with ANCHO CHILI AND AVOCADO

If you've never tasted sprouted mung beans, you are in for a real treat: they're crunchy, kinda sweet, and rather addictive, and they can be tossed into a myriad of dishes. Bursting with life-force energy, alkaline minerals, vitamins, and proteins, they are amazing for your body! It's worth the effort to sprout them yourself, and it's sooo cool to see them wake up! Kids love watching them grow. This recipe makes about 1 cup more sprouts than you'll need, so refrigerate them in an airtight container for up to 5 days. Add these nutritious sprouts to any salad or just munch on them as a snack like my daughter loves to do!

SERVES 4–6
(AS A SIDE SALAD)

3 Tbsp raw almond butter

1 Tbsp extra-virgin olive oil

2 Tbsp filtered, alkaline water

½ tsp grated ginger

½ tsp grated or finely minced garlic

½ tsp ancho chili powder

1 Tbsp lemon juice

 2 cups sprouted mung beans (1 cup dry)

1 cup thinly sliced red cabbage

1 cup finely diced jicama

8 radishes, thinly sliced

1 avocado, diced

* **DO AHEAD**: Soak 1 cup of mung beans in enough filtered, alkaline water to cover them by 3–4 inches overnight. Rinse the beans under cold running water, then allow them to sprout in a warm place for 8–12 hours (page 96).

Place the almond butter in a small bowl. Using a fork or a whisk, slowly work in the olive oil until you have a uniform mixture. Add the water and stir until well combined. Mix in the ginger, garlic, and chili powder. Add the lemon juice last to ensure the almond butter does not seize up. You should have a nice creamy, pourable sauce.

Place the sprouts in a medium bowl and add the cabbage, jicama, and radishes. Pour the dressing over top and toss gently so as to not harm the wee sprouts. Top with avocado or have guests add their own.

CAULIFLOWER **TABBOULEH**

**SERVES 2–3 (AS A MAIN)
OR 4–6 (AS A SIDE)**

¼ cup extra-virgin olive oil

juice of 1 large lemon

1 clove garlic, finely minced

½ tsp Himalayan salt

1 small head cauliflower,
roughly chopped

1 cup diced, scrubbed
English cucumber

1 cup diced tomatoes

2 green onions, green and
white parts, thinly sliced

1 cup minced fresh parsley

1 cup minced fresh mint + a
few leaves for garnish

12 cherry tomatoes, halved

12–18 olives, preferably
cured, dried black or
your faves

Traditional tabbouleh is often made with bulgur wheat, and I initially made this salad with more alkaline millet. One summer I had a desire for lighter fare and replaced cooked millet with an equivalent amount of crumbled cauliflower. It was deelish. Try this salad both ways, maybe with millet in the winter and cauliflower in the summer. If you are cleansing, choose cauliflower and save the millet until you are balanced—although millet is pretty close to being neutral on the pH scale, it isn't a high-water-content food.

In a glass measuring cup, whisk together the olive oil, lemon juice, garlic, and salt, and set it aside to allow the flavors to mingle.

Place the cauliflower in a food processor and pulse until you have a fine, even crumble. (You should have about 3 cups.) Pour it into a medium bowl, add the cucumber and diced tomatoes, green onions, parsley, and mint, and toss to combine.

Pour the dressing over the salad, combine gently, and top with cherry tomatoes, olives, and a few more mint leaves.

KANIWA TOMATO STACK

When our local greenhouses open in the spring, I get all excited about tomatoes. Although my faves are heirlooms grown under the sun, my next favorites are these juicy organic ones, especially since I'm starved for a decent tomato by the time March arrives! These tomatoes are even more divine when paired with this versatile nutty-tasting micro seed called kaniwa. It's a cousin of quinoa, and often called baby quinoa, but it comes from a different plant and does not have the saponins that make quinoa bitter. Kaniwa is a great source of protein and is rich in calcium, iron, zinc, and fiber. Try it as a porridge. Serve this dish with a side salad for some chlorophyll!

SERVES 2–4

Pistachio Crumble

½ cup pistachios

sea salt

freshly ground black pepper

pinch cayenne pepper

Kaniwa Salad

 ½ cup soaked kaniwa, drained and rinsed well

1 cup organic veggie broth

1 clove garlic, minced

1 large carrot, scrubbed, finely diced

½ large watermelon radish, scrubbed, finely diced

2 Tbsp finely minced parsley

2 Tbsp finely minced basil

1 Tbsp extra-virgin olive oil

Himalayan salt

freshly ground black pepper

3 large tomatoes, cut into ⅜-inch-thick slices

✳ DO AHEAD: Soak ½ cup kaniwa in 2 cups filtered, alkaline water overnight.

CRUMBLE: In a food processor, mix the pistachios, sea salt, pepper, and cayenne pepper until crumbled. Pour into a small pretty bowl and set aside.

SALAD: Place the kaniwa in a medium pot, add the veggie broth, and bring to a boil, uncovered, over high heat. Turn down the heat to low and allow to simmer for 10–15 minutes. (Keep a close eye on the pot because the water evaporates quickly.) Remove from the heat, stir in the garlic, cover, and allow to stand for 10 minutes.

Pour the kaniwa into a medium bowl and add the carrot, radishes, parsley, basil, and olive oil. Season to taste with salt and pepper.

Arrange 1 slice of tomato on each plate. Scoop a generous serving of the kaniwa mixture over top and cover with another slice of tomato. Spoon over more kaniwa, cover with 1 more slice of tomato, and finish with a final pile of kaniwa. Sprinkle each stack with the pistachio crumble and dig in!

SOUPS AND WRAPS

What I love most about soups and wraps is that you can pretty much toss in any ingredients you like and they will taste delicious. I have never had any real disasters that couldn't be redeemed by adjusting the herbs or spices. It usually turns out better than I imagined and I only wish I had written down the recipe. I hope these soup recipes inspire you to be creative! Serve warmed soups with a salad so that you get the nutritional benefits of both raw and cooked veggies. A wrap made with a big fresh green leaf of lettuce, chard, or collard greens tucked full of colorful vegetables and seasoned with dips and sauces nicely rounds out a warm bowl of soup or stands quite well on its own. The tasty combinations are endless.

Wrap it up—

RAW GREEN SOUP *with* AVOCADO AND BASIL

SERVES 4

2 cups raw spinach

2 stalks celery, chopped

1 avocado

1 small zucchini, chopped

¼ green bell pepper

2 Tbsp chopped onion

1 small clove garlic

½ cup fresh basil

¼ cup fresh parsley

❋ ¼ cup almonds

1½ cups filtered, alkalized water

¼ tsp sea salt or ½ tsp Bragg Liquid Aminos + ⅛ tsp sea salt

juice of ½–1 lime or lemon

dried black olives for garnish

diced tomatoes for garnish

fresh mixed herbs for garnish

4 nasturtium flowers for garnish (optional)

Since beginning this alkaline lifestyle I've become quite accustomed to raw soups. It just makes perfect sense to enjoy the veggies in their raw state and consume them blended, which makes them easier for your body to assimilate and gives your digestive tract a mini-vacation. If you aren't fond of cold soups, heat them gently until warm (piping hot will damage the enzymes in the veggies). This soup is perfect for the veggie feast or for detoxing at any time.

In a blender or a Vitamix, combine the spinach, celery, avocado, zucchini, bell pepper, onion, garlic, basil, parsley, almonds, and water. Process until well mixed. If you prefer the soup warm, blend it longer in the Vitamix or transfer it to a saucepan and warm it gently over low heat.

Season with sea salt and lime or lemon juice. Ladle into individual bowls and garnish as preferred.

> ❋ DO AHEAD: Soak ¼ cup almonds in 1 cup filtered, alkaline water overnight and rinse.

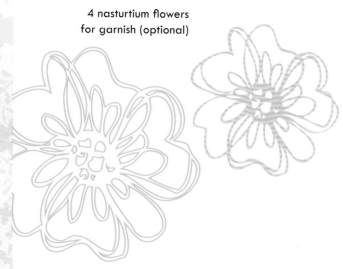

SERVES 1

CREAMY DILL AND
SPINACH **DETOX SOUP**

1 long English
cucumber, scrubbed,
roughly chopped

1–3 Tbsp coconut water or
filtered, alkaline water

1 cup spinach, packed

1 avocado

1 scallion, roughly chopped

½ clove garlic

1-inch piece
ginger, scrubbed

3 Tbsp roughly chopped
fresh dill or 3 tsp
freeze-dried dill weed

3 Tbsp roughly
chopped cilantro

Himalayan salt

extra-virgin olive oil
for drizzling

handful of mixed finely
diced veggies (carrots,
radishes, scallions, celery,
and/or jicama)

Packed full of green chlorophyll goodness and healthy fats, this raw soup is a surefire way to help release those nasty acids and toxins! It's not just for veggie-feasting, so give this a go any time you feel like you need a balancing boost. Liquefying the cucumber here is the trick to lots of flavor, as it saves diluting with water to facilitate blending. Be sure to add the minced veggie garnish— what I like to call vegetable confetti—for added crunch and a burst of flavor.

Place the cucumber in a blender and process until well liquefied. (You may need to scrape down the sides and encourage it!) Use the coconut water if necessary. Add the spinach, avocado, scallion, garlic, ginger, dill, and cilantro, and blend until smooth. Season to taste with salt. Ladle into a bowl and drizzle generously with olive oil. Sprinkle with vegetable confetti and then find a pretty spoon!

CREAMY CELERY AND CANNELLINI BEAN SOUP

I get sooo excited when a recipe passes the kid test! I can't say it happens all the time, but this one was a definite winner! I grew up eating cream of celery soup poured over steamed carrots—and I loved it. This soup kinda reminds me of the celery flavor that I liked, and I am so pleased that I can use it to mask (hide from the kiddos) the cannellini beans while creating a creamy rich texture that is filling and nourishing. If you soak your own dry beans and cook them up in advance, you will be rewarded with the most outstanding flavor.

However, in a pinch, by all means use organic canned beans. Serve this soup with a tossed salad, such as The Seriously Alkaline Salad (page 163), and/or veggie sticks to ramp up your alkaline balance.

SERVES 6–8

* 2 cups soaked white cannellini beans, drained and rinsed well, + kombu

1 Tbsp coconut oil

6 stalks celery, diced

1 onion, diced

3 cloves garlic, minced

4 cups vegetable broth (use 3 Veggie Bouillon Cubes (page 277) + 4 cups filtered, alkaline water)

1½ cups finely diced celeriac

¼ tsp ground celery seeds

sea salt

freshly ground black pepper

extra-virgin olive oil, for drizzling

> *** DO AHEAD:** Soak 1 cup dried cannellini beans in 3 inches filtered, alkaline water with a 3-inch piece of kombu at room temperature for 12 hours. If you have time, rinse the beans, cover them with another 3 inches of filtered, alkaline water and the kombu, and allow them to soak for another 12 hours (page 94).

Place the beans and the kombu in a medium pot and add enough filtered, alkaline water to cover them by ½ inch. Bring to a boil, uncovered, and then turn down the heat to a simmer for 20–30 minutes. They are ready when you test 5 beans and all are tender. Drain and reserve any excess liquid.

Heat the coconut oil in a large pot over low heat. Add the celery, onion, and garlic and sauté for about 5 minutes, until softened. Add the veggie broth and celeriac and simmer until the vegetables are tender, 8–10 minutes.

Place ½ the vegetables and ½ the broth in a blender with ½ of the cooked beans and process until smooth. Pour the blended mixture into another large pot. Add the remaining vegetables, broth, and beans to the blender with the celery seeds and process until smooth. (Alternatively, add the beans to the pot and use an immersion blender.) Add this to the blended soup already in the pot and heat it all through. Season with salt, pepper, and a good drizzle of olive oil.

Ladle the soup into bowls and finish with another drizzle of olive oil and a grind of pepper.

SERVES 4–6

HEALING SEASONAL VEGETABLE SOUP

* ¾ cup brown lentils, soaked, rinsed, and drained, + kombu

4½ cups + 2 Tbsp filtered, alkalized water

1 medium onion, minced

2 cloves garlic, minced

1 recipe 8-Veg juice (page 104) or 6 cups vegetable broth

2 stalks celery, sliced into ½-inch pieces

1 sweet potato, scrubbed, cut into ½-inch dice (optional)

2 carrots, scrubbed, sliced into ½-inch pieces

10 green beans, trimmed and sliced into 1-inch pieces

1 red bell pepper, cut into ½-inch dice

6-inch zucchini, scrubbed, sliced into ¼-inch rounds

1 medium crown of broccoli, chopped into bite-sized florets

6 asparagus, trimmed and sliced into 1-inch pieces

10 cherry tomatoes, halved

Himalayan salt

small handful of chopped fresh parsley

small handful of chopped cilantro

fresh oregano and thyme leaves

drizzle of extra-virgin olive oil

This soup is a great way to ease back into solid purely alkaline foods on your first day off the veggie feast. Have it for breakfast—and for lunch and dinner too, like I did! Just skip the lentils and the sweet potato and add or subtract alkaline vegetables at will. *Mise en place* means "putting in place," or chopping and measuring all your ingredients into individual bowls so everything is ready to go when you start cooking, and it's the secret to making this soup. You'll feel like a pro when you begin to cook in this manner, so break out the tall, white chef's hat! Serve this soup with any salad and perhaps Socca (page 250), Broccoli and Onion Breakfast Bites (page 141), or Yeast-free Spelt Focaccia Bread with Olives and Rosemary (page 252).

Place the lentils and kombu in a medium pot with 1½ cups of the water. Bring to a boil, uncovered, over medium-high heat, then turn down the heat to low, cover, and simmer until the lentils are tender but not mushy or splitting, 25–35 minutes. Drain off any excess water and set aside.

> *** DO AHEAD**: Soak ¾ cup lentils with a 3-inch piece of kombu in 3 cups filtered, alkaline water overnight.

In a large soup pot, combine the onion, garlic, and 2 Tbsp of the water and steam-fry over medium-high heat until the onion is translucent, 2–3 minutes. Add the remaining 3 cups water and the 8-Veg juice to create a broth and heat until it just begins to simmer. Stir in the veggies, following the order in which they are listed in the ingredient list. Allow each vegetable to cook for 1–2 minutes before adding the next one. Once you've added the cherry tomatoes, test the veggies for doneness and gently stir in the lentils. Season to taste with salt.

Ladle the soup into individual bowls and top with parsley, cilantro, oregano, and thyme and a generous drizzle of olive oil.

SOUP OF CELERIAC, SWEET ONION, AND FRESH MINT

Celeriac, also known as celery root, doesn't look like celery—it's a brown, rather unattractive knob—but it *is* related. It's the root of a particular variety of celery and it tastes like a cross between celery and parsley. As you dice the root, be sure to trim ¼–½ inch of the skin's thick outer layer or it may taste bitter. Since this soup is cooked, save it for the Aspire phase if you are cleansing.

SERVES 4

3½ cups diced celery root (½ large root)

¾ tsp Himalayan salt

2 Tbsp coconut oil

1½ cups diced sweet onions

1 cup spinach, packed

24 mint leaves + 4 for garnish

freshly ground black pepper

drizzle of extra-virgin olive oil

Place the celery root in a medium pot and cover with filtered, alkalized water by about 1 inch. Add ½ tsp of the salt and bring to a boil. Turn down the heat to medium and cook until tender, 10–15 minutes. Drain the celery root, saving ½ cup of the cooking water, and set aside ¼ cup of the diced root in a small bowl. Transfer the remaining celery root (without the cooking water) to a blender. Set aside.

Heat the coconut oil in a small pan over medium-low heat. Add the onion and sauté until translucent. Cook for another 5 minutes to allow the onion to sweeten. If it begins to brown, add 1 Tbsp filtered, alkalized water. Spoon ¼ cup of the onion into the reserved ¼ cup celery root, then add the remainder to the blender with the spinach and mint. Process until completely smooth, slowly adding the reserved cooking water as needed, until you have a nice thick, creamy consistency. Season to taste with a little salt and black pepper. For a warmer soup, pour the soup into a medium pot and heat it gently over low heat.

To serve, ladle the soup into individual bowls or mugs. Mix together the reserved celery root and onion, add a drizzle of olive oil, and season with a pinch of salt and a grind of pepper. Gently float a spoonful of this mixture on top of each bowl of soup, and finish with a little more olive oil, a bit more pepper, and a sprig of mint. *Voilà!*

UDON SOUP *with* SPELT NOODLES AND BOK CHOY

SERVES 4

4 cups filtered, alkaline water

3 Tbsp Bragg Liquid Aminos, or to taste

1 clove garlic, finely grated or pressed

1 tsp finely grated ginger

⅛ tsp Celtic sea salt

1½ cups shelled organic edamame beans or 4 oz organic tofu, cut into ½-inch cubes

8 oz package spelt udon noodles or 2–3 bundles of buckwheat soba noodles

2–3 cups chopped baby bok choy, leaves + stalks

finely chopped chives or green onions for garnish (optional)

What I love about this soup is that it's a good balance of greens to noodles, it provides vegetable protein (the edamame or tofu), and it's *easier* than pie! If you boil extra noodles and double the broth, you can refrigerate them separately and then just reheat the broth, add the veggies, and drop in the noodles at the last minute to heat them through. I do this in the morning and pop the soup in a thermos so it's nice and warm for my kids' lunch. My daughter usually comes home bragging that she has eaten every bit! Serve this soup with a side salad of lightly dressed mixed greens or some raw veggie sticks to increase the alkalinity of your meal.

In a medium pot, combine the water, Bragg, garlic, ginger, and salt and stir well. Add the edamame and cook over medium heat for 4–5 minutes. (If using tofu, add and warm through for about 3 minutes.)

While the beans are heating, bring a large pot of filtered, alkalized water to a boil over high heat and add the noodles. Cook according to the package directions until al dente. Drain and rinse well under warm water. Divide the noodles evenly among 4 soup bowls.

Add the bok choy to the pot, cooking for just 1 minute to wilt it. Using a slotted spoon, scoop the beans and bok choy from the broth and divide them among the bowls of noodles. Then pour the remaining broth over each serving. If desired, garnish with finely chopped chives or green onions.

SPROUTED GRAIN WRAPS
with ROASTED ROOTS, GREENS, AND CHIPOTLE DIP

SERVES 4–6

Chipotle Dip

1 cup soaked almonds, rinsed well and drained

1 clove garlic, crushed

1¼ tsp smoked paprika

½ tsp Celtic sea salt

¼ tsp chipotle pepper

½ cup filtered, alkalized water + 1–2 Tbsp more, if needed

juice of 1 lemon

2 Tbsp extra-virgin olive oil

Wraps with Roasted Roots and Greens

1 large sweet potato, peeled and cut into small dice

1 parsnip, peeled and cut into ½-inch dice

1 yellow beet, peeled and cut into small dice

2 medium purple beets, peeled and cut into small dice

3–4 Tbsp grapeseed oil

1 tsp sea salt

4–6 sprouted-grain tortilla wraps (or rotis, page 196)

4–6 handfuls of mixed greens

4–6 large handfuls of fresh pea shoots

2 avocados, sliced (optional)

Sprouted grain wraps are a great way to take your veggies to go, as are rotis (page 196) and large green leaves (try collards, chard, or kale). Don't fret if you don't have any of these wraps—just turn the filling into a simple salad in a bowl and thin the dip with a bit of almond mylk or water to make a dressing. If you are making this dish as a takeaway lunch, remember to keep the dip (or dressing) on the side to avoid sogginess. Be generous with the greens to get a good alkaline balance for this meal. And roast the root veggies just until they are al dente rather than soft right through to help them maintain more nutrients.

DIP: Place all the ingredients in a blender and combine until creamy and smooth. If the dip is too thick to spread, add 1–2 Tbsp water and blend again.

> *** DO AHEAD:** Soak 1 cup almonds in 2 cups filtered, alkaline water for 30–60 minutes (but ideally overnight).

WRAPS: Preheat the oven to 350°F. Line a baking sheet with parchment paper.

In a bowl, combine the sweet potato, parsnip, and yellow beet. Place the purple beets in a separate bowl. Add grapeseed oil and salt to both bowls and toss well to coat the vegetables. Spoon the mixed vegetables onto the baking sheet, arranging them in a single layer. Sprinkle the purple beets on top. (This step is just so the dish looks prettier; it stops the purple beets from bleeding on the other veggies. If you aren't fussed by how the veggies look, just mix 'em all together.) Roast for 20–25 minutes, or until just barely tender. Remove from the oven and allow to cool to room temperature.

Place a wrap in the middle of a plate. Arrange a generous layer of mixed greens on top and spoon some of the roasted roots down the center. Dollop the chipotle dip over the roots and cover with pea shoots and avocado (if using). Fold the bottom ⅓ of the wrap over the filling, then fold in the sides to completely encase the contents. Use a toothpick to hold everything in place. Cut the wrap in half or leave it whole. Serve with extra dip.

ROSEMARY KAMUT ROTIS
with ROASTED RATATOUILLE

MAKES 10 WRAPS

Roasted Ratatouille

1 small eggplant, cut into 1-inch dice

2 cups cauliflower, chopped into 1-inch pieces

1 medium zucchini, cut into 1-inch dice

1 red bell pepper, cut into 1-inch dice

1 yellow bell pepper, cut into 1-inch dice

1 large red onion, cut into 1-inch dice

24 whole cherry tomatoes

6 Tbsp coconut oil, melted

Celtic sea salt

1 recipe Oregano and Sundried Tomato Marinara (page 231)

2 cups fresh sprouts (optional)

Kamut Rosemary Rotis

2 cups whole kamut flour (or sprouted kamut flour, if you can find it)

1 Tbsp finely chopped fresh rosemary or ½ tsp crumbled dried rosemary

1 cup warm filtered, alkaline water + up to 2 Tbsp more

1 tsp grapeseed oil or coconut oil, melted

I love the smell of roasting veggies wafting through the house. If you use good-quality fresh veggies, they taste so yummy that they don't need a lot of adornment. Here they are naked, save for a wee bit of coconut oil and good salt, stuffed into a roti. This is perfect with Oregano and Sundried Tomato Marinara (page 231).

Kamut is an ancient grain related to the wheat family. It is not a GMO crop and it is high in potassium and magnesium. If it is sprouted, it is much more easily digested than wheat, but if you are highly sensitive, do be aware that it contains gluten. You can sprout your own kamut to make flour but you need to plan ahead: soak the grain for 24 hours to allow it to sprout, then dehydrate it overnight, and grind it in the dry vessel of your Vitamix.

RATATOUILLE: Preheat the oven to 325°F. Line 2 baking sheets with parchment paper.

Arrange the eggplant and cauliflower in a single layer on 1 baking sheet. On the second sheet, spread out the zucchini, bell peppers, and onion. Put the tomatoes in a small baking dish. Drizzle each baking sheet/dish with 2 Tbsp melted coconut oil and sprinkle liberally with sea salt.

Place the eggplant and cauliflower in the oven and bake for 10 minutes, then stir. Add the second baking sheet to the oven and bake for 5 minutes, then stir. Finally, place the tomatoes in the oven alongside the other roasting veggies and bake for 15–20 minutes. After a total of 30–35 minutes, check that the eggplant and cauliflower are tender but not soft. Remove all the pans from the oven and allow to cool slightly.

Pour the eggplant, cauliflower, zucchini, bell peppers, and onion into a large bowl and toss them gently to combine. Carefully fold in the tomatoes.

ROTIS: While the veggies are baking, prepare a clean work surface for rolling rotis. Have on hand a small dish of extra flour, a wee bit of water, and your rolling pin. Maybe don a pretty apron too—and dust some flour on your face!

Place the 2 cups kamut flour in a medium bowl and create a well in

the center. Add the rosemary, water, and oil. Using your hands, work the wet ingredients into the flour, a bit at a time, until you have a slightly sticky dough with which you can form a ball.

Sprinkle a little of the extra flour on your work surface and place the dough on top. Knead the dough, using a pinch of flour here and there (or a few drops of water), until it is smooth and non-sticky. You want it to be soft and pliable. Knead for about 2 minutes more. Place the dough in a clean bowl, cover it with a tea towel, and allow it to rest for 10 minutes.

Divide the dough in 2 equal halves. Separate the first ½ into 5 equal pieces and roll it into balls. Cover the remaining dough with a tea towel until you are ready to roll it. Roll each of the 5 balls into a round, 6–7 inches in diameter. Repeat with the remaining dough.

Heat a cast-iron griddle pan over medium-high heat. Line a plate with a tea towel. Set the rounds in the pan, 1 at a time, and heat for 30–40 seconds per side. They may puff up a wee bit. As you remove them from the pan, place them on the plate and wrap the tea towel around them to keep them moist and warm.

To assemble, place a generous scoop of veggies down the center of the roti and spoon Oregano and Sundried Tomato Marinara on top. Add a handful of fresh sprouts and roll up (or serve with a salad to get your greens in!).

RICE WRAPS *with* CILANTRO CREAM AND PONZU SAUCE

SERVES 4

Creamy Cilantro Dressing

½ cup roughly chopped raw zucchini

* ¼ cup soaked cashews, rinsed well and drained

¼ cup cilantro leaves (no stems)

½ clove garlic

¼ tsp Himalayan salt

freshly ground black pepper

2 Tbsp filtered, alkaline water

2 Tbsp extra-virgin olive oil

2 tsp lemon juice

Ponzu Sauce

6 Tbsp Bragg Liquid Aminos

3 Tbsp filtered, alkaline water

2 Tbsp lemon juice

juice of 1 lime

2 drops liquid stevia

½ tsp minced garlic

½ tsp minced ginger

½ tsp finely chopped chives

cayenne pepper

* **DO AHEAD**: Soak ¼ cup cashews in 1 cup filtered, alkaline water for 20 minutes.

Every time I make these wraps, I think about Copenhagen, which is one of my favorite travel destinations because it's so darn charming. On my last visit, I was lucky enough to share a marvelous lunch with the wonderful Sarah B of the My New Roots blog. We chatted about our passion for sharing healthy food and wisdom and could have talked until sundown—and we nearly did! The food at the raw restaurant Sarah chose was scrumptious, and these wraps are similar to the lettuce rolls with lovely dipping sauces that we ate there. I couldn't help but try to mark the happy memory with a recipe of my own and share it with you.

If you haven't used rice paper wraps before, you're in for a real treat: they're fast, simple, and deelish! Or make this dish purely alkaline by substituting coconut wraps (see Resources). And feel free to play with the filling: use your favorite veggies or whichever ones are in season.

DRESSING: Place all the ingredients in a blender and combine until smooth and creamy. This will keep refrigerated in an airtight container for up to 3 days.

SAUCE: In a small bowl, whisk together all the ingredients until well combined. Pour into a dipping bowl for serving. This will keep refrigerated in an airtight container for up to 3 days (a few days longer without the chives).

Rice Wraps

2 rice paper sheets, each
about 8½ inches in
diameter

3 carrots, scrubbed, julienned

1 large red bell pepper,
thinly slivered

6-inch piece of daikon radish,
peeled and julienned

1 bunch watercress

1 head curly leaf lettuce,
separated into leaves

other veggies you enjoy,
julienned, or perhaps
sprouts, jicama, or avocado

WRAPS: Fill a large bowl or pot with water at room temperature (or according to the package directions). Immerse a sheet of rice paper in the water, then set it on a dinner plate and allow it to soften for 1–2 minutes.

Arrange some of the carrots, bell pepper, and radish down the center of the rice paper sheet, drizzle these with cilantro cream, and top with some sprigs of watercress and leaves of curly lettuce. Starting at 1 edge, tightly but gently roll the rice paper around the filling. Don't try to close the ends. Let the lettuce and watercress stick out, but be sure the overlapping seam down the length of the wrap forms a tight seal. Cut the wrap into 4 sections and stand them on end on a serving platter. Repeat with the remaining sheet of rice paper, veggies, and cilantro cream. Serve with the ponzu dipping sauce.

HUMMUS AND VEGGIES
WRAPPED IN CHARD LEAVES

SERVES 4–6

4–6 large chard leaves

1 recipe Lemony Garlic Hummus (page 277)

1 cup thinly sliced red cabbage

1 red bell pepper, thinly sliced

4–6 radishes, thinly sliced

8–10 cherry tomatoes, each cut into 3 slices

½ English cucumber, scrubbed, thinly sliced, and halved lengthwise

broccoli sprouts or radish sprouts

sprigs of fresh herbs (optional)

Large rainbow chard leaves are the perfect canvas for these simple wraps full of raw vegetables that deliver lots of flavor and crunch. Use this recipe as a starting point and customize your wraps according to your preferences and what you have on hand: try using collard leaves and your fave veggies. I love julienned jicama as well as grated carrots, and I sometimes change up the hummus by adding parsley or substituting another dip such as the Spring Pea and Edamame Spread (page 278). Have ready 8–12 toothpicks to secure the wraps.

Lay the chard leaves flat on a clean work surface with the stem facing you. Using a sharp knife, cut out and discard the tough stem from each leaf. Spread the hummus generously down the spine of each leaf, and then top with cabbage, bell peppers, radish slices, tomato slices, cucumber slices, sprouts, and herbs (if using).

Turn each leaf 90 degrees so the spine is parallel to the edge of the counter. Starting at the bottom, roll up the chard leaf, tightly encasing the filling, and secure the wrap at either end with a toothpick. Cut the wraps in half, arrange on a serving platter, and serve.

ALKALINE BALANCED
PURELY ALKALINE
(WITHOUT THE BREAD)

AVOCADO TOMATO **TOAST**

SERVES 1–2

1 avocado, diced

8 cherry tomatoes, halved

1 clove garlic, grated on a
rasp or finely minced

1 Tbsp minced white onion
(optional)

2 Tbsp hemp hearts

1 Tbsp chopped fresh basil
(optional but so yummy!)

1 Tbsp extra-virgin olive oil

2–4 slices Broccoli and Onion
Bread (page 141)

Himalayan salt or crunchy
sea salt

freshly ground black pepper

Avocado is a meal in itself and hardly needs adornment, unless you have a few minutes to chop it up and toss it with the goodies below. Sometimes I don't even bother with the bread—I just grab a spoon and dig right in!

In a bowl, combine the avocado with the tomatoes, garlic, onion, hemp hearts, basil, and olive oil until well mixed. Spread the mixture on the bread, season with salt and pepper, and, *presto*, instant comfort food!

AVOCADOS ARE ONE OF NATURE'S PERFECT FOODS

These creamy fats are delicious, satiating, healthy comfort food and ideally should make up about 20% of your daily calories. They alkalize, energize, and hydrate your body. My motto is: An avocado a day helps keep the doctor away! Healthy fats are vital for optimal wellness, even if you are looking to lose weight, as they accelerate metabolism and also help to release stored acids found tucked inside fat cells. Healthy fats in turn help to shed those very fat cells. Remember, 77% of an avocado's calories come from beneficial fats—over 50% of which are oleic fats that provide anti-inflammatory benefits.

Look for fruit with a smooth, dark green skin. I buy at least 6–8 at a time at varying degrees of ripeness and store any perfectly ripe ones (yield to slight pressure) in the fridge if need be. Cut out any browned bruises or veining, which contain oxidized/rancid oils. Enjoy them often!

CHICKPEA DILL CREPES

SERVES 4

This seriously yummy recipe uses ingredients that will energize you. It is delicious for either lunch or dinner. I've even served these crepes, to rave reviews, for a healthy Sunday brunch. This is not a tricky recipe. Blend, pour, and flip—it's that simple! Try swapping out the broccolini with asparagus or zucchini. To save time, double the recipe and store the extra crepes separately from the veggies and the sauce so you can just warm them up the next day.

Chickpea Dill Crepes

2 cups unsweetened almond mylk (page 122)

⅓ cup diced white onion

1⅓ cups chickpea flour

2 Tbsp tapioca starch

½ tsp sea salt

⅓ cup chopped fresh dill or 5 tsp freeze-dried dill weed

coconut oil, for cooking

CREPES: In a blender, purée the almond mylk and onion until smooth. Add the chickpea flour, tapioca starch, and sea salt, and blend again until combined. Pour the batter into a large bowl and allow to stand for 20–30 minutes while you prepare the filling and the cream sauce.

Veggie Filling

1–2 tsp coconut oil

1 cup diced white onion

2 cups diced broccolini

2 Tbsp filtered, alkalized water

1 cup fresh or frozen peas

drizzle of extra-virgin olive oil

sea salt

FILLING: Heat the coconut oil in a sauté pan. Add the diced onion and heat over medium heat until translucent, 3–4 minutes. Scoop ½ the onions into a small bowl and reserve them for the pea cream sauce.

Add the broccolini and sauté for 1 minute, then pour in the water and allow to steam-fry, stirring, for 1 minute more or until bright green. Add the peas and sauté for another minute or 2. Remove from the heat and set aside in the pan.

Pea Cream Sauce

½ cup sautéed onions (reserved from vegetable filling)

½ cup frozen peas, rinsed under warm water

1 Tbsp lemon juice

2 Tbsp extra-virgin olive oil

1 Tbsp filtered, alkalized water, if needed

1 drop liquid stevia

sea salt

SAUCE: In a blender, combine the sautéed onions, peas, lemon juice, and olive oil, and blend until smooth and creamy. (If the sauce is very thick, add a wee bit of water.) Season to taste with stevia and/or salt. Spoon and scrape the mixture into a piping bag or a small resealable plastic bag.

TO FINISH: Line a plate with a tea towel. Stir the dill into the crepe batter and blend just until mixed (the batter will become greenish if overmixed).

Heat an 8- to 10-inch non-stick pan over low heat for 1–2 minutes. Add 1 tsp coconut oil and allow it to melt. Ladle ⅔ cup batter into the pan, swirling it to create a 7- to 8-inch circle. Cook until the surface loses its gloss and looks dry, 2–3 minutes, then carefully loosen the edges with a butter knife and gently flip the crepe over with a spatula. Cook for 30–60 seconds more, then transfer to a plate and cover with a tea towel.

Repeat with the remaining batter. This recipe makes 5 crepes—one to practice with, since the first is usually a flop!

TO ASSEMBLE: When the crepes are ready, quickly reheat the vegetable filling on medium-low heat for 1 minute, then remove from the heat and drizzle with olive oil and sea salt.

Place 1 crepe on a plate and cover 1 half with an even layer of the veggie mixture. Generously pipe (or snip a small hole in a corner of the bag) cream sauce over the veggies. Fold the other half of the crepe over the filling and then gently fold in half once again to create a pie-shaped wedge. Drizzle with more cream sauce and garnish with dill. Repeat with the remaining crepes, filling, and cream sauce. Serve warm or at room temperature.

WARMED VEGETABLES, LEGUMES, AND GRAINS

Raw foods are ideal for alkaline health, but some plants benefit from being warmed, as it enhances their nutritional benefits and our ability to metabolize them. Many of these are delicious comfort foods in cooler weather. Planning ahead is the key, though now and then you'll find me quick-soaking lentils at the last minute while I make the rest of the meal. If you prepare foods spontaneously like I often do, try to always be soaking or sprouting something so you have options. In a pinch, open a can of organic beans or pick up sprouted legumes at the market. Alternatively, I find that batch-soaking, batch-cooking, and then freezing beans and legumes works quite nicely.

If you can't soak, don't fret: digestive enzymes are your friend and can assist in digestion. However, once you form a habit of soaking/sprouting regularly, you won't go back. For a change of pace, look for the salmon recipe that I've snuck into this section too!

STEAMED ASPARAGUS AND SNOWPEAS *with* LEMON PARSLEY GREMOLATA

SERVES 4

I often enjoy my veggies simply drizzled with olive oil and a pinch of sea salt, but sometimes I feel like switching it up. Inspired by my holistic nutritionist pal, Kathleen, this gremolata can take a simple dish from ordinary to extraordinary with just a bit of garlic, lemon, and parsley—all of which are so alkalizing for the body. Keep this handy for days when you feel the need to jazz up your steamed broccoli, cabbage, or Brussels sprouts. It's also yummy stirred into lentils or beans!

Lemon Parsley Gremolata

½ cup fresh parsley

1 clove garlic

2 Tbsp extra-virgin olive oil

2 tsp lemon juice

2 tsp lemon zest

sea salt

freshly ground black pepper

GREMOLATA: Place all the ingredients in a food processor and combine until well chopped but not puréed. (Or very finely chop the parsley and garlic, or use a mortar and pestle to combine them, and then mix with the remaining ingredients.) Season to taste. Spoon the gremolata into a small bowl.

Steamed Veggies

1 bunch asparagus, about 12 stalks, trimmed and sliced lengthwise

24 snowpeas

1 medium red onion, slivered

4 cups mixed baby greens

2 Tbsp hemp hearts

chive flowers and finely chopped chives for garnish (optional)

VEGGIES: Fill a pot or the bottom of a steamer with water and bring to a boil over high heat. Place the asparagus, snowpeas, and onion in a steaming basket and cook until the asparagus and snowpeas are crisp-tender, 2–4 minutes. Remove from the heat.

Arrange 1 cup of baby greens on each plate. Divide the warm veggies evenly over top and spoon the gremolata over them. Sprinkle with hemp hearts and garnish with pretty chives and chive flowers if you have them.

CRUSHED EDAMAME, PEAS, AND MINT *over* SPRING GREEN BEANS

SERVES 4–6

3 cups green beans, trimmed, or 36 green beans, each 6 inches long, trimmed

2 cups frozen shelled organic edamame beans

2 cups frozen or fresh green peas

½ cup extra-virgin olive oil

juice of 1½ limes

2 drops liquid stevia

12–14 large mint leaves

sea salt

7 chives, chopped, or 1 green onion, green and white parts, chopped

1 good-sized bunch of pea shoots

slices of pink watermelon radish for garnish (optional)

In the spring, we gorge ourselves on the most beautiful green beans from our local greenhouse. We have to call ahead to reserve as they are so popular! Fresh beans are quite amazing just lightly steamed, but this recipe provides a little variety. Adding the edamame and peas turns it into more of a main dish providing added protein.

Fill the sink or a large bowl with cold water. Fill a pot or the bottom of a steamer with water and bring to a boil over high heat. Place the green beans in a steaming basket, cover, and cook for 3 minutes. Using tongs, transfer the beans to the cold water to halt the cooking. Place in a bowl, cover to keep warm, and set aside.

Place the edamame in the steaming basket, cover, and cook for 1 minute. Add the peas and steam for 2 more minutes. Pour the edamame and peas into a colander and run cold water over them to stop the cooking. Shake the colander gently and allow it to drain well.

In a food processor, pulse the edamame and peas with the olive oil, lime juice, stevia, mint, and sea salt just until crushed and roughly combined. You should have some large pieces of edamame. Add the chives and pulse again to mix them in.

Divide the pea shoots between 4–6 plates and top each with beans. Divide the edamame and pea mixture among the plates, setting it over the beans. Garnish with some pretty pink watermelon radish slivers. Alternatively, layer this on a nice oval platter and serve family-style.

SOY PRODUCTS

Choosing healthy alkaline foods means being informed about where they come from. Eat soy and wheat only very, very occasionally.

As much as 95% of the world's soybeans are said to be genetically modified, and fermented soy, as in miso and tempeh, is acidic and contains yeast, fungus, and mold. When soy is highly processed to become vegan faux meats, it's jammed with additives and preservatives. So always choose organic whole, unsprouted beans, such as edamame; fresh tofu (unfermented bean curd); unsweetened organic soy mylk without additives; and GMO-free soy lecithin granules and soybean oils. Sprouting soybeans, which you can do in 4–5 days, dramatically increases their life force and nutritional value (see sprouting chart on page 96).

LENTILS *with* CREAMY EGGPLANT

SERVES 4

Lentils were a new food for me when I became an alkavorian. Now I often pack these proteins into soups and stews. Though the kids aren't big on eggplant—yet!—they do appreciate lentils. So the kids could have the lentils while the adults indulge in the creamy eggplant, but it's tempting to just sneakily mix the eggplant in with the lentils and see how that goes over. When I eat this dish, I love scooping up the eggplant with heaps of lentils. I also serve it with a mixed green salad to add some raw to the meal and balance out the cooked. I usually prepare the lentils and the crumble while the eggplant is cooking.

Creamy Eggplant

2 large eggplants

coconut oil

¼ tsp sea salt + more for sprinkling

freshly ground black pepper

2 large bulbs garlic

3 Tbsp extra-virgin olive oil

Mediterranean Lentils

1 cup black lentils, soaked, drained, and rinsed

½ red onion, diced

1 bay leaf

2½ cups filtered, alkaline water

½ cup diced red bell pepper

10–12 cherry tomatoes, quartered

¼ cup minced parsley

¼ tsp sea salt

freshly ground black pepper

1 recipe Garlic Walnut Cheeze (page 283)

EGGPLANT: Preheat the oven to 350°F. Slice the eggplants in half lengthwise and score on the diagonal in 2 directions. Place them on a baking sheet, cut side up. Rub the cut sides with coconut oil and sprinkle with some salt and pepper.

Slice the tops off the garlic and smear a bit of coconut oil over them. Add them to the tray with the eggplants and roast for 40–50 minutes, until soft. Set aside until cool enough to handle.

> *** DO AHEAD:**
> Soak 1 cup black lentils in 3 cups filtered, alkaline water for 8–12 hours.

LENTILS: Place the lentils, onion, and bay leaf in a medium pot with the water and bring to a boil, uncovered, over high heat. Turn down the heat to low, cover, and simmer until the lentils are tender but not mushy or split, 20–30 minutes. Drain off any excess water. Stir in the bell pepper, tomatoes, parsley, salt, and some black pepper.

TO FINISH: Scoop the flesh from the eggplant into the bowl of a food processor (discard the skins) and squeeze the roasted garlic from the bulbs (discard the husks) into the same bowl. Add the ¼ tsp salt and the olive oil and process until smooth.

To serve, spread a generous layer of creamy eggplant onto 4 plates. Then pile a big scoop of the lentil mixture on top. Sprinkle with the Garlic Walnut Cheeze and dig in.

AVOCADO CREAMED KALE
with PUY LENTIL PILAF

SERVES 6

Lentil Pilaf

* 1 cup soaked Puy lentils, rinsed and drained well

1¾ cups vegetable broth (or 1½ Veggie Bouillon Cubes (page 277) + 1¾ cups filtered, alkaline water) + 3 Tbsp for steam-frying

1 Tbsp coconut oil

½ red onion, minced

1 clove garlic, minced

2 stalks celery, cut into small dice

6 baby carrots, thinly sliced

½ red bell pepper, cut into small dice

½ yellow bell pepper, cut into small dice

8 asparagus stalks, trimmed and chopped into 1-inch rounds, tips left intact

Himalayan salt

freshly ground black pepper

6 radishes for garnish

Creamed Kale

6 packed cups finely chopped kale, ribs removed

¼ cup extra-virgin olive oil

juice of 1 lime

1 avocado, diced

¼ tsp chipotle chili pepper

½ tsp smoked paprika

¼ tsp Himalayan salt

2–3 drops liquid stevia or 1 tsp pure maple syrup

This is kinda 2 recipes in 1. Each can certainly stand on its own but they are marvelous together. An added bonus of this recipe is a wonderful hand treatment: avocado massaged into your hands makes them nice and soft! The kale becomes even more tender after marinating overnight, so pack any leftovers separately and take them for lunch. If you can't eat that much kale in 2 days, massage just enough for 1 meal and refrigerate the kale and the dressing separately for up to 3 days.

PILAF: Place the lentils and broth in a medium pot over high heat and bring to a boil. Cover, turn down the heat to medium-low, and simmer for 20–25 minutes, or until the lentils are tender and most of the liquid has been absorbed. Remove from the heat and allow to rest for at least 10 minutes. Drain any excess liquid.

While the lentils are cooking, heat the coconut oil in a sauté pan over medium-low heat. Add the onion, garlic, and celery and sauté until the onion is translucent, 2–3 minutes. Add the carrots, bell peppers, and the 3 Tbsp of vegetable broth and steam-fry for 2 minutes. Stir in the asparagus and steam-fry until bright green and tender crisp, 2–3 minutes. If the pan becomes dry, add a wee bit more broth. Stir in the lentils and season to taste with salt and pepper.

KALE: In a large, deep bowl, toss the kale with the olive oil and lime juice. Using your hands, massage the liquid into the kale for about 1 minute. Add the remaining ingredients and massage them into the kale for 1–2 minutes, or until the avocado is completely creamed through the greens and the greens have softened.

To serve, divide the kale among 6 plates and top each serving with lentil pilaf and a radish for garnish. Deelish!

> **✳ DO AHEAD**: Soak 1 cup Puy lentils in 3 cups filtered, alkaline water for 8–12 hours.

STEAM-FRIED VEGGIE RICE

SERVES 8

When my herniated disk was at its very worst, my daughter was only a year old. I was so blessed to have a nanny, Flordeliza, who also prepared many alkaline meals for me, including this recipe that is still a family favorite. I jazz it up by replacing 1 cup of the rice with ½ cup soaked quinoa and ½ cup soaked buckwheat, or by replacing the black rice with brown. Served with a nice big green salad, this makes a nice big batch for a crowd, or for packing in lunches the next day. Note that this dish is steam-fried with broth to avoid frying the olive oil, which is added once the cooking is complete.

* 1½ cups soaked black rice + kombu

3¼ cups vegetable stock (or use 2 Veggie Bouillon Cubes (page 277) + 3¼ cups water)

1 white onion, diced

4 cloves garlic, minced, separated

2 large carrots, scrubbed, finely diced

2 stalks celery, finely diced

1 red bell pepper, diced

1 cup finely diced zucchini

6 fresh asparagus stalks or 10 fresh green beans, trimmed and sliced into ¼-inch rounds

1 cup frozen peas

2–3 Tbsp extra-virgin olive oil

2 Tbsp Bragg Liquid Aminos

1 Tbsp grated ginger

Himalayan salt to taste

¼ cup diced watermelon radish (optional)

Place the rice, kombu, and 3 cups of the stock in a rice cooker and set it to cook. (Alternatively, place the rice, kombu, and stock in a large pot and bring to a boil over high heat. Turn down the heat to low, cover, and simmer for 30–40 minutes, or until almost all of the liquid has been absorbed. Remove from the heat and allow to stand, covered, for 10 minutes.) Remove and discard the kombu.

Turn the rice out onto a large platter and fluff it with a fork to allow it to cool somewhat. (You want the rice to be fluffy and not stick together too much.) The more it cools, the more it gains this fall-apart consistency, which is why many people use day-old rice, fluffed and then refrigerated overnight.

Heat the onion and the remaining ¼ cup stock in a medium pot over medium heat and steam-fry for 1–2 minutes. Add ¾ of the garlic and continue to steam-fry until the onion is translucent, about 2 minutes more. Stir in the carrots and celery and cook for 1–2 minutes. Add the bell pepper, zucchini, and asparagus and steam-fry for another minute or 2. Pour in the frozen peas, cover, and cook for 1 more minute. Remove from the heat.

Add the rice, using 2 large spoons to toss and combine it. Gently stir in the olive oil, Bragg, ginger, and the remaining garlic. Season to taste with salt. Pour onto a serving platter and garnish with slices of radish (if using). This will keep refrigerated for up to 3 days and even freezes well. To reheat, place in a sauté pan with a couple of tablespoons of water or broth and stir until warm.

* DO AHEAD: Soak 1½ cups black rice and a 4-inch piece of kombu in 4 cups filtered, alkaline water overnight. Rinse well and save the kombu for cooking.

CREAMY CANNELLINI BEAN SAUCE *over* **SPELT FETTUCCINE**

SERVES 6–8

Pistachio Cheeze Crumble

½ cup raw or lightly toasted pistachios

finely grated zest of ¼ lemon

⅛ tsp fine sea salt

pinch chili flakes

Who doesn't love a bowl of creamy pasta? My kids sure love it, which is why I recreated the typical Alfredo sauce—minus the butter and the rich cream—in this tasty number. You'll enjoy this garlicky sauce just as much as the original but you'll feel so much better for it. The pistachio cheeze is also delicious sprinkled over rice or salads. Remember to serve this with a green salad to ensure a balanced meal. If you wish, take an enzyme with your meal to help digest the beans if you don't soak and cook your own.

CRUMBLE: Combine all the ingredients in a blender or food processor and grind until chopped but not completely uniform. This will keep refrigerated in an airtight container for up to 3 days.

Bean Sauce

✳ ¾ cup dry cannellini beans, soaked, rinsed, and drained + kombu

4¼ cups filtered, alkaline water

½ onion, diced

2 whole cloves garlic

1 stalk celery, diced

3 Tbsp grapeseed oil

10 cloves garlic, halved

¼ cup extra-virgin olive oil

1 Tbsp lemon juice

1½ tsp chopped fresh rosemary + more for garnish

1 Tbsp + ¼ tsp Celtic sea salt

¼–⅓ cup unsweetened almond mylk (page 122)

Spelt fettuccine and veggies

1 pkg (16 oz) spelt fettuccine noodles (or about 4 cups cooked noodles)

18 sugar snap peas, trimmed

2 carrots, scrubbed, thinly sliced on the diagonal

1 small crown cauliflower, cut into bite-sized florets

1 small crown broccoli, cut into bite-sized florets

1 red bell pepper, cut into 1-inch pieces

1 yellow bell pepper, cut into 1-inch pieces

SAUCE: Place the cannellini beans and kombu in a medium pot with the water. Add the onion, 2 whole cloves garlic, and celery, and bring to a boil, uncovered, over medium-high heat. Turn down the heat to low and simmer for 40 minutes, stirring periodically. If the beans are tender but not mushy, remove them from the heat. If they are not yet tender, cook them for up to 20 more minutes, checking regularly. Remove from the heat and allow to cool somewhat. Drain the beans, reserving any cooking liquid for soup.

Heat the grapeseed oil in a small sauté pan over low heat, add the garlic halves, and cook for 3–5 minutes, until soft or translucent. Remove from the heat and allow to cool.

In a blender, combine the cannellini beans with the sautéed garlic, olive oil, lemon juice, rosemary, and ¼ tsp sea salt and process until silky smooth. Season to taste and adjust the thickness, adding ¼–⅓ cup of almond mylk until you have a heavy but pourable sauce. If you need more liquid, use a few spoonfuls of the reserved bean liquid (or almond mylk if you didn't have any bean liquid left). Set aside.

FETTUCCINE AND VEGGIES: Cook the pasta until al dente, 8–10 minutes.

Set all the veggies in a steamer basket. Place the steamer basket over a pot of boiling water and steam the veggies for 3–4 minutes. Be careful not to overcook them: they should be firm but slightly tender.

Drain the pasta into a large colander—no need to rinse it as the sauce will adhere better if you don't.

To serve, scoop the pasta into a large serving dish, add the steamed veggies, and gently pour the creamy bean sauce over top. Toss carefully, but thoroughly, before dividing among individual bowls. Serve with pistachio cheeze.

> **✳ DO AHEAD:** Soak ¾ cup cannellini beans with a 4-inch piece of kombu in 4 cups filtered, alkaline water overnight.

STEAMED BRUSSELS SPROUTS AND QUINOA SALAD

Did you like Brussels sprouts as a kid? I sure didn't! I remember them as khaki balls of mush but we *had* to eat them. It's taken me a while to embrace these lovely miniature cabbages, but now I love them. Not only are they alkaline-forming, but studies show that by consuming 1¼ cups every single day you'd improve the stability of the DNA in your white blood cells. And a few 1½-cup servings a week of cruciferous vegetables can make a world of difference in protecting you against cancer and helping to release toxins. If you're short on time, cut the Brussels sprouts into ¼-inch slices rather than peeling them.

SERVES 6–8

Hazelnut-peppercorn Crumble

¾ cup hazelnuts, soaked, rinsed, and patted dry

1 Tbsp pink peppercorns

½ tsp sea salt

CRUMBLE: In a food processor or blender, pulse the hazelnuts, peppercorns, and salt until you have a rough crumble. Set aside.

> **✳ DO AHEAD:** Soak 1½ cups quinoa in 3 cups filtered, alkaline water + 1 Tbsp lemon juice overnight. Soak ¾ cup hazelnuts in 1½ cups filtered, alkaline water overnight.

Brussels Sprouts Salad

1 small white onion, cut into ¼-inch dice

1 stalk celery, diced

6 Tbsp filtered, alkaline water

✳ 1½ cups soaked quinoa, drained and rinsed well

¾ cup yeast-free vegetable broth

30 Brussels sprouts, leaves peeled off from the tiny inner cores

1 clove garlic, minced

3 Tbsp extra-virgin olive oil

¼ tsp sea salt

SALAD: In a blender, purée 2 Tbsp of the onion and 2 Tbsp of the celery with the water until smooth. Set aside this onion broth.

Place the quinoa and vegetable broth in a large pot and bring to a boil, uncovered, over medium-high heat. Turn down the heat to low and allow to simmer for 5–7 minutes, or until the broth is absorbed. Cover and remove from the heat.

Halve the Brussels sprout cores. In a large sauté pan, place the remaining onion and celery, the garlic, Brussel sprout cores, and 2 Tbsp of the onion broth over medium-high heat and steam-fry until translucent, 3–4 minutes. Add the remaining onion broth and Brussels sprout leaves and stir to coat the leaves. Cover and steam for 1 minute, then stir and steam for 1 more minute.

Place the quinoa in a serving bowl, add the Brussels sprouts, olive oil, and sea salt, and toss to combine.

To serve, spoon into individual bowls and top with hazelnut-peppercorn crumble.

THAI SPAGHETTI SQUASH NOODLES *with* SWEET CHILI SAUCE

SERVES 6

Sweet Chili Sauce

¾ cup filtered, alkaline water

juice of 1 lemon

4 drops liquid stevia

1 Tbsp tapioca starch

1 tsp coconut oil

½ cup finely minced sweet onion

2 garlic cloves, finely minced

½ cup finely minced red bell pepper

½ Thai bird's-eye chili pepper, seeded and finely chopped (⅛–¼ tsp)

sea salt

2 tsp maple syrup (optional) or more stevia

Whereas butternut, acorn, kabocha, and other popular winter squash are not considered alkaline, spaghetti squash is non-starchy and definitely alkalizing! You could say this is your pasta replacement if you are crazy for pasta but would rather avoid it. Making your own chili sauce lets you control the sweetness and the heat. Just remember that the oils in chili peppers can burn your skin, so wear gloves when handling them and don't rub your eyes after chopping! If you can't find a Thai bird's-eye chili, a milder green jalapeño pepper will do. In a pinch, I sometimes just use a vegetable peeler to cut the vegetables into long, thin strips.

SAUCE: In a glass measuring cup, whisk together the water, lemon juice, stevia, and tapioca starch until well combined. Set aside.

Heat the coconut oil in a small saucepan over medium heat. Add the onion and sauté for 1 minute. Stir in the garlic, bell pepper, and chili pepper, and sauté for 1 more minute. Whisk the tapioca mixture again and pour it into the pan. Cook, stirring to combine, for 3–5 minutes, until the mixture turns from cloudy to clear. Add the salt and stir in the maple syrup (if using). Remove from the heat, allow to cool slightly, and pour into a sauceboat. (The sauce will set up as it chills. To thin it, whisk in a drizzle of warm water.)

Thai Noodles

1 large spaghetti squash (do not substitute)

1 Tbsp coconut oil

¼ cup sliced yellow onion

3 Tbsp finely chopped fresh lemongrass

1 Tbsp finely chopped garlic

1 Tbsp finely chopped ginger

½ cup julienned, scrubbed carrot

½ cup julienned, scrubbed daikon radish

½ cup julienned red bell pepper

½ cup julienned, scrubbed zucchini

1 Tbsp Bragg Liquid Aminos

¼ tsp sea salt

5 Tbsp finely chopped cilantro

3 Tbsp thinly sliced fresh mint

3 Tbsp thinly sliced fresh basil

3 Tbsp finely chopped fresh green onions

juice from ½ lime

hemp hearts for garnish

NOODLES: Preheat the oven to 350°F. Line a baking sheet with parchment paper.

Halve the squash lengthwise and place it, cut sides down, on the baking sheet. (Do not add water or the squash will be too soft.) Bake for 30–40 minutes, or until fork-tender and the "spaghetti" strings pull freely from the skin. Remove from the heat and allow to cool.

Heat the coconut oil in a sauté pan on medium-low heat. Add the onion, lemongrass, garlic, and ginger, and sauté for 1–2 minutes. Stir in the carrot, daikon, bell pepper, and zucchini for 1–2 minutes. Season with Bragg and salt. Remove from the heat, then add the cilantro, mint, basil, green onions, and lime juice and toss well to combine.

Using a fork, loosen the strands of spaghetti squash from the skin by dragging it lengthwise with the strands. Divide the squash among 6 plates into nice heaps. Discard the skins. Pile the Thai-spiced veggie noodles over the squash and serve with sweet chili sauce on the side. Garnish with hemp hearts.

SPROUTED QUINOA CROQUETTES *with* SMOKED PAPRIKA ALMOND CREAM

**SERVES 8–16
(1–2 PER PERSON)**

Smoked Paprika Almond Cream

1 cup soaked almonds, patted dry and roughly chopped (if using an immersion blender)

1 clove garlic, chopped

½ cup filtered, alkaline water

juice of 1 lemon

2 Tbsp extra-virgin olive oil

1¼ tsp smoked paprika

½ tsp Celtic sea salt

cayenne pepper (optional)

Just thinking about these tasty morsels makes me want to run and soak some black beans and quinoa! This dish is great to make ahead, and the croquettes freeze well, so you can pull out the delicious patties and serve up a quick, satisfying meal with a salad just like that! Alternatively, you can save a step by not forming the mixture into patties. Just heap the croquette mixture, warm or cold, into wraps with avocado, greens, and a dollop of almond cream. This one will definitely have you coming back for more!

CREAM: Place all the ingredients in a high-speed blender and combine until creamy and smooth. (Or use an immersion blender and a deep bowl, if you prefer.) If the cream is too thick to pour, add 1–2 Tbsp more water and blend again.

cont. next page . . .

WHAT ABOUT WHEAT?

Gluten-free grains are becoming more of a staple as many people discover sensitivity to the gluten in wheat. Wheat crops are often genetically modified and stored for long periods of time, which can cause molds to spread throughout the grains. If you are not celiac, choose heirloom wheat grains or kamut (an heirloom cousin to wheat) and sprout these to reduce the gluten content. If you are celiac or gluten-sensitive, consume only organic wheatgrass, which is completely gluten-free.

Sprouted Quinoa Croquettes

1 cup quinoa, soaked, cooked, and cooled (about 3 cups cooked)

1 very large sweet potato, peeled, chopped, steamed, and mashed (2 cups mashed)

2 Tbsp coconut oil

1 cup finely diced red onion

4 cloves garlic, crushed

½ cup finely diced red bell pepper

 1¾ cups soaked and cooked pinto beans or 1 can (14 oz) pinto beans, drained and rinsed

½ cup hemp hearts

1½ Tbsp ground white chia seeds

½ cup chopped cilantro

1 tsp freeze-dried oregano

1 tsp ground cumin

juice of 1 large lime

1 tsp Celtic sea salt

cayenne pepper (optional)

CROQUETTES: In large bowl, combine the quinoa and sweet potato and set aside.

Heat 1 Tbsp of the coconut oil in a small saucepan over medium-low heat. Add the onion, garlic, and bell pepper, and sauté for 2–3 minutes, or until translucent but not browned. Allow to cool and then add these veggies to the quinoa mixture.

Add the remaining ingredients to the bowl. Use your hands or a wooden spoon to combine the mixture. Using a tablespoon, gather 3 Tbsp of mixture into your hands, form it into a ball, and flatten it into an oval patty about ¾ inches thick and 4 inches across.

Heat the remaining 1 Tbsp coconut oil in a sauté pan on medium-low heat. Gently set the patties in the pan, cooking them in batches if necessary, and heat through on both sides, about 2 minutes per side. Remove the croquettes from the heat and carefully arrange them on a serving plate.

To serve, arrange 1 or 2 croquettes on each plate. Drizzle with the cream or serve it on the side. Enjoy.

> *** DO AHEAD:** Soak 1¾ cups pinto beans in 8 cups filtered, alkaline water overnight, then cook (page 92). Soak 1 cup almonds in 3 cups filtered, alkaline water overnight. Soak 1 cup quinoa in 2 cups filtered, alkaline water overnight, then cook in 2 cups filtered, alkaline water with 2 Veggie Bouillon Cubes (page 277) and allow to cool.

SPROUTED LENTIL AND BUCKWHEAT SLIDERS *with* SPICED SAUCY VEGGIES

SERVES 4–6 (ABOUT 12 SLIDER PATTIES)

Lentil and Buckwheat Sliders

* 1 cup sprouted brown lentils, rinsed and drained well

⅓ cup soaked buckwheat, drained and rinsed

1 Tbsp coconut oil

½ red onion, finely diced

½ green bell pepper, finely diced

2 cloves garlic, diced

3 Tbsp soaked ground chia seeds

2 Tbsp minced fresh parsley

1½ tsp minced jalapeño peppers or ¼ tsp chili powder

¼ tsp Himalayan salt

1 Tbsp Bragg Liquid Aminos

3 Tbsp spelt or buckwheat flour

2–3 large Savoy cabbage leaves, cut into 3-inch rounds or squares

broccoli or other fave sprouts for garnish

There's just something so cute about mini things. And making small bites is a good way to get kids to eat new foods: it makes the foods more exciting and gives the kids a chance to try them in small, manageable portions. These sliders are great for an appie gathering because they're easy to serve, even at room temperature, and they look fantastic on the serving plate. (Make the parts ahead of time and assemble the sliders at the last minute.) Packed with some serious nutrition from the sprouted lentils and buckwheat, they provide protein, iron, fiber, and lots of vitamins and minerals. These are power sliders for sure! Serve these with a mixed green salad and Green Bean Fries (page 244).

SLIDERS: Place the lentils in a medium pot, add 2 cups filtered, alkaline water, and bring to a boil, uncovered, over high heat. Turn down the heat to low, cover, and simmer for 25–30 minutes, or until all the water is absorbed. (You should have about 2¼ cups cooked lentils.) Allow to stand, covered, for 5–10 minutes.

Place the buckwheat in a small pot, add ⅔ cup filtered water, and bring to a boil, uncovered, over high heat. Turn down the heat to low, cover, and simmer for 7–10 minutes, or until the water is nearly all absorbed. Watch carefully to avoid burning. Allow to stand, covered, for 10 minutes.

Heat the coconut oil in a sauté pan over medium-low heat. Add the onion, bell pepper, and garlic and sauté until softened, 2–3 minutes. Set aside.

> * **DO AHEAD:** Soak 1 cup brown lentils in 3 cups filtered, alkaline water overnight. Rinse and transfer them to a jar and allow them to sprout for 12–48 hours. Soak ⅓ cup buckwheat in 2 cups filtered, alkaline water overnight. Soak 1 Tbsp ground chia seeds in 3 Tbsp filtered, alkaline water for 20–30 minutes.

cont. next page . . .

Saucy Spiced Veggies

6 large cherry tomatoes or 1 medium Roma tomato, roughly chopped

6 sundried tomatoes in oil, chopped

1 small clove garlic, roughly chopped

½ red bell pepper, roughly chopped

¼ small onion, roughly chopped

¼ cup roughly chopped, scrubbed zucchini

8 basil leaves

2 Tbsp ground chia seeds + more if needed

1½ tsp roughly chopped jalapeño pepper

¼ tsp Himalayan salt

2 Tbsp extra-virgin olive oil

3 drops liquid stevia

In a food processor, pulse the lentils, buckwheat, chia, parsley, jalapeño pepper, salt, Bragg, and the onion—bell pepper mixture 12–15 times, or until it starts to come together but still retains some texture. Add the spelt flour and pulse a couple more times until mixed in. Spoon the slider mixture into a large bowl and set aside to cool while you make the saucy veggies. This will keep refrigerated in an airtight container for up to 3 days.

VEGGIES: Place all the ingredients in a food processor and combine until saucy but not puréed. Be sure to leave some texture. Season to taste and pour into a bowl. Set aside. If the mixture is watery add 1–2 more tsp of chia to thicken. This will keep refrigerated in an airtight container for 2 days.

TO FINISH: Preheat the oven to 325°F and line a baking sheet with parchment paper. Using a tablespoon, gather 2 heaping Tbsp of the slider mixture into your hands, roll it into a ball, and flatten to form a patty ¾ inch thick and about 1¾ inches across. Set the patty on the baking sheet. Repeat with the remaining slider mixture. Bake the patties for 12–15 minutes, until warmed through.

To assemble, place a small piece of cabbage on a plate, then top it with a slider and some of the saucy spiced veggies. Top with sprouts and serve as open-face sliders or use a larger cabbage leaf and make a wrap.

WHERE ARE THE CORN AND POTATOES?

Corn and potatoes are a natural with sliders (and many other dishes), but even some alkaline foods are best eaten only very, very occasionally.

- **Corn.** Fresh ears of corn make me think of corn roasts and late-summer harvest, but this is a complicated food. For one thing, roughly 95% of the world's corn crops are genetically modified, and for another, this veggie harbors more mold and pathogens than most. It's hard for our digestive tract to break down, yet it shows up in nearly every processed food. If you choose to eat corn, buy freshly picked, organic cobs from your local farmer and eat them right away, no more than a few times each season.

- **Potatoes.** In North America, potatoes are so abundant that it's hard to imagine not eating them. However, crops, including potatoes, that remain in storage beyond their growing season contain mold spores that will eventually spread throughout the bag or barrel. Potatoes are also high in starch, which breaks down into sugar in the body. If you choose to eat potatoes now and then, buy freshly picked, organic new or red potatoes from your local farmer and eat them within 6 weeks. If this just isn't possible, use your nose to detect any presence of mold on storebought organic ones. Keep them in a cool, dark place to prevent greening, which can be toxic.

RED QUINOA BITES
with OREGANO AND SUNDRIED TOMATO MARINARA SAUCE

SERVES 4–6

Marinara Sauce

1 large tomato

½ cup sundried tomatoes in olive oil or dried ones, soaked for 30 minutes

½ cup chopped red bell pepper

1 clove garlic, roughly chopped

2 Tbsp extra-virgin olive oil

1 Tbsp chopped fresh basil or 2 tsp freeze-dried basil

2 tsp chopped fresh oregano or 1 tsp freeze-dried oregano

Red Quinoa Bites

2½ cups filtered, alkaline water

½ cup chopped white onion

1 stalk celery, chopped

1 clove garlic

3 sprigs oregano

1 cup soaked red quinoa, rinsed and drained well

2 Tbsp chia seeds

¼ cup finely diced red bell pepper

2 Tbsp chopped fresh parsley

⅛ tsp ground celery seeds

¼ tsp Himalayan salt

½ tsp Bragg Liquid Aminos

½ cup chickpea flour, preferably sprouted flour

Enjoy these bites with some fresh greens, and how about some steamed broccoli? Kids love picking these up with toothpicks and dipping them in the marinara sauce. Alternatively, you can try making the mixture into meat-ball-shapes and bake as directed in the recipe—then serve with zucchini noodles and the marinara sauce for Spaghetti and Quinoa Balls!

> *** DO AHEAD**: Soak 1 cup red quinoa in 4 cups filtered, alkaline water for 24 hours or more.

SAUCE: Place all the ingredients in a food processor and combine until fairly smooth. This will keep refrigerated in an airtight container for up to 3 days.

QUINOA BITES: Place 2 cups of the water in a blender with the onion, celery, garlic, and oregano, and combine until puréed. Pour it into a medium saucepan, add the quinoa, and bring to a boil, uncovered, over high heat. Turn down the heat to low, cover, and simmer for 20–25 minutes, or until almost all the water has been absorbed. Remove from the heat and allow to stand, covered, for 10 minutes. (If the water is not fully absorbed, return the quinoa to the heat for a few minutes and repeat the standing time.) Fluff with a fork.

In a small bowl, whisk the chia seeds with the ½ cup water for 30 seconds. Set this mixture aside to thicken for 20–30 minutes, stirring occasionally.

In a large bowl, combine the bell pepper, parsley, celery seeds, salt, Bragg, and chia gel. Add the quinoa and toss well to combine. Add the flour and combine again.

Preheat the oven to 325°F. Line a baking sheet with parchment paper. Wet your hands. Using a tablespoon, scoop 1½ Tbsp of the mixture into your hands and form it into a ball. Set the ball on the baking sheet. Repeat with the remaining quinoa mixture. Bake for 15–20 minutes, or until heated through and dry on the outside. Serve hot or at room temperature with the marinara sauce.

SAVORY BITES AND HEALTHY SWEET TREATS

Just because you've cleared your pantry of all the nasty processed snacks doesn't mean you won't be enjoying delicious nibblies! I've created a whole host of nutritious recipes including celebratory cakes (birthdays come but once a year!) to keep you happy for a long, long time—even when you're selecting purely alkaline recipes. You shouldn't ever feel as though you can't eat when you are hungry nor that you have to go without a little something sweet with your afternoon herbal tea if you wish. Remember, this lifestyle isn't based on calories. You know the alkaline-balancing rules by now: enjoy the mildly acidic treats in moderation . . . Now snack away, my friend!

Amaranth

AMARANTH CRISPS
with SWEET ONION AND CHIVES

MAKES 36+ CRISPS

1 cup soaked amaranth, rinsed and drained well

2 cups filtered, alkaline water

¼ cup chopped sweet onion

¼ tsp coarse sea salt + more for sprinkling

2 Tbsp chopped fresh chives or 1 Tbsp dried chives

Or try one of these other variations instead of the chives:

1 Tbsp finely chopped fresh rosemary + sea salt

¼ tsp smoked paprika + 1½ tsp lime zest + sea salt

2 cloves garlic, finely grated + 2 Tbsp finely chopped basil + sea salt

2 tsp grated ginger + 2 cloves garlic, finely grated + 4 drops stevia + ½ Tbsp Bragg Liquid Aminos

¾ tsp ground cinnamon + 5 drops stevia + good pinch of allspice

My kids are serious cracker kids! After school, they go hunting for something crunchy, and these nutritious, wafer-thin crisps are the perfect answer. They're so light that they're strictly a munching cracker—no dips or spreads with these—and they're especially wonderful for toddlers because they require very little chewing. Got the munchies? Give these a shot and see how you like them!

* DO AHEAD: Soak 1 cup amaranth in 4 cups filtered, alkaline water overnight.

Place the amaranth and the water in a medium pot over medium-high heat. Bring to a boil, cover, and cook for 12–15 minutes, or until the water has been absorbed. Remove from the heat and allow to stand, covered, for 10 minutes.

Preheat the oven to 300°F. Line a baking sheet with parchment paper.

Place the onion, then sea salt, then ½ the cooked amaranth in a blender and combine until smooth and creamy. If the mixture seems too thick, add 1–2 Tbsp water and process again. Be patient and refrain from adding more water, just scrape down the sides of the blender and keep blending. Pour this mixture into the rest of the cooked amaranth, stirring until well combined. Stir in the chives.

Use the back of a tablespoon to smear 1 Tbsp of the amaranth mixture onto the parchment paper, forming it into a very thin, long oval (try to keep the thickness consistent so they cook evenly and do not burn). (Alternatively, make them into 2-inch rounds.) Make as many crackers as will fit on the tray, leaving lots of space around each cracker.

Bake the crackers for 10 minutes. Sprinkle with salt and bake for another 15–20 minutes. Watch them closely, especially if you made the smaller crackers. They should be just slightly brown with a nice even light crunch, not a soft chew. Allow the crackers to cool completely on a wire rack before you pack them away.

These will keep in an airtight container at room temperature for up to 4 months, though they are sooo addictive that they probably won't last that long!

GREEN BEAN **FRIES**

SERVES 4

Looking for a guilt-free, addictive snack? These could be it! I could eat an entire batch myself. Since they are so easy to whip up, these non-fried fries make a yummy pre-dinner snack for a gathering or for the kids while you prep dinner. They are also a yummy side dish for the Sprouted Lentil and Buckwheat Sliders (page 227), or any veggie burger.

Almond Flour Parmesan

½ cup almond flour
(or ¾ cup almonds,
finely ground, soaked,
and dehydrated)

½ tsp garlic powder

½ tsp onion powder

½ tsp Himalayan salt

freshly ground
black pepper

Green Bean Fries

36 fresh green beans

2 tsp extra-virgin olive oil

1 tsp Bragg Liquid Aminos

PARMESAN: Place all the ingredients in a small bowl and mix until well combined. This will keep refrigerated in an airtight container for 2 weeks.

FRIES: Fill the bottom half of a steamer with water and bring to a boil over high heat. Place the beans in a steaming basket and steam for 4–6 minutes, or until tender, being careful not to overcook. Remove from the heat, drain well, and transfer to a medium bowl. (If they are really wet, lightly pat them dry with a towel.)

Pour in the olive oil and Bragg and toss gently. Add ½ the parmesan mixture and toss gently again. Pour the beans into a serving dish and sprinkle with a little more parmesan. Serve with the remaining parmesan. Enjoy.

COOKING WITH HEALTHY OILS

To protect your health and investment, be sure to avoid damaging your nutrient-dense cold-pressed oils and only heat the two heat-tolerant ones: coconut and grapeseed. With others, heat breaks the oil down into potentially harmful and possibly carcinogenic materials containing free radicals that can do some serious damage within the body! Use extra-virgin coconut oil when you don't mind a hint of coconut (it works more often than not) and grapeseed oil when you do.

Olive oil is best not heated but is such a welcome flavor, you can always add a good drizzle after cooking. Play with delicious cold-pressed nut oils for drizzles on soups and in dressings, and don't forget about flax and hemp oils in your dressings too—but never ever heat them! And remember that steam frying also works like a charm!

Hemp Chipotle Kale Chips
(page 246)

HEMP CHIPOTLE KALE CHIPS (+ KALE CAESAR)

SERVES 6

2 large bunches curly kale
(10 large leaves + stalks)

1 cup sunflower seeds

⅓ cup hemp hearts

3 cloves garlic

¾ tsp sea salt

½–¾ tsp smoked paprika

⅛ tsp chipotle pepper

1¼ cups filtered,
alkaline water

2 Tbsp extra-virgin olive oil

1½ tsp maple syrup or 4–6
drops stevia or a
combination of both

Kale chips are all the rage, and you can even find them in the chip aisle of supermarkets now. But read the label! Most of them are full of nutritional yeast, which is best avoided altogether. This recipe is packed with such a powerhouse of nutrients from the kale, sunflower seeds, and hemp hearts that you'll be making these often. Make them ahead and then hide them for movie night! And here's a bonus: this is the same recipe I use for my Kale Caesar Salad. Just skip the baking/dehydrating step and enjoy these ingredients as a raw salad (one of my faves!) with any nuts tossed in fresh grated garlic, a dash of olive oil, and a pinch of sea salt as your croutons.

Preheat your oven to its lowest setting or set up your dehydrator. Line your trays with Teflex sheets or parchment paper.

Wash and pat dry the kale leaves, discarding the tough center rib. Tear each leaf into 2 or 3 large pieces (they shrink a lot as they dry) and place them in a very large bowl.

Place the remaining ingredients in a blender and combine until creamy and smooth. Pour ½ the mixture over the kale leaves. Using 2 spoons or your hands, toss the kale until well coated. Add the remaining spice mixture and toss again to ensure it gets into all the folds and curls.

Arrange the kale in a single layer on your trays. Bake in the oven, with the door cracked open, for 3–4 hours, or until dry and crispy. Rotate the trays once or twice during cooking. Or dehydrate them for 8 hours, or until crisp. These will keep in an airtight container or a resealable plastic bag for up to 2 weeks.

photo on previous page · · ·

MINT AND LIME EDAMAME SNACK

SERVES 4–6

2½ Tbsp coarse sea salt

1 bag (16 oz) frozen whole edamame bean pods

extra-virgin olive oil

juice and zest of 1 lime

3 Tbsp finely chopped fresh mint

This yummy, nutritious snack is a great way to enjoy edamame beans. Be sure to choose organic fresh or frozen beans to avoid pesticides and GMOs. The kids really love opening up the pods, and the seasoning is tasty too! Serve these warm, at room temperature, or even chilled.

Bring a large pot of filtered, alkaline water to a boil on high heat, then add 2 Tbsp of the sea salt and the edamame. Cook for about 3 minutes, or until the beans are bright green. Drain the beans into a strainer, run them under cool water to stop them cooking, then drain well again.

Pour the edamame into a bowl and add a drizzle of olive oil and the lime juice and zest, mint, and remaining ½ Tbsp salt. Toss well to combine. Serve warm.

ROASTED CHICKPEAS, 3 WAYS

SERVES 8 (ABOUT 4 CUPS)

4 cups soaked dried organic chickpeas, cooked, drained, and cooled

If you are looking for a crunchy snack to replace chips or corn nuts, this is it! These roasted chickpeas are very nutritious compared to packaged snacks, and my kids love them. A large proportion of the carbs in chickpeas are complex carbs, which are mildly acidic as they break down. So, as yummy as these are, just make sure you share. Another reason not to overindulge: you might become a real tootster for a while. Use dried chickpeas rather than canned in this recipe for best flavor results and for economy. They will double in volume as they cook, so you'll have about 4 cups—enough to try each of the flavor variations (each makes enough for 2 cups of roasted chickpeas). Serve roasted chickpeas with a glass of green juice or lemon water to balance and help to rehydrate them in your tummy!

> *** DO AHEAD:** Soak 2 cups dried chickpeas in 6 cups filtered, alkaline water overnight. Drain and rinse well. Cook in 8 cups filtered, alkaline water for 60–90 minutes, until nice and tender, not al dente (page 94).

Preheat the oven to 325°F. Spread out the chickpeas in a single layer on a baking sheet and roast for about 90 minutes, stirring occasionally, until dry and crunchy.

While the chickpeas are drying, prepare each of the seasonings below in a separate bowl. Pour ⅓ of the hot roasted chickpeas into each bowl and toss well. Allow to cool. These will keep in airtight containers at room temperature for up to 3 weeks—if you can keep them that long!

1. SWEET CINNAMON

1 Tbsp grapeseed oil (or extra-virgin olive oil)

1½ tsp ground cinnamon

8–10 drops liquid stevia, or to taste

½ tsp Himalayan sea salt

2. SALTY GARLIC

1 Tbsp extra-virgin olive oil

2 cloves garlic, grated on a rasp

½ tsp Himalayan salt or good-quality fine sea salt

3. TERIYAKI

1 Tbsp extra-virgin olive oil

½ tsp toasted sesame oil (optional)

2 Tbsp grated ginger

2 tsp Bragg Liquid Aminos

6 drops liquid stevia

½ tsp Himalayan salt or good-quality fine sea salt

SOCCA

1 cup sprouted chickpea flour (or regular, unsprouted)

1 cup filtered, alkaline water

¼ medium white onion, roughly chopped

2 cloves garlic, chopped

2 Tbsp grapeseed oil

¾ tsp fine Himalayan salt

freshly ground black pepper

3–4 Tbsp fresh herbs or 2–3 tsp dried

10 cherry tomatoes, halved (optional)

2–3 Tbsp extra-virgin olive oil

coarse sea salt

Socca is a popular, incredibly versatile French flatbread made from chickpeas. It's packed with protein and nutrients, especially if you can find sprouted chickpea flour or if you make your own (sprout, dehydrate, and grind!). Firm but soft, crispy at the edges, and a titch sweet but still savory, socca is delicious naked or topped with goodies. Serve it as an appetizer with olives or alongside a soup or salad. Swap out the herbs (I like dill, rosemary, basil, thyme, or a blend like herbes de Provence) to sway it Mexican, chocolately, or chai (see variations on opposite page). Be sure to start this recipe early in the day so the batter has time to soak before you cook it.

Place the chickpea flour in a medium bowl and make a well in the center. Set aside.

Place the water in a blender with the onion, garlic, grapeseed oil, Himalayan salt, and pepper and combine until puréed. Pour this mixture into the chickpea flour and combine until mixed. If using dried herbs, stir them into the batter now. Cover and allow to soak for 1–2 hours.

Preheat the oven to 325°F. Line the bottom of two 9-inch round pans with parchment paper (or use springform pans).

If using fresh herbs, stir them into the batter now. Divide the batter evenly between the pans. Top with tomato halves (if using) and bake for 25–30 minutes, or until set. A skewer inserted in the center should come out clean or with only a few crumbs attached. Remove from the oven, allow to cool slightly, then place a wire rack on top of the pan and invert the socca onto it. (If you used a springform pan, just release and remove the sides, sneak a knife under the socca to loosen the parchment, and lift it onto a serving plate.) Carefully peel away and discard the parchment. Invert the socca onto a plate and drizzle with the olive oil and a sprinkle of coarse sea salt.

VARIATION: MEXICAN

Replace the herbs with 1 tsp ground cumin, ¼ tsp chili powder, and ¼ cup chopped cilantro.

VARIATION: CHAI

Replace the herbs with ½ cup puréed sweet potato and 1 tsp chai spice. Add ¼ cup more water plus 5–8 drops stevia or 1 Tbsp pure maple syrup. Serve sprinkled with ground cinnamon and finely chopped pecans.

VARIATION: CHOCOLATELY

Replace the herbs with ¼ cup raw cacao or carob powder (or an equal mix of both) and 1 Tbsp lucuma powder. Add an extra ¼ cup water plus 5–8 drops stevia. Serve sprinkled with raw palm sugar crystals and ground cinnamon (optional).

YEAST-FREE SPELT FOCACCIA BREAD *with* OLIVES AND ROSEMARY

SERVES 6–8

2 cups whole spelt flour

2 tsp baking powder

2 Tbsp finely chopped fresh rosemary + more leaves for topping

1 Tbsp freeze-dried oregano or 1 tsp dried (optional)

1 tsp sea salt

1 cup almond mylk (page 122)

1 tsp agar agar powder

2 cloves garlic, minced

1 Tbsp grapeseed oil

dried cured olives

coarse sea salt

Spelt is highly nutritious: it has more protein, fiber, and healthy fats than wheat and very little gluten, which makes it a better option for those with mild gluten sensitivities so long as one isn't a celiac. It is also high in vitamin B17, which is excellent for warding off cancer. Although spelt is almost neutral on the pH scale, it should be in the 25% portion of your alkaline/acidic ratio. Try to seek out sprouted spelt flour. Serve this with the Healing Seasonal Vegetable Soup (page 188) or spread it with the Tomato Pesto (page 280). Because this focaccia is unleavened, this recipe is really quick to make.

Preheat the oven to 300°F. In a large bowl, combine the flour, baking powder, rosemary, oregano, and salt, and set aside.

Place the almond mylk in a small saucepan and whisk in the agar agar. Bring to a boil over high heat and simmer for 2–3 minutes to allow the agar agar to dissolve. Remove from the heat and allow to cool for 10 minutes.

Stir in the garlic and grapeseed oil, then pour the wet ingredients into the dry ingredients, mixing carefully until just combined. Scoop the dough into a 10- to 12-inch round cast-iron pan or pat it into a 9- to 10-inch circle on a baking sheet, about ¾ inch thick. Press the olives into the top of the dough, sprinkle with salt and rosemary leaves, and bake for 30–40 minutes. Remove from the oven and allow to cool slightly on a wire rack. Drizzle with olive oil and sprinkle a little coarse salt over top.

FRESH STRAWBERRY AND MINT JELLY DESSERT

Jell-O was a tradition for the kids in my husband's family. It was a seasonal treat that Great-Grandma, and years later Grandma, would make only at Christmas. With this in mind, here is a recipe for special occasions or when berries are in their prime. Using stevia as a sweetener keeps this dish as healthy as just eating the fruit off the plant, and the agar agar adds a few minerals and a lot of fiber. You can easily swap out the strawberries for raspberries or blackberries (just strain the seeds after blending) or melon, and then incorporate them into the mix. Serve this as an afternoon snack or dessert with the Whipped Coconut Cream (page 286).

**SERVES 4
(MAKES 2½ CUPS)**

2 generous cups fresh organic strawberries, roughly chopped, save a few for garnish

8 finely chopped large mint leaves

juice of 1 small lemon

½ tsp pure vanilla extract

12 drops liquid stevia

½ cup filtered, alkalized water

2 tsp agar agar powder

4 edible flowers for garnish (optional)

Unearth 4 of your prettiest 4 oz ramekins and set aside.

Place the strawberries, mint, lemon juice, vanilla, and stevia in a blender and process until liquefied. If the mixture is too thick to blend, add 1–2 Tbsp filtered, alkalized water and blend again. Set aside.

In a small saucepan, whisk together the water and agar agar to combine. Place the pot over medium-low heat and boil for 3 full minutes, whisking constantly. Remove from the heat and whisk for 2–3 minutes more, allowing it to cool to the touch. Add this thickening mixture to the blender with the strawberries and immediately blend until completely smooth.

Pour the jelly into the ramekins, scraping down the sides of the blender as you go. Shimmy the dishes to slightly level out the tops or use the back of a spoon to smooth. Allow to cool on the counter or refrigerate for 10 to 20 minutes, or until set. Garnish with a strawberry and an edible flower, or try it with Whipped Coconut Cream (page 286).

WILD SUMMER BERRIES
with VANILLA ALMOND LEMON CREAM

SERVES 4–6

 1 cup soaked almonds (or 1 cup soaked cashews), rinsed and drained well

juice of 1½ lemons

zest of 1 lemon

5 Tbsp coconut water + more as needed

6 drops liquid stevia

1 tsp pure vanilla extract

2–3 cups mixed summer berries

We share the berries near our cottage with several resident bears, but they can't possibly eat them all, so there are always lots for us too! We especially love the huckleberries, and we add them to blackberries and any other berries we can forage or seek at the markets. To enhance them, all we do is top them with this luscious nut cream or the Non-Fermented Vegan Vanilla Bean Yogurt (page 286) and dig in. This is a great combination with Breakfast Seednola (page 140) or Chia Seed Breakfast Porridges (page 134). You can also use cashews, instead of almonds, for a creamier texture (as shown in the photos opposite).

> **＊ DO AHEAD**: Soak 1 cup almonds in 2 cups filtered, alkaline water overnight (or 1 cup cashews in 2 cups filtered, alkaline water for 1–2 hours).

Place the almonds, lemon juice and zest, coconut water, and stevia in a high-speed blender and process until smooth and creamy. If the mixture is too thick, add 1–2 Tbsp more coconut water and blend again. (You want it to be like heavy whipping cream, not a thick spread.)

To serve, divide the berries among 4–6 bowls, spoon the lemon cream on top, and enjoy.

VARIATION:
BLACKBERRY COCONUT CREAMSICLES

2 cups blackberries, preferably wild-foraged or organic

13½ oz (1 can) thick organic coconut mylk (+ 1¾ tsp agar agar dissolved as above if not using ice cream maker)

10–12 drops liquid stevia

1 tsp pure vanilla extract

Place the blackberries in a blender and combine until puréed. Press the fruit through a fine-mesh strainer into a small bowl. Discard the seeds.

Rinse the blender and pour in the blackberry purée. Add the coconut mylk/agar agar mixture (if using), stevia, and vanilla and process to combine until smooth. Divide among the molds and freeze.

ROASTED GREEN APPLE, LIME, AND AVOCADO CREAMSICLES

SERVES 6

3 green organic apples, peel on; 2 juiced, 1 cut into ¼-inch dice

13½ oz (1 can) full-fat coconut mylk + ½ can for dipping (optional)

1¾ tsp agar agar powder

1 small avocado

6-inch zucchini, diced

1 tsp ground cinnamon

sea salt

14–16 drops liquid stevia

juice of 1 lime

6 cinnamon sticks

⅔ cup finely shredded unsweetened raw coconut (optional)

1 green organic apple, peel on, sliced for garnish (optional)

Who doesn't love a creamy frozen treat? Since these creamsicles are full of good fats from the avocado and even contain a vegetable (shhh …), don't be afraid to let your kids have them, even for breakfast or lunch! If you have an ice cream maker, these will be creamy and smooth and you can skip the agar agar step; if not, the agar agar will help to give these a similar creaminess with less iciness.

Preheat the oven to 350°F. Line a baking sheet with parchment paper. Have ready a 6-hole popsicle mold and an ice cream maker, if you have one.

Arrange the diced apple on the baking sheet and roast for 15 minutes. Set aside and allow to cool.

Warm 13½ oz coconut mylk in a small saucepan over medium heat. Whisk in the agar agar and bring to a boil for a full 3 minutes, whisking constantly. Remove from the heat and allow to cool just until warm or it will set up. Reheat if it sets up. The mixture should be thickened but not stiff.

Place the apple juice, agar mixture, avocado, zucchini, ground cinnamon, sea salt to taste, stevia, and lime juice into a blender and combine until smooth. Divide this mixture evenly among the molds. Gently sprinkle roasted apple into each mold, using a knife to submerge some pieces. (If you have an ice cream maker, churn it as per the manufacturer's directions. Stir in the roasted apple and then divide among the molds.) Pop a cinnamon stick in the middle of each mold as a handle. Allow to freeze for 3 hours or overnight.

To make dipped popsicles, pour the 6½ oz full-fat coconut mylk into a mason jar. Pour the shredded coconut onto a flat plate.

To remove the popsicles, hold the mold under warm running water, allowing it to flow along the bottom and sides of each mold. Gently wiggle the cinnamon sticks and the popsicles should slide out. Dip the popsicles in the coconut mylk, roll them in coconut, and serve with a slice of apple. Or wrap them individually in plastic wrap and freeze. These will keep frozen for up to 2 months.

VANILLA FENNEL KANTEN
with RED CURRANTS

Kanten, which is Japanese for agar agar, is a very popular Asian dessert made from several species of seaweed—eeek! A cross between pudding and jelly with quite a firm texture, kanten is vegan and very neutral in flavor. It's a good source of calcium, iron, and iodine, as well as insoluble fiber to carry toxic waste from the body and act as a mild laxative. Agar agar is not recommended if you are pregnant or nursing or if you have weak bowels.

SERVES 8

Almond Flour Crust

1½ cups almond flour

⅔ cup coconut oil

1 tsp pure vanilla extract

10–12 drops liquid stevia

sea salt

Kanten Filling

1¾ cups coconut mylk or 13½ oz (1 can) coconut mylk

1½ tsp fennel seeds

1¾ tsp agar agar powder

½ cup almond mylk (page 122)

1 bulb fennel, juiced

¼ cup chicory root powder (inulin)

seeds scraped from ½ vanilla pod or ¾ tsp pure vanilla extract

10–12 drops liquid stevia

sea salt

1 cup fresh red currants, destemmed, + some for garnish

CRUST: Cut 2 sheets of parchment paper, each about 16 inches long. Set the first sheet in the bottom of an 8-inch square pan, allowing the edges of the paper to hang over both sides of the pan. Place the second sheet at 90 degrees to the first sheet. This will allow you to easily remove the squares.

In a food processor, combine the crust ingredients until well mixed. Spoon the mixture into the pan, pushing it into the corners and pressing it down so it is evenly distributed. Refrigerate for 30 minutes, or until chilled.

FILLING: Place a fine-mesh sieve over a small bowl.

Place the coconut mylk and fennel seeds in a small saucepan and stir in the agar agar. Bring to a boil over medium-high heat for 30–40 seconds to dissolve the agar agar, turn down the heat to low, and simmer for 3–4 minutes to allow the fennel to infuse. Remove from the heat and quickly strain this mixture through the sieve. Discard the fennel seeds. Stir in the almond mylk, fennel juice, inulin, vanilla, stevia, and a pinch of salt. (If you allow this mixture to cool too much, it will set, making it difficult to spread. If it is extremely hot, it will melt the crust. If it sets up by accident, reheat the mixture and stir to melt it (but be sure to let it cool somewhat before continuing).)

Remove the crust from the fridge, sprinkle with the currants, and pour the kanten filling over top, quickly smoothing the surface with a spatula. Allow to chill for 20–30 minutes until set.

To serve, carefully lift the parchment paper and place on a large cutting board. Cut into squares, place on pretty plates, garnish with fresh currants, and enjoy. This will keep chilled for up to 3 days in an airtight container lined with parchment.

SIMPLE BERRY TARTS (OR CRUMBLE)

If you are looking for a wow-wee response from friends at a gathering, these are the cutest and tastiest wee tarts! Pretty them up with fresh berries and mint leaves. These are very easy to make and you may be tempted to eat the whole batch, but the rich, creamy nut filling and natural sugar from the dates make them a sweet treat to share with as many people as possible! Make them ahead, freeze them, and pull them out for a special event. Instead of making tart shells, you can blend the almonds with ½ cup dates (skip the coconut oil) to create a crumble to spoon into serving dishes, topped with berries and fresh Whipped Coconut Cream (page 286). Yum!

MAKES 16 MINI TARTS

* 1¼ cups soaked almonds, rinsed, drained well, and patted dry

¾ cup soft dried organic dates, seeded and roughly chopped

3 Tbsp extra-virgin coconut oil

1 Tbsp filtered, alkaline water (if needed)

1 recipe Vanilla Almond Lemon Cream (page 257) or Non-Fermented Vegan Vanilla Bean Yogurt (page 286), chilled for 30 minutes

2 pints fresh strawberries or blackberries, or your favorite combination

fresh stevia leaves or mint leaves for garnish

* **DO AHEAD**: Soak 1¼ cups almonds in 3 cups filtered, alkaline water overnight.

Set out a 16-cup mini-tart pan.

Place the almonds, dates, and coconut oil in a blender and pulse until the mixture becomes crumbly then comes together and forms a ball. Add a little water, if needed. Using a tablespoon, scoop a generous spoonful of this pastry into your hands, roll it into a ball, and place it in the tart pan. Using the end of a wooden spoon, gently press the pastry from the center toward the sides so it evenly covers the pan. Repeat with the remaining pastry. Chill or freeze the tart shells for 15 minutes.

To assemble, run a butter knife around the edge of each tart shell and gently lift them onto a serving platter. Divide the lemon cream among the tart shells, heaping it in the center. Top each tart with fresh berries and a garnish of fresh stevia or mint leaves. Serve immediately.

These will keep refrigerated for up to 1 day (or without the fruit topping for up to 3 days). They will keep frozen, wrapped individually in plastic without the fruit garnish, for up to 1 month. Just thaw and add fresh fruit to serve.

LEMON THYME–STRAWBERRY BLOSSOM TART

SERVES 8 (MAKES ONE 9-INCH TART)

Nutty Crust

¾ cup soaked Brazil nuts, rinsed and drained well

½ cup soaked buckwheat, rinsed, drained well, and patted dry with paper towels

3 soft dried dates, roughly chopped

2 Tbsp chia seeds

2 Tbsp coconut oil

⅛ tsp ground vanilla powder or ½ tsp pure vanilla extract

sea salt

Lemon Thyme–Strawberry Filling

13½ oz (1 can) full-fat coconut mylk

2 tsp agar agar powder

2 cups fresh strawberries, rinsed and hulled

6 sprigs lemon thyme or 4 sprigs regular thyme

juice of 1 medium lemon

1 tsp pure vanilla extract

24 drops liquid stevia (not powder as will discolor the cake)

edible blossoms for garnish

Birthdays come but once a year, and our gang loves to make a big deal out of them. I made this tart for my alkaline sister and also for my daughter, making it as mildly acidic as possible. I used fresh local strawberries that we had just harvested, but you can substitute raspberries or blackberries (blend them on their own first and pour them through a fine-mesh sieve to remove the seeds). Whichever berries you choose, be sure they are fresh and organic, and wash them well to remove any powdery molds. If you are cleansing, try the alkaline Coconut, Lime, and Basil Tarts (page 267) instead.

> **✳ DO AHEAD**: Soak ¾ cup Brazil nuts in 2 cups filtered, alkaline water for 2 hours. Soak ½ cup buckwheat in 2 cups filtered, alkaline water for 2–8 hours.

CRUST: Line a 9-inch springform pan with parchment paper.

Place the Brazil nuts in a food processor and process until a crumble forms. Add the remaining crust ingredients and process until the mixture forms a ball. Press the crust into the pan and freeze for 30 minutes.

FILLING: Warm ½ of the coconut mylk in a small saucepan over medium heat. Whisk in the agar agar and bring to a boil over medium-high heat. Turn down the heat to low and simmer for 3–4 minutes, whisking constantly. Remove from the heat and whisk in the rest of the coconut mylk, allowing it to cool enough to touch.

Remove the crust from the freezer. Place the strawberries, lemon thyme, lemon juice, vanilla, and stevia in a high-speed blender and quickly blend until smooth. Stop the blender and carefully and quickly add the warm, thickening agar agar mixture and process just until creamy and smooth. Quickly pour the filling into the crust, scraping down the sides of the blender, as this sets up very fast. Smooth the top, if needed, or just tap the pan on the counter to minimize air bubbles. Refrigerate for 20–30 minutes until chilled.

To serve, release the bottom of the springform pan and slide the tart onto a serving platter, discarding the parchment paper. Decorate with edible blossoms before slicing.

COCONUT, LIME, AND BASIL **TARTS**

SERVES 3–4 (MAKES ONE 8-INCH TART OR THREE 4-INCH TARTS)

Another purely alkaline dessert! How about that? As long as you are not veggie-feasting, you can enjoy these tarts no matter what stage you are at in alkalizing your lifestyle. Dried coconut is susceptible to mold, so be sure to buy the freshest you can find. Check the expiry date on the package and, if possible, purchase from a vendor that refrigerates these kinds of dried goods. Also look for the best-quality extra-virgin coconut oil you can find, as you'll taste the difference here. Serve with purely alkaline Whipped Coconut Cream (page 286).

Coconut-sesame Crust

2 cups finely shredded unsweetened coconut

2 Tbsp sesame seeds

⅓ cup extra-virgin coconut oil (solid)

½ tsp pure vanilla extract

8 drops liquid stevia

CRUST: Line an 8-inch springform or tart pan (or three 4-inch tart pans with removable bottoms) with parchment paper.

Place the coconut and sesame seeds in a food processor and pulse until crumbly and well combined. Add the coconut oil, vanilla, and stevia and process until well combined, scraping down the sides of the food processor if needed. Press the mixture into the tart pan(s) and refrigerate for 20–30 minutes while you prepare the filling. Over-mixing will release oils and result in a soft, creamy mass. (If this occurs, fill the pan(s), chill, and press into place.)

Coconut, Lime, and Basil Filling

1 avocado

⅔ cup diced green zucchini, scrubbed

10 small basil leaves + 3–4 more for garnish

2 tsp lime zest

½ cup lime juice

14 drops liquid stevia

1 tsp pure vanilla extract

½ cup coconut mylk

1 tsp agar agar powder

lime slices for garnish

FILLING: Place the avocado, zucchini, basil, lime zest and juice, stevia, and vanilla in a blender and combine. Set aside.

In a small saucepan, whisk together the coconut mylk and agar agar to combine. Place the pot over medium heat and bring to a boil for a full 1 minute, whisking constantly. Remove from the heat and allow to cool slightly. This ensures that the mixture isn't hot enough to spoil the enzymes and vitamins in the filling.

Add this thickening mixture to the blender with the zucchini and avocado filling and process immediately until smooth. Quickly pour the filling into the tart pan(s) as you only have a minute before it begins to set up. Refrigerate for 15–20 minutes until set. Let stand for 15 minutes before slicing. Garnish with slices of lime and basil leaves.

SERVES 10–12 (MAKES ONE 6-LAYER, 6-INCH ROUND CAKE)

PANCAKE CAKE

Pancake Cake

2 cups oat flour (or very finely ground old-fashioned oats)

2 cups almond flour

1½ cups spelt flour

¼ cup arrowroot flour

2 Tbsp baking powder

2 tsp baking soda

1 tsp Himalayan salt

2 cups unsweetened almond mylk (page 122)

13½ oz (1 can) full-fat coconut mylk

1½ tsp pure vanilla extract

½ tsp pure almond extract

32 drops liquid stevia

This cake is perfect for celebrating summer, birthdays, or just being vibrant and healthy! Kris Carr, author of *Crazy Sexy Diet* (and my alkaline mentor), would say "LIVE like you MEAN IT!" and this cake is all of that and more! It takes a bit of time to make the 6 layers (having a couple of pans going at the same time helps), but it comes together pretty quickly after that and it will knock the socks off your family and friends, particularly if you decorate it with a nice pile of seasonal berries and some edible flowers. If you can find it, sprouted spelt flour contains less gluten and is more alkaline. I've incorporated the oats for flavor and to minimize the gluten in the recipe, and for a completely gluten-free version see the variation below. The bottom line is that for a healthy yet lovely dessert, this recipe pretty much takes the cake!

CAKE: Heat 2 pancake griddles over low heat.

In a large bowl, combine the oat, almond, spelt, and arrowroot flours, baking powder, baking soda, and salt and set aside. In a separate bowl, combine the almond and coconut mylks, vanilla and almond extracts, and stevia until well mixed. Pour the wet ingredients into the dry and combine just until moistened.

Ladle enough batter onto the griddle to form a thin 6-inch round pancake. (You can use a springform pan or an embroidery hoop as a guide if you want to be particular, otherwise just eyeball it.) Flip the pancake only when the top is full of bubbles and loses its shine and the bottom is lightly browned. Cook for a few minutes more, then transfer to a wire cooling rack. Repeat until you have 6 pancakes to layer.

cont. next page . . .

GLUTEN-FREE VARIATION

For a gluten-free alternative, double the recipe for Sprouted Buckwheat Silver Dollar Pancakes (page 148, being sure to include the optional almond extract) and use this instead of the Pancake Cake recipe above.

Lemon Coconut Icing

13½ oz (1 can) coconut mylk, stirred

✱ 1 cup soaked cashews, rinsed and drained well

juice of 2 large lemons

1 Tbsp lemon zest

1 tsp pure vanilla extract

12–16 drops liquid stevia or 2 tsp pure maple syrup

sea salt

1 tsp agar agar powder

berries and edible flowers for garnish

ICING: Combine ½ of the coconut mylk, the cashews, lemon juice and zest, vanilla, stevia, and salt in a blender and process until as smooth as possible. Set aside.

Pour the remaining coconut mylk into a small saucepan. Whisk in the agar agar and bring to a boil over medium-high heat. Turn down the heat to low and simmer for 3–4 minutes, whisking constantly. Remove from the heat and allow to cool for 3–4 minutes, whisking occasionally to prevent a film from forming on top.

Quickly add the warm, thickening agar agar mixture to the blender and process until creamy. Pour it into a bowl and refrigerate for 30–60 minutes to allow it to set up.

To assemble, set 1 pancake on a serving platter. Using a spatula, slather ⅙ of the icing on top. Cover with another pancake and repeat, layering pancakes and icing until you have 6 layers. Finish with a final layer of icing, and decorate with berries and edible flowers.

> ✱ DO AHEAD: Soak 1 cup cashews in 2 cups filtered, alkaline water for 30 minutes.

NO BUTTER, SUGAR, OR EGGS?

As a busy mom, I savor quiet moments with a mug of herbal tea and a sweet treat. Since most baking involves a mix of butter, sugar, and eggs, I had to learn some new tricks when I began to alkalize my lifestyle. These healthful plant-based ingredients are the starting blocks for some pretty yummy, nourishing snacks, including lovely desserts for special occasions. Check your health food store for these ingredients.

agar agar powder: a seaweed that is ground into a powder and used in place of gelatin to set liquids or create some softness in non-yeasted breads.

cacao powder (raw chocolate powder): the ground beans of the cacao plant, which are partially fermented and contain caffeine—both of which are toxic and acidic—as well as some healthy nutrients. Not even an Alkaline Sister can resist a teensy bit of chocolate now and then.

carob powder: a chocolate substitute made by grinding the bean-shaped pods of the carob plant; it contains polyphenols, which are powerful antioxidants, is rich in calcium, and is also a good source of selenium.

chicory root: a mild sugar substitute, also called inulin, made by roasting and grinding the roots of the chicory plant; it is low-alkaline and rich in fiber.

coconut mylk: a healthy fat used to replace butter and oils made by soaking the grated flesh of fresh brown coconuts in hot water, skimming off the cream, and then pressing the remaining liquid through cheesecloth. Use only full-fat milk for the best flavor and nutrient profile.

coconut nectar: a sugar substitute derived from the sap of coconut blossoms that is very low in fructose and sucrose and that barely affects blood sugar levels. Use only when not cleansing.

lucuma: a caramel flavoring made by drying and grinding the pulp of the lucuma fruit into a powder; it is sweet and chock-full of nutrients.

stevia: a sugar substitute made from the leaves of the stevia plant that is 100s of times sweeter than sugar but does not spike blood sugar levels; it comes in powdered or liquid form. Read the labels carefully and choose alcohol-free liquids and green-leaf powders. Use sparingly.

tapioca starch or arrowroot powder: thickeners made from the root of the cassava plant and the root of the arrowroot plant, both of which often replace cornstarch.

yacón syrup: a sweet syrup extracted from the tuberous roots of the yacón plant that is low in fructose and has little effect on blood sugar levels. Use only when not cleansing.

BLACK BEAN AND LAVENDER
BLOSSOM BITES

SERVES 8–10

1½ cups cooked black beans OR ¾ can (15 oz) organic black beans, rinsed and drained well

2 Tbsp cacao powder

2 Tbsp carob powder

4 tsp lucuma

½ cup coconut oil

1 tsp pure vanilla extract

⅛ tsp ground vanilla seeds

18 drops liquid stevia

½ cup unsweetened, finely shredded coconut for dusting

1½ tsp dried culinary lavender blossoms OR 18–20 edible flowers, such as pansies or rose petals

I created these truffles for moments when you want something sweet for your tea but you don't want to mess up your perfectly balanced alkaline day! These are totally deelish, and because they are made with black beans, they fill you up and give you sustainable energy. They also make amazing gifts. If you're a chocoholic, start with this version where carob powder makes up half the chocolaty flavor, but gradually aim to replace more of the cacao powder, which is acidic, with carob. If you are making these bites out of lavender season, look for dried lavender in the spice section of your health food store.

✳ DO AHEAD: Soak ¾ cup dry black beans in 2½ cups filtered, alkaline water overnight. Rinse and drain well. Place in a medium saucepan with 3 cups filtered, alkaline water over high heat, bring to a boil, turn down the heat to low, and simmer for 30–40 minutes or until tender, then drain. Be sure to measure it as this may yield more than the recipe requires.

Place the black beans, cacao and carob powders, lucuma, coconut oil, vanilla extract and vanilla seeds, and stevia in a food processor and combine, scraping down the sides a few times, until thick and smooth. Scoop the dough into a bowl.

Line a baking sheet with parchment paper. Arrange the shredded coconut on a large, flat plate.

Using a teaspoon, scoop a spoonful of the dough into your hands, form it into a ball, and roll it in the coconut to coat. Press a few lavender blossoms (and/or edible flowers) into the top and set on a serving platter. Refrigerate for 20–30 minutes, or until firm. Serve chilled or at room temperature. These will keep refrigerated in an airtight container for up to 10 days.

SALTED PECAN CARAMEL BUTTER CUPS

If you were a fan of peanut butter cups as a kid, this is the healthy adult version you can enjoy without the guilt. Although the cacao powder is not exactly ideal, it is okay in moderation if you are alkaline balanced. And lucuma, a slightly sweet powder ground from the lucuma nut, boosts the natural caramel flavor of the pecans. Keep these cups chilled, as the nutrient-rich coconut oil softens and melts easily: you may have to pop them in your mouth after only 1 or 2 bites! The salted pecan caramel filling is delicious as a dip on its own—try it with crisp, crunchy slices of jicama and pinches of coarse sea salt.

MAKES 10–12 PECAN BUTTER CUPS

Salted Pecan Caramel Filling

1 cup soaked pecans, rinsed and drained well

1½ tsp filtered, alkalized water

1½ Tbsp lucuma

2½ Tbsp flax oil

½ tsp pure vanilla extract

5–8 drops liquid stevia

Chocolate Cups

½ cup cold-pressed, extra-virgin coconut oil

¼ cup raw cacao powder

¼ cup carob powder

1 tsp pure vanilla extract

1 tsp pure maple syrup (optional)

4–6 drops liquid stevia

coarse sea salt

FILLING: Place the pecans in a food processor and process until the nuts form a butter. If the mixture is too thick, add the water and blend again. You should end up with a soft, smooth, rather creamy butter that doesn't appear oily. Add the lucuma, flax oil, vanilla, and stevia and blend again to combine.

✻ DO AHEAD: Soak 1 cup pecans in 2 cups filtered, alkaline water for 1–2 hours.

CUPS: Line a 12-cup muffin tin with paper cupcake liners.

Melt the coconut oil in a medium saucepan over very, very low heat. Stir in the cacao and carob powders, vanilla, maple syrup (if using), and stevia.

Fill a 2-cup measuring cup with hot tap water, pour out the water, and then dry the cup with paper towel. Pour the chocolate mixture into the measuring cup.

TO ASSEMBLE: Pour a teaspoonful of the melted chocolate mixture into each cupcake liner. Add a heaping teaspoonful of the pecan filling, smooth it out a little with the back of the teaspoon, and top with 2 tsp of the chocolate to cover. Repeat until you run out of filling or chocolate. (If the chocolate starts to solidify, fill a large bowl with hot water and set the measuring cup in it.) Sprinkle with coarse sea salt. Refrigerate for 20 minutes, or until cool and set. Then try to share these insanely yummy treats instead of eating the whole batch!

HOMEMADE STAPLES

Ever notice how many more veggies you can
eat when they're served with a delicious spread
or a yummy sauce? Here are my go-to dressings,
dips, and crumbles for times when I want a
healthy meal without a lot of prep. I often
spend a few hours on a Sunday making up a
couple of these recipes for the week. And these
are so versatile that I can use them with a
range of salads and raw vegetables, tuck them
into wraps, or sprinkle them over warm dishes.
Add to and change these options to suit your
tastes—these are easy building blocks
for alkalizing meals.

FLAVORED SALTS

MAKES 1 CUP

The body needs and craves salt, so don't be afraid of it. Choose mineral salts, though, such as unrefined sea salt, Himalayan salt, or Celtic sea salt, which are full of trace minerals that our body needs. Whiz the following combinations in your food processor. The proportions may vary, according to your taste and tolerance for spice, but aim for 1 cup of salt with 1–2 tsp of each flavor and 2–3 Tbsp of any nut or seed suggested and adjust as you like. Store the salt in a pretty jar with a small scoop or in a spice jar with a sprinkle lid. Salt is a natural preservative, so most of these will keep in an airtight container at room temperature for 3–4 months. Refrigerate those with nuts or seeds for up to 1 month.

1.

salt, lime zest, pistachio, fresh chili pepper

2.

salt, lemon zest, mixed whole peppercorns

3.

salt, roasted garlic (finely minced and slowly dry-roasted until golden), rosemary, hemp hearts

4.

pinches of salt, stevia, lemon verbena, lemon zest, unsoaked raw cashews

5.

salt, lemon zest, fresh herbs, Brazil nuts

6.

salt, olives, rosemary, pumpkin seeds

7.

salt, lemon zest, fresh dill, unsoaked raw almonds or sprouted dry almonds

HEALTHY VEGAN BUTTER

MAKES 1¾ CUPS

1 medium sweet onion, diced

10 cloves garlic, minced

1–2 Tbsp filtered, alkaline water

1 cup extra-virgin coconut oil

¼ cup extra-virgin olive oil

¼ cup flax oil

½ tsp fine Himalayan salt

If you're finding it tricky to let go of butter, schmear this delicious version on Broccoli and Onion Bread (page 141) or steamed veggies, or stir it into whole grains or legumes. Please don't use it for cooking (the oils can become toxic) or sweet baked recipes (the salt will change the flavor). Try naked extra-virgin coconut oil for baking instead.

Place the onion, garlic, and 1–2 Tbsp filtered, alkalized water in a sauté pan over medium-high heat and steam-fry for 2–3 minutes, or until the water has evaporated. Remove from the heat, add the coconut oil, and allow it to melt.

Pour the mixture into a blender and pulse gently until smooth. Add the olive oil, flax oil, and salt and blend just to combine. Pour the butter into an airtight jar and refrigerate for about 30 minutes to set up. This will keep refrigerated for about 2 weeks, or frozen for up to 3 months.

**MAKES FIFTEEN
1-INCH CUBES**

3 stalks celery,
roughly chopped

2 carrots, roughly chopped

1 yellow onion,
roughly chopped

12 cloves garlic

3-inch piece ginger, scrubbed

3-inch piece fresh turmeric or
1 tsp ground turmeric

1 cup chopped fresh parsley

⅓ cup chopped fresh dill (or
your favorite herb)

⅓ cup chopped fresh basil (or
your favorite herb)

3 Tbsp fine Himalayan salt

VEGGIE **BOUILLON CUBES**

When added to water, these healthy, unprocessed cubes make an instant, flavorful broth to enhance rice, quinoa, buckwheat, millet, or beans as well as
any soup. Make these up while veggies and herbs are abundant from the
garden so you can avoid having to buy Tetra-Paks of broth or bouillon cubes
made with yeast and corn. Use 1 cube for every 1¼ cups of water.

Fit your food processor with the S-blade. Add all the ingredients and combine
until very finely puréed. Spoon the mixture into ice cube trays and freeze
overnight.

Because of the salt, these will not freeze super hard but they will be plenty
firm to pop out and transfer to a glass mason jar. Use a spoon or tongs
when handling the cubes, as the salt allows the cubes to freeze to a lower
temperature than regular ice. These will keep frozen for up to 6 months.

photo on next page · · ·

MILDLY ACIDIC (WITHOUT AVOCADO)
ALKALINE BALANCED
(WITH AVOCADO)

**MAKES ABOUT
1½ CUPS**

* 1¾ cups soaked and cooked
chickpeas or 1 can (15 oz)
organic chickpeas

1 avocado (optional)

2 cloves fresh garlic,
roughly chopped

2 Tbsp raw sesame tahini
(optional)

¼ cup extra-virgin olive oil +
more if needed for
consistency

juice of 1 lemon, or to taste

1 Tbsp lemon zest

⅓ cup chopped cilantro
(optional)

½ tsp Himalayan salt

½ tsp ground cumin

LEMONY **GARLIC HUMMUS**

The best hummus is made with soaked and
homecooked chickpeas, no contest. But in a
pinch, use a can of organic chickpeas
instead. Basic hummus is slightly acidic,
but adding avocado and ⅛ cup of cilantro
brings this spread back to alkaline balance.
Serve with your favorite raw veggies or the
Juicy Raw Herbed Crackers (page 282), or in the chard wrap (page 200).

* **DO AHEAD:** Soak 1 cup
dry chickpeas in 3 cups filtered,
alkaline water overnight. Drain and
rinse well. Cook in 6 cups water for
60–80 minutes, until tender
(page 94).

Place all the ingredients in a food processor and combine until crushed and well
mixed but not completely puréed. A little texture is kind of nice. Season to taste
and scoop into a serving bowl. Will keep refrigerated in an airtight container
for up to 5 days.

photo on page 281

SPRING PEA AND EDAMAME **SPREAD**

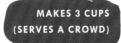

MAKES 3 CUPS (SERVES A CROWD)

1½ cups frozen organic, shelled edamame beans

1½ cups fresh or frozen peas

⅓ cup extra-virgin olive oil

juice and zest of 1 lime

3 stems fresh mint, leaves removed, + some leaves for garnish

½ tsp coarse sea salt

I know it's green, but kids seem to like this spread because the peas sweeten it nicely. Unfermented organic soy (like the edamame) in moderation, 1–3 times per week, is a healthy addition to your diet. Serve this spread with raw veggies, like cucumber slices, or Juicy Raw Herbed Crackers (page 282).

Bring a medium pot of filtered, alkaline water to a boil over high heat. Pour in the edamame beans and cook for 3–4 minutes, until bright green but still firm. Using a slotted spoon, transfer the beans to a colander and run them under cold water to stop the cooking.

Return the pot of salted boiling water to the stove, add the peas, and cook for 1 minute. Drain them in a colander and run under cold water to stop the cooking.

Place the beans, peas, olive oil, lime juice and zest, mint, and salt in a food processor. Combine until slightly chunky but thoroughly mixed. Season to taste and scoop the spread into a serving bowl. Garnish with mint leaves and a drizzle of olive oil. This will keep refrigerated in an airtight container for about 3 days.

MAKES ABOUT 1 CUP

¼ cup extra-virgin olive oil

¼ cup soaked cashews, rinsed and drained well

¼ cup diced zucchini, peeled if you want a white dip

¼ cup diced celery

2 Tbsp hemp hearts

1 clove garlic, roughly chopped

½ tsp ground celery seed

¼ tsp Himalayan salt

1½ Tbsp lemon juice

2 Tbsp chopped fresh dill

1 Tbsp chopped chives

ALKALINE BALANCED
PURELY ALKALINE
(WITH SOAKED ALMONDS)

CREAMY **HERB DIP**

Kids are all about dips, and frankly so am I! In a pinch, I sometimes buy a non-dairy storebought dip, but generally we make our own. Here's a healthy creamy, herby, and garlicky dip to serve with raw veggies: it's quick to prepare if you have some cashews or almonds already soaked.

Place all the ingredients, except the dill and chives, in a blender and process until creamy. If the dip is too thick, add 1–2 Tbsp water and blend again. Pour the dip into an airtight jar, stir in the chopped herbs, and refrigerate for a few minutes to allow the flavors to mingle. This will keep refrigerated for about 3 days.

CRUSHED CHICKPEA AND ROASTED TOMATO ANTIPASTO

MAKES ABOUT 2¼ CUPS

* 2 cups soaked and cooked chickpeas or 1 can (15 oz) chickpeas, drained and rinsed + kombu, if you like

20 cherry tomatoes

8 cloves garlic, sliced

¼ tsp smoked paprika

¼–½ tsp Himalayan salt

2 Tbsp grapeseed oil

2 Tbsp extra-virgin olive oil

When spring beckons you for a picnic, a jar of this smoky tomato antipasto is the perfect accompaniment. The sweet roasted cherry tomatoes paired with the smoky paprika and chickpeas are super deelish wrapped in a big leafy green like Swiss chard or collard greens. It also makes a great topping for cucumber slices or slathered on the Socca (page 250) or Juicy Raw Herbed Crackers (page 282). Now all you need is a pretty picnic basket and some good company.

* DO AHEAD: Soak ¾ cups dried chickpeas in 3 cups filtered, alkaline water overnight. Drain and rinse well. Cook the chickpeas in 4 cups filtered, alkaline water with a 4-inch piece of kombu for 60–80 minutes, or until tender (page 94).

Preheat the oven to 300°F. Place all the ingredients, except the olive oil, in a large baking dish, toss to combine, and bake for 25–30 minutes, or until the tomatoes and garlic have just softened. Remove from the oven and allow to cool for 10 minutes.

Transfer the contents of the baking dish to a food processor, add the olive oil, and pulse ever so gently, just to break up the tomatoes and slightly crush the chickpeas and garlic. Season to taste. Pour into an airtight jar. This will keep refrigerated for up to 3 days.

Crushed Chickpea and Roasted Tomato Antipasto

Veggie Bouillion Cubes (page 277)

PESTO OF HERBS, NUTS, AND SEEDS

MAKES 1½ CUPS

2 cups fresh basil

1 cup fresh mint

⅓ cup soaked almonds, rinsed, drained well, and patted dry (dehydrated, if desired)

⅓ cup soaked pecans, rinsed, drained well, and patted dry (dehydrated, if desired)

3 large cloves garlic

½ tsp Himalayan salt

½ cup extra-virgin olive oil

I could eat this tasty pesto in a box, with a fox, in a house, with a mouse, here, there, and anywhere! It is almost always in my fridge because it's delicious slathered on Socca (page 250), Cauliflower Pizzettes (page 236), spelt or zucchini noodles, diced tomatoes, or avocado, or, as a treat, with steamed organic red potatoes. Try it without the mint but with more basil, or with spinach or kale. It's so packed with chlorophyll and healthy fats that you can't get too much of this good thing!

✳ DO AHEAD: Soak ⅓ cup almonds in 1 cup filtered, alkaline water and ⅓ cup pecans in 1 cup filtered, alkaline water overnight.

Combine all the ingredients in a food processor and grind until well combined but with a bit of texture. Season to taste with salt, if needed. Spoon this pesto into an airtight container or ice cube trays. This will keep refrigerated for 3 days or frozen for up to 2 months.

MAKES 2 CUPS

PURELY ALKALINE

¼ cup hemp hearts

¼ cup soaked almonds, rinsed, drained well, and patted dry

6 soaked sundried tomatoes, drained, or 6 sundried tomatoes in olive oil

12 olives, pitted, dry-cured if possible

3 cloves garlic

2 Tbsp chopped fresh rosemary or 1½ tsp dried rosemary

10 basil leaves

⅓ cup extra-virgin olive oil

1 Tbsp lemon juice

8 drops liquid stevia

12 large cherry tomatoes, quartered

Himalayan salt (optional)

TOMATO PESTO

I'm a huge fan of Mediterranean flavors and this pesto really sums them up. It is delicious on Cauliflower Pizzettes (page 236), or spread on wraps, veggie noodles, or crunchy raw veggie sticks, or on soups as an accent. Any which way you serve it, this pesto rocks!

✳ DO AHEAD: Soak ¼ cup almonds overnight in 1 cup filtered, alkaline water. Soak 6 sundried tomatoes in 1 cup warm filtered, alkaline water for 30 minutes.

Place all the ingredients, except the cherry tomatoes and the salt, in a food processor and pulse until combined but still slightly textured. Add the tomatoes and pulse just a few times to chop and combine them so they cream up the mixture. Season to taste with salt, if needed. This will keep refrigerated in an airtight container for 2–3 days (or up to 7 days if you omit the tomatoes and add them when you use the pesto).

SAVORY **NUT SPRINKLE**

MAKES 1½ CUPS

* ½ cup almonds (preferably dried, sprouted almonds)

½ cup raw walnuts (preferably dried, sprouted walnuts)

½ cup pumpkin seeds

¼ cup hemp hearts

2 cloves garlic

3 Tbsp roughly chopped fresh parsley

3 sprigs thyme

1 Tbsp chopped fresh rosemary leaves

1 tsp Himalayan salt

½ tsp lemon zest

¼ tsp freshly ground black pepper

When salad greens are so amazingly fresh from the garden that they need nothing more than a light dressing of good oil and lemon juice, a nut crumble adds texture and substance. It's also a good way to increase your intake of healthy fats and proteins and ensure your body's assimilation of chlorophyll and carotenoids. Always chew well to liquefy your greens and reduce the burden on your digestive tract. If you have time, soak the nuts for up to 24 hours to sprout them and then dry them in a dehydrator. Otherwise, soak and air-dry them, or use them unsoaked in a pinch.

* DO AHEAD: Soak ½ cup almonds in 1 cup filtered, alkaline water and ½ cup walnuts in 1 cup filtered, alkaline water for 12–24 hours. Rinse and drain well, then transfer to a wire rack and allow to air-dry for 24 hours, or place them in a dehydrator overnight.

Place all the ingredients in a food processor and combine until the mixture forms a coarse crumble (do not overprocess it or it will become a butter or a spread). This will keep refrigerated in an airtight container for about 7 days.

Lemony Garlic Hummus (with and without avocado, page 277)

Savory Nut Sprinkle

Pesto of Herbs, Nuts and Seeds

Tomato Pesto

JUICY RAW HERBED CRACKERS

MAKES ABOUT 2 DOZEN CRACKERS

2½ cups vegetable pulp

¼ cup + 1 Tbsp freshly ground chia seeds

¼ cup + 1 Tbsp freshly ground flax seeds

3 Tbsp minced fresh dill

3 Tbsp minced cilantro

3 Tbsp minced green onions

2 Tbsp sunflower seeds

½ tsp onion powder

2 tsp Bragg Liquid Aminos

½ cup filtered, alkaline water

coarse Celtic sea salt

Don't let the pulp from your juicer go to waste! I use the pulp from 1 recipe of 8-Veg Juice (page 104) (+ 3 kale leaves, but minus the tomatoes) when I make these crackers, but you can experiment with different combinations. They're a crunchy alkalizing base for any dip or spread or for slices of creamy avocado. Or serve them with soups and salads. Enjoy these with a glass of water so they rehydrate without causing you a stomachache.

Have ready 2 large baking sheets, 4 sheets of parchment paper (cut to the size of the pans), a rolling pin, and a pizza cutter (or long sharp knife).

In a large bowl, stir together the vegetable pulp, chia and flax seeds, dill, cilantro, green onions, 1 Tbsp of the sunflower seeds, onion powder, and Bragg until well combined. Slowly add the water, stirring to moisten all the ingredients. Allow to stand for 5 minutes.

Preheat the oven to 150°F or lower, if possible. Place a sheet of parchment paper on a clean work surface and scoop ½ the mixture into the center of it. Using a fork, flatten the mixture into a large, even rectangle. Cover with a second piece of parchment, and use the rolling pin to roll the mixture to about an even ½-inch thickness. Remove and discard the top layer of parchment. Score the mixture into crackers with a pizza cutter or a long knife. Sprinkle with the 2 Tbsp of sunflower seeds. Repeat with the remaining pulp mixture.

Place the baking sheets in the oven with the door slightly ajar and dry for 2–3 hours, or until crispy but not browned. (Or place them on parchment paper in a dehydrator at 115°F for 12–24 hours, or until crisp.) Remove from the oven, sprinkle with some coarse sea salt, transfer to a wire rack to cool, and then break into crackers following the outline you made. These will keep in an airtight container for up to 2 weeks.

MACADAMIA **CHEEZE**

MAKES 1 CUP

* 1 cup soaked macadamia nuts, rinsed and drained well

1 green onion, chopped, white and green parts separated

¼ tsp minced garlic

¼ tsp sea salt

¼ tsp Bragg Liquid Aminos

This nice, mild, creamy mixture is free of fermentation including yeast. It is delicious crumbled over Cauliflower Pizzettes (page 236) or Greek Salad (page 160), tucked into wraps, or spread on cucumber slices.

Place all the ingredients, except the green parts of the onion, in a food processor and process until the mixture comes together like soft cheese curds. This may take a few minutes. If needed, add 1 tsp of water to encourage the curds to form. Add the green parts of the onion and process just until flecks are scattered through the cheese—don't let the batch turn green! This will keep refrigerated in an airtight container for about 3 days.

* DO AHEAD: Soak 1 cup macadamia nuts in 2 cups filtered, alkaline water overnight.

GARLIC **WALNUT CHEEZE**

MAKES 1 CUP

* 1 cup soaked walnuts, rinsed, drained well, and patted dry

2 cloves garlic

½ tsp sea salt

freshly ground black pepper

Once you've soaked the nuts, this cheese comes together in no time! Make it ahead so it's handy to sprinkle on salads and warmed dishes to add another texture and flavor. For a purely alkaline version, substitute almonds for the walnuts.

Place the walnuts, garlic, salt, and pepper in a food processor and pulse until the mixture forms a fine crumble. Pour into a bowl to serve. This will keep refrigerated in an airtight container for up to 2 weeks.

* DO AHEAD: Soak 1 cup walnuts in 1½ cups filtered, alkaline water overnight.

ESSENTIAL SALAD DRESSINGS

Homemade dressings make your salad rock! Increase your repertoire by blending seeds, nuts, and veggies for new flavors—and save the plain lemon juice and olive oil for when you are dining out so that simple dressing tastes yummy instead of boring. Most of these only take a few minutes to whip up, so start with some of my favorites and then get creative on your own. You'll find other options in the salad section too! These will keep refrigerated in an airtight container for 2–3 days.

CREAMY MINT AND LIME DRESSING

ALKALINE BALANCED

I like it with a little papaya and greens, but try it with some of *your* favorite salads. Blend.

MAKES ABOUT 1¼ CUPS

½ avocado

5 mint leaves + stems

sea salt

¼ cup extra-virgin olive oil

juice of ½ lemon

juice and zest of 1 lime

2–3 Tbsp filtered, alkalized water, as needed

2 tsp coconut nectar or 3 drops liquid stevia

CAESAR DRESSING

PURELY ALKALINE

Best on romaine lettuce but nice on mixed greens too. Blend.

MAKES 1½ CUPS

½ small zucchini, peeled and roughly chopped

1 clove fresh garlic

1 Tbsp hemp hearts

½ cup extra-virgin olive oil

juice of 1 lemon

2 tsp raw tahini

1½ Tbsp Bragg Liquid Aminos

Celtic sea salt

SWEET COCONUT CURRY DRESSING

PURELY ALKALINE

Delicious on mild greens like butter lettuce with a teensy bit of finely diced fresh mango. Blend.

MAKES ½ CUP

¼ cup avocado oil or grapeseed oil

¼ cup thick, full-fat coconut mylk

juice of ½ lime

2 drops liquid stevia

2 tsp Madras curry powder (or your choice of mild curry powder)

Celtic sea salt

SWEET SLAW DRESSING

ALKALINE BALANCED

A great dressing for a mix of crunchy greens and cabbages, with bell peppers and jicama. Whisk.

MAKES ABOUT ¾ CUP

¼ cup extra-virgin olive oil

juice of 1 lime

2 Tbsp coconut nectar or 4–6 drops liquid stevia

1 large clove garlic, crushed

½ cup finely chopped cilantro

½ tsp ground cumin

¼ tsp cayenne pepper

⅛ tsp sea salt

LIME AND GINGER SALAD DRESSING

ALKALINE BALANCED

I make this dressing often. It's lovely on greens or with a little diced mango or papaya with avocado and nuts or in a slaw of Savoy cabbage. Whisk.

MAKES ¾ CUP

⅓ cup sunflower oil

juice of ½ lemon

juice of 2 limes

1–2 Tbsp pure maple syrup or 5–6 drops liquid stevia (or a combination like I usually do)

1 Tbsp very finely grated ginger

½ tsp vinegar-free Dijon mustard or ¼ tsp dried mustard

Himalayan salt

freshly ground black pepper

ASIAN DRESSING

PURELY ALKALINE

Great for coleslaws but yummy over fresh sprouts too. Whisk.

MAKES ½ CUP

juice of ½ lemon

2 Tbsp Bragg Liquid Aminos

2 Tbsp extra-virgin olive oil

1 Tbsp toasted sesame oil

2 tsp grated ginger

2 tsp raw tahini

Celtic sea salt

GINGER AND HEMP DRESSING

PURELY ALKALINE

Otherwise known as liquid gold, this is my all-time favorite dressing. It's especially good on mixed veggie salads. Blend.

MAKES 1 CUP

⅓ cup hemp hearts

1 tsp finely grated ginger

juice of 1½ lemons

½ cup extra-virgin olive oil

2 Tbsp Udo's omega oil (or more if you like)

2 Tbsp Bragg Liquid Aminos

1 Tbsp filtered, alkalized water

1 Tbsp raw tahini

CREAMY LEMON PEPPER DRESSING

ALKALINE BALANCED

Nice with walnuts, grapefruit, and greens. Blend.

MAKES ABOUT 1 CUP

½ cup peeled and diced zucchini

⅓ cup Brazil nuts, soaked for 2 hours, rinsed and drained well

1 very small clove garlic

⅓ cup extra-virgin olive oil

juice and zest of 1 lemon

1 Tbsp filtered, alkaline water (optional)

¾ tsp coconut nectar or 1–2 drops liquid stevia

¼ tsp Himalayan sea salt

¼ tsp freshly ground black pepper

TRIPLE CITRUS DRESSING

ALKALINE BALANCED

Great with greens, avocado slices, grapefruit, walnuts, and a stack of sprouts on top. Skip the orange juice if you have a medical condition. Whisk.

MAKES 1 CUP

juice of 1 large white grapefruit

juice of ½ navel orange

juice of 1 large lemon

⅓ cup raw cold-pressed sunflower oil (or flax or extra-virgin olive oil or a combination)

2 Tbsp coconut nectar or 5–6 drops liquid stevia (or a combination)

¼ tsp vinegar-free Dijon mustard

¼ tsp grated ginger

Celtic sea salt

WHIPPED **COCONUT CREAM**

MAKES 1¾ CUPS

13½ oz (1 can) organic
full-fat coconut mylk,
chilled 4 hours
or overnight

1 tsp pure vanilla extract

3 drops liquid stevia
(or 1 Tbsp coconut nectar
or a combination)

This easy-peasy recipe will have you coming back for more! This is a soft whipped cream that melts easily, so be sure to keep it well chilled. If you need a temperature-stable cream for piping or for hot days, try the lemon coconut icing in the Pancake Cake recipe (page 268). For a lemon version of this cream, add 1 tsp lemon zest and 1 Tbsp lemon juice in addition to the vanilla.

Open the tin of coconut mylk from the bottom and carefully drain the coconut water into a bowl. Reserve it for another use, perhaps a smoothie. Scoop the coconut cream into a blender, add the vanilla and stevia and mix until verrrrry, verrrrry creamy and well combined, 30–60 seconds. Keep chilled until needed. This will keep refrigerated in an airtight container for up to 5 days.

NON-FERMENTED **VEGAN VANILLA BEAN YOGURT**

MAKES ABOUT 2 CUPS

2 young coconuts

½ vanilla bean pod,
scraped or ½ tsp ground
vanilla bean powder

juice of ½ lemon

3–6 drops stevia

This is definitely a staple in my kitchen as it is so versatile and can be eaten on its own any time, even while veggie-feasting! It's sublime on so many recipes—from chia porridge to warm buckwheat porridge or just topped with a few berries for breakfast or dessert! Only in a pinch use liquid vanilla as the bean imparts a truer flavor that is perfect in this recipe.

Open both young coconuts, pour the water into a bowl, and set aside. You should have around 2½ cups of coconut water. Scoop the coconut flesh into a small colander, rinse, and discard any bits of hard shell. Place the coconut in a high-speed blender, and add ½ of the coconut water (or a bit less if the coconut meat is very thin) along with the vanilla, lemon juice, and stevia. Blend on very low speed, and very gradually increase the speed, scraping down the sides as needed, to get the creamiest texture possible. The cream should be pourable but not runny, so add a bit more coconut water if necessary (reserve the rest for smoothies or drink it straight up—deelish!). This will keep refrigerated in an airtight container for up to 4 days.

photo on opposite page

Resources

Alkaline Sister
www.alkalinesister.com
Instagram: @alkalinesister
Twitter: @alkalinesister
Pinterest: alkalinesister
Facebook: alkalinesister
#alkalizeyourlifestyle
#eatbetterlivebetterfeelbetter

Supplements
Alkaline supplements, products,
  cookbook, and courses
  www.energizeforlife.com
Alkaline supplements, products, and
  health retreats
  www.phmiracleliving.com
Alkaline supplements and colloidal
  supplements
  www.phmlife.com
Digestive health supplements
  www.renewlife.com
Aloe vera
  www.andrasina.com/nutrition
Chlorophyll
  www.desouzas.com
Dried sweet wheatgrass juice capsules
  www.brightcorenutrition.com
Enzymes
  www.enzymedica.com
Essential omega oils—fish
  www.ascentahealth.com
Essential omega oils—plant-based
  www.udoerasmus.com
Greens powder
  www.phmiracleliving.com
  www.phmlife.com
Probiotics
  www.natren.com
Salts, mineral and flavor
  www.phmiracleliving.com
  www.phmlife.com

Water
Alkaline water filtration
  www.santevia.com
  www.jupiterionizers.com
pH drops
  www.liveenergized.com

Foods
Coffee replacement
  www.teeccino.com
Coconut wraps
  www.upayanaturals.com
Ezekiel 4:9 sprouted grain wraps
  www.foodforlife.com
Organic soaked beans, BPA-free tins
  www.edenfoods.com
Sprouting seeds and kits
  www.sproutpeople.org
Whole Foods Markets, for most
  everything
  www.wholefoods.com

Blenders
For everyday, high-speed blenders
  www.vitamix.com
  www.blendtec.com
  www.omniblendkitchenblenders.
  co.uk
  www.nutribullet.com
Travel blender—Magic Bullet
  www.buythebullet.com

Juicers
www.angel-juicer.com/en
www.breville.ca
www.greenstarjuicer.com
www.omegajuicers.com
www.hurom.com

Other Products
Assorted
  www.navitasnaturals.com
Almond milk machines
  www.tribestlife.com
  www.soymilkmaker.com
Easy coconut opener
  www.coco-jack.com
Food grater (strip slicer for making
  veggie noodles)
  www.oxo.com
Julienne peeler
  www.oxo.com
Mandoline V-blade slicer
  www.oxo.com
Veggie spiralizer or grater
  www.buyspirooli.com
Vegetable storage bags
  www.debbiemeyer.com

Healing Practices
Alkaline coaching via Skype
  www.intrinsicprinciples.ca
At-home colon cleansing—colema
  board
  www.colema.com/products.html
Colon hydrotherapy: colon therapist
  network
  www.colonhealth.net/
  therapist-search
Gaiam TV for Yoga (online yoga
  videos and products, by subscription)
  www.gaiamtv.com
Live blood analysis: microscopist and
  alkaline consultant directory
  www.phmiracleliving.com/
  t-Microscopist-List.aspx
Living Health Coaching Program
  (CDs)
  www.tonyrobbins.com

Meditation
www.chopracentermeditation.com
Online support for alkaline cleanses
www.liveenergized.com
www.phmiraclecleanse.com
Online support for *Candida* cleanses
www.thewholejourney.com

Further Reading and Connecting

Blogs/Websites
Blog of Robert O. Young, DSc, PhD
www.articlesofhealth.blogspot.ca
Food investigator
www.foodbabe.com
Healthy, sustainable, humane, and conscious food for all
www.foodrevolution.org
Information about the whole food, plant-based movement
www.thechinastudy.com
Kris Carr's alkaline approach to health
www.kriscarr.com

Books

Alkaline information, diet, and lifestyle
Alkaline Cook Book by Dr. Annie Guillet
Back to the House of Health I and *Back to the House of Health II* by Shelley Redford
The Biology of Belief by Bruce Lipton
Conscious Eating by Gabriel Cousens, MD
Crazy Sexy Cancer and *Crazy Sexy Diet* by Kris Carr
Crazy Sexy Kitchen by Kris Carr and Chad Sarno
Fats that Heal, Fats that Kill by Udo Erasmus

Honestly Healthy and *Honestly Healthy For Life* by Natasha Corrett and Vicki Edgson
Honestly Healthy Cleanse by Natasha Corrett
I Quit Sugar by Sarah Wilson
Joshi's Alkaline Diet by Nish Joshi
May Cause Miracles by Gabrielle Bernstein
The Alkaline Diet Recipe Book II by Ross Bridgeford
The Beauty Detox Solution and *The Beauty Detox Foods*, by Kimberly Snyder, CN
The Blender Girl: Super-Easy, Super-Healthy Meals, Snacks, Desserts, and Drinks—100 Gluten-Free, Vegan Recipes by Tess Masters
The China Study by T. Colin Campbell and Thomas M. Campbell II
The Food Babe Way by Vani Hari
The Food Revolution by John Robbins
The pH Miracle for Diabetes, The pH Miracle for Weight Loss, The pH Miracle for Cancer, and *Sick and Tired* by Robert O. Young, DSc, PhD
The pH Miracle, Revised & Updated (also available in audio format) by Robert O. Young, DSc, PhD and Shelley Redford
Understanding the Messages of Your Body: How to Interpret Physical and Emotional Signals to Achieve Optimal Health by Jean-Pierre Barral, DO

Enzymes
The Enzyme Factor by Hiromi Shinya, MD

Food Combining
Food Combining and Digestion: 101 Ways to Improve Digestion by Steve Meyerowitz
The Complete Book of Food Combining by Kathryn Marsden

Style Props
ABC Home, NYC
Anthropologie
Fishs Eddy, NYC
Grønlykke, Denmark
Plint, Denmark
West Elm

Fabrics
Drygoods Design, Seattle
Liberty, London, UK
Purl Soho, NYC

Love + Gratitude

Acknowledgments
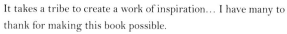

It takes a tribe to create a work of inspiration… I have many to thank for making this book possible.

First, **my husband**, for his consistent help with our young family while most of my days were consumed with recipe creation, styling, photos, writing, and editing for what seemed like forever! I love you dearly.

And to **my family**, for their patience and understanding of how very important it is for the Aries in me to "shout from the mountaintop" and share my passion for this alkaline lifestyle. You mean the world to me.

To my Alkaline Sister, **Yvonne**, for always being there, especially when I needed you most on our first veggie feast together and for being my cheerleader from day 1 with the blog and this book. I don't know what I'd do without you.

Marilyn Lister, for being my alkaline hero and mentor. I am so inspired by you! Your extensive alkaline wisdom is invaluable; your generosity, a gift. Thank you, my Aries twin!

Krystianna and **Angelique Queensley**, my alkaline coaches, for setting me on this alkaline journey and showing me the way. I am forever grateful.

Kathleen Cabral, my comrade in everything holistic, for getting creative in the kitchen with me, reading my chicken scratch, and sharing your wisdom. You made it way more fun!

Leslie Shewring, for always shining the light for me when things get dim. Your intuition, your wisdom, and your own personal journey have motivated me ever since I drank my first green juice and have carried me right through this book project. I'm ready to skip off to Copenhagen again. Are you in?

Karen Elgersma, for being my Oprah and my Maya Angelou. Thanks for always peeling that dang gremlin off my back! Your wise words of encouragement, compassion, endless support, and unwavering friendship inspire me to reach for the stars!

Holly Becker, my blog boss! I probably would never have written this book without having created my blog, so thanks to your inspiring blog workshop eons ago.

Aran Goyoga, **Mikkel Vang**, and **Helen Dujardin** for sharing your enduring passion for food photography and styling that continue to inspire me with every photo shoot. This book wouldn't be nearly as pretty without the lessons I learned from each of you.

Sherri Strong, thank you kindly for leading me to Robert at Random House. The match was perfect!

Robert McCullough of Appetite by Random House, for seeing my potential and believing in my alkaline message and journey enough to print it! It's been an absolute pleasure.

Lucy Kenward and **Lindsay Paterson**, your patience with my first book ever and your editorial wizardry are what make this book sing! Thank you for guiding me and my words and for making magic out of mincemeat!

Lesley Cameron, for ensuring we crossed all of our t's and that we didn't miss a pinch of sea salt! Thank you for tweaking the wee bits and pieces. :)

Rose Cowles, you always amaze me with your artistic genius! Thank you for tying all the pretty pieces together and adding your sparkle to these pages.

Kris Carr, your contagious spark for living a vibrant healthy life has become a part of my world since I read your *Crazy Sexy Diet* way back when! I sooo look forward to seeing your colorful unicorns in my inbox every week. You've paved the yellow brick road for those of us who are also eager to inspire alkaline wellness. Thank you!

Anthony Robbins, your empowering words of alkaline wisdom came when I needed them most and helped to affirm that I was absolutely on the exact right path with my wellness plan. From walking on hot coals to listening to the health tapes a hundred times over, your inspiration is everlasting and life changing.

Dr. Robert O. Young, your guiding light will be shining forever with the valuable pioneering knowledge you have bravely imparted that has helped millions, including me, to heal from overacidity. You have mentored my personal alkaline journey and continue to inspire me to share the healing alkaline lifestyle with others. I am forever grateful.

I can't help but acknowledge the folks that I don't even know. When I'm standing in the grocery line or waiting at the airport, I often overhear strangers' stories of woe as they chat about their ailments, medications, and worries. It inspires me to no end to continue to learn and explore day after day while sharing and willing this knowledge to them, in the hope that it reaches and touches their lives to help them through.

Last but certainly not least … **YOU**, the readers of my blog and this book, of course! For being brave and taking the first step to optimal wellness by getting curious and reading about, experimenting with, and embracing the alkaline lifestyle to take charge of your health. You are the undying inspiration that fuels every recipe I create, every word I write, and every photo I take. Thank you. I'm so proud of you! Keep up the good work!

Index

The End